Laughter in Middle-earth:
Humour in and around the Works of JRR Tolkien

Laughter in Middle-earth: Humour in and around the Works of J.R.R. Tolkien

edited by
Thomas Honegger & Maureen F. Mann

2016

Cormarë Series No. 35

Series Editors: Peter Buchs • Thomas Honegger • Andrew Moglestue • Johanna Schön

Series Editor responsible for this volume: Thomas Honegger

Library of Congress Cataloging-in-Publication Data

Thomas Honegger & Maureen F. Mann (eds.):
Laughter in Middle-earth: Humour in and around the Works of J.R.R. Tolkien
ISBN 978-3-905703-35-1

Subject headings:
Tolkien, J.R.R. (John Ronald Reuel), 1892-1973
Humour
Middle-earth
The Lord of the Rings
The Hobbit
The Silmarillion

Cormarë Series No. 35

First published 2016

© Walking Tree Publishers, Zurich and Jena, 2016

All rights reserved. No portion of this book may be reproduced, by any process or technique, without the express written consent of the publisher

Set in Adobe Garamond Pro and Shannon by Walking Tree Publishers
Printed by Lightning Source in the United Kingdom and United States

Cover Photograph Copyright 1973 by Douglas R. Gilbert

Board of Advisors

Academic Advisors

Douglas A. Anderson (independent scholar)

Dieter Bachmann (Universität Zürich)

Patrick Curry (independent scholar)

Michael D.C. Drout (Wheaton College)

Vincent Ferré (Université de Paris-Est Créteil UPEC)

Dimitra Fimi (Cardiff Metropolitan University)

Verlyn Flieger (University of Maryland)

Thomas Fornet-Ponse (Rheinische Friedrich-Wilhelms-Universität Bonn)

Christopher Garbowski (University of Lublin, Poland)

Mark T. Hooker (Indiana University)

Andrew James Johnston (Freie Universität Berlin)

Rainer Nagel (Johannes Gutenberg-Universität Mainz)

Helmut W. Pesch (independent scholar)

Tom Shippey (University of Winchester)

Allan Turner (Friedrich-Schiller-Universität Jena)

Frank Weinreich (independent scholar)

General Readers

Johan Boots

Jean Chausse

Friedhelm Schneidewind

Isaac Juan Tomas

Patrick Van den hole

Johan Vanhecke (Letterenhuis, Antwerp)

Acknowledgments

Many thanks to all those who worked with us to make this volume possible – most prominently, of course, the contributors!

Special thank you to Becky Dillon for putting us onto the track for the humorous Tolkien illustrations – which opened up an entire new world.

A great 'thank you' also to Tamara Schmidt and Maryna Tymoshchuk who helped with the layouting and proofreading of the text.

    Thomas Honegger & Maureen F. Mann

Contents

Tom Shippey
Foreword … 1

Maureen F. Mann
"Certainly not our sense": Tolkien and Nonsense … 9

Alastair Whyte
A Fountain of Mirth: Laughter in Arda … 39

Jennifer Raimundo
Mirth's Might:
The Tenacity of Humour in the Works of J.R.R. Tolkien … 61

Łukasz Neubauer
Plain Ignorance in the Vulgar Form:
Tolkien's Onomastic Humour in *Farmer Giles of Ham* … 89

Laura Lee Smith
"This of course is the way to talk to dragons":
Etiquette-Based Humour in *The Hobbit* … 107

Evelyn Koch
Parodies of the Works of J.R.R. Tolkien … 135

Sherrylyn Branchaw
Strategies of Humour in *The Stupid Ring Parody* … 155

Davide Martini
Humour in Art Depicting Middle-earth … 179

Jared Lobdell
Humour, Comedy, the Comic, Comicality, Puns,
Wordplay, 'Fantastication', and 'English Humour' in and
around Tolkien and His Work, and among the Inklings … 213

List of illustrations in order of appearance in the volume

All copyrights remain with the artists; reproduction by permission of the artists.

Page 7: Chris Riddell, *The Author Hanging Out With the Wise Wizard Gaiman*

Page 37: Jef Murray, *The Balrog Hanging up His Wings*

Page 59: Ulla Thynell, *Tom Bombadil* (2016)

Page 87: Ted Nasmith, *Lalaith* (2016)

Pages 105f: Anke Eissmann, *You Cannot Pass* (2016) & *New Hat* (2016)

Pages 133f: Graeme Skinner, *The Doors of Durin* (2016) & *The Force* (2016)

Pages 152f: Kay Woollard, *Party Piece* (1992)

Pages 210f: Patrick Wynne, *Mordor Lemonade* (1989) & *Grendel's Mom* (1987)

Page 245: Tim Kirk, *Homeless Orc* (2016)

About the artists

ANKE KATRIN EISSMANN (*1977) is a German artist and graphic designer who studied at the Bauhaus-Universität Weimar (Thuringia, Germany) and the Colchester Institute (Colchester, UK). She is best known for her paintings inspired by and illustrations of Tolkien's works and works of other fantasy authors.
Official webpage: http://anke.edoras-art.de/d_anke_home.html

TIM KIRK is an American artist who worked as a senior designer at Tokyo DisneySea, as an imageer for Walt Disney. He earned his Bachelor's Degree in Fine Arts with an emphasis in Commercial Art, and his Master's Degree in Illustration from California State University, Long Beach. His thesis project consisted of a series of paintings for *The Lord of the Rings*, thirteen of which were published as the 1975 Tolkien Calendar.

JEF MURRAY (1960-2015) was a fantasy artist and author. He is best known for his illustrations of the works of J.R.R. Tolkien and C.S. Lewis, which were published regularly in publications focussing on Tolkien, the Inklings and other mythopoeic authors.
Official webpage: http://gallery.jefmurray.com

TED NASMITH (*1956) is a Canadian artist and illustrator, probably best known for his illustrations of *The Silmarillion* (1998) and contributions to several Tolkien Calendars. More recently, he has illustrated George R.R. Martin's epic *Song of Ice and Fire*. He is also a gifted songwriter and singer.
Official webpage: http://www.tednasmith.com

CHRIS RIDDELL (*1962) is a British illustrator and occasional writer of children's books and a political cartoonist for *The Observer*. He has won two Kate Greenaway Medals, the British librarians' annual award for the best-illustrated children's book, and two of his works were commended runners-up, a distinction dropped after 2002. Books that he wrote or illustrated have won three Nestlé Smarties Book Prizes and have been silver or bronze runners-up four times. In 2015 he was appointed the UK Children's Laureate.
Official webpage: http://www.chrisriddell.co.uk

GRAEME SKINNER is a Cumbrian artist and photographer who was influenced by Tolkien's work at an early age. Now he spends his time either painting landscapes or illustrating fantasy and science fiction. More of his work can be found at his Official webpage: http://www.graeme-skinner.com

ULLA THYNELL is an artist and professional illustrator based in Helsinki, Finland. She studied philosophy and aesthetics at Helsinki University and graphic desing at Helsinki Metropolia UAS and started working with fantasy and children's books in 2013.
Official webpage: http://www.ullathynell.com

KAY WOOLLARD (aka Dora Baggins) (1924-2008) was born in the Pennine town of Halifax. She studied at the Halifax School of Art, where she qualified as a pictorial designer and went to the Royal College of Arts in London, where she studied stained glass and illustration with, amongst others, Eduardo Ardizzone. In 1979, on reading for the first time the works of Professor Tolkien, she became an instant devotee, joined the Tolkien Society the following winter and contributed many drawings to the publications of the Tolkien Society. The drawing printed on pages 152-53 in this volume was the centre piece to the Programme Book for the 1992 Tolkien Centenary Conference, held at Keble College, Oxford in August 1992, and constituted the conclusion to a series of Progress Report covers that Dora had been commissioned to produce. Two of her richly illustrated stories, *The Terror of Tatty Walk* (2000) and *Wilmot's Very Strange Stone* (2001), were published by Walking Tree Publishers.

PATRICK WYNNE has authored numerous articles on Tolkien's invented languages for the journals *Parma Eldalamberon*, *Vinyar Tengwar*, and *Mythlore* and is a member of a project to order, transcribe, and edit Tolkien's unpublished linguistic papers. His artwork has been published in numerous Tolkien journals and other publications, and he has illustrated several books, including *Fish Soup* by Ursula K. Le Guin.
Official webpage: http://pa2rick.com

Tom Shippey

Foreword

In Roald Dahl's *Matilda*, the title-heroine (a child prodigy who has taught herself to read) remarks that she liked C.S. Lewis's *The Lion, the Witch, and the Wardrobe*, but that Mr Lewis "has one failing. There are no funny bits in his books". She reflects a moment and adds, "There aren't many funny bits in Mr Tolkien either". Evidence might appear to be against Matilda here, for (as Alastair Whyte points out) there are some two hundred and forty mentions of laughter in *The Lord of the Rings*, and, one might add, fifty or so in *The Hobbit* and even about thirty in the dark pages of *The Silmarillion*.

Laughter, however, is not the same as "funny bits". Matilda would be right in saying that there are few comic scenes in Mr Tolkien. *The Hobbit* certainly starts with one, in the "socially-coded humour" of Gandalf's first encounter with Bilbo (for which see Laura Lee Smith's essay here), and it continues similarly as Bilbo tries to remember his manners and his "duty as a host" to the intrusive dwarves. Bilbo's party, at the start of *The Lord of the Rings*, contains humour in the same vein. While *The Hobbit* at least ends with a laugh, however – Bilbo handing Gandalf the tobacco-jar – *The Lord of the Rings* ends with what has been called the most heartbreaking line in all of modern fantasy", Sam saying, "Well, I'm back" (Swanwick 45). It is certainly one of the most emotionally complex. What does Sam mean by this apparently non-committal and even pointless remark?

One could argue that Tolkien's mood darkened as he wrote his way through both *The Hobbit* and *The Lord of the Rings*, but that is not the case if one considers his career-trajectory. *Farmer Giles of Ham* (an early work at least in conception) is comic all the way through, and *Leaf by Niggle* (which we can date to the late 1930s) ends with laughter till "the Mountains rang". On the other hand "The Story of Kullervo", which we can date as early as 1914, and which is the first element of what came to be *The Silmarillion*, could hardly be sadder in tale or in tone. One has to conclude, as always, that Tolkien was too complex a writer to be readily reduced to order.

One way of considering his oeuvre is to look at the traditions affecting him, one of which is the powerful Victorian tradition of "nonsense" (discussed in different ways both by Maureen Mann and Jared Lobdell), which one might call more broadly a tradition of light-hearted fantasy, with a strong element of verbal humour (for which see further Łukasz Neubauer): it shows in the jokes about "golf" and "Bounders" at the start of *The Hobbit* and the "Prologue" to *The Lord of the Rings* respectively, though this was a technique which Tolkien rapidly dropped. As Mann points out, this kind of humour often contained an element of subversion, poking fun at the established certainties of the Victorian world. It may be that it is Tolkien's own subversion which has made him such a target for parody in the modern world, though what he chose to subvert were the established certainties of irony, modernism, and the world-view of his lifelong enemies, the literary critics. Some of the parodies aimed at him are friendly – I would pick out the scenes involving the dragon and "the last arrow" in Terry Pratchett's *Guards! Guards!* – but not all of them. Tolkien's re-assertion of the modes and values of epic, romance and even myth upset some people very badly, and one reaction was indeed derisive (if unavailing) parody, as detailed by both Evelyn Koch and Sherrylyn Branchaw.

The other tradition one should keep in mind is, however, the extraordinarily strong tradition of Old Northern literature, to which Tolkien devoted much of his professional life: and this takes us back to the theme of laughter. When this tradition was rediscovered, from the 17th century on, it too shocked the learned men of Europe all but out of their powdered wigs, though at the same time they (or some of them) found it inspiring. Old Norse literature in particular was marked by scenes of ferocious laughter. Brynhild arranges the murder of her treacherous lover Sigurd, but what makes her laugh is not his death, but the sound of his wife Gudrún weeping. Tolkien, in his *The Legend of Sigurd and Gudrún* (174), translated the scene, staying very close to his original, as:

> Then laughed Brynhild
> in her bed listening,
> with whole heart once –
> the house shuddered –
> Gudrún hearing
> in grief's torment.

One could not find a more extreme example of triumphant laughter.

Another example, this time more nuanced, would be the end of the poem often translated as "The Death-Song of Ragnar Lodbrog" (for early reactions to this see Shippey). Here the hero is dying alone and helpless in the snake-pit into which he has been thrown by King Ella, but his last words – after a long and boastful account of his victories – are, word for word, "laughing shall I die". What in the world has Ragnar got to laugh about? He is sure of his entry into Valhalla. Sure also of the terrible vengeance his sons will take for him. But there must also be a strong element of what the English call "bloody-mindedness". He will not give his enemies the satisfaction of seeing him defeated. This is not triumphant laughter, but it is last-ditch defiant.

All these and many other scenes were familiar to Tolkien, who surely appreciated (as more modern scholars often have not) their frequent emotional complexity. He did his best to recreate them. Almost all the laughter in *The Silmarillion* is of this general kind, the cruel humour of superiority. I would pick out, for instance, Sauron laughing at Gorlim, in "The Tale of Beren and Lúthien" (mockery), Beren laughing at Thingol (contempt, expressed from a position of weakness), Glaurung laughing at Túrin (secret knowledge), and Túrin laughing "as one fey" just before his suicide (a scene which escapes analysis).

There is then a harsh and bitter element in a great deal of Tolkienian laughter. Can this be called comic? Or even funny? It is well known that nothing shakes the nerve of the modern academic person more than the sharp remark (so often heard), "That's not funny!" Of course the remark is never true. If one decodes its social coding, taking a lead again from Alastair Whyte, what it means is, in succession:

- "you have said what you have said in the belief that it is funny"
- "I, however, do not find it so" (almost always because the joke turns on some assumption of superiority)
- "I, therefore, am a more sensitive person than you and accordingly morally superior."

One claims superiority by rejecting superiority, which is quite funny in itself. What such exchanges ignore is the fact that humour is culturally diverse. And this is one area where it is allowable to be culturally "judgmental".

I have to say (and this is speaking personally) that I find modern judgements less than nuanced. Years ago I remarked that one of the more human features of the orcs was that they were great jokers. They are caught laughing at least a dozen times in *The Lord of the Rings*. Of course, what they laugh at is other people's pain, which we have been culturally programmed since the Enlightenment to disapprove of (no more public executions, bull-baiting etc.). The programming hasn't always worked. I can vividly recall, as I was being carried off from a rugby field on a stretcher, with a broken tibia and fibula and my foot at right angles to my leg, the faces of my team-mates looking down at me. They were all laughing, and competing for who could think of the funniest thing to say. One offered me a very low price for my ticket to the evening dance. Another berated me for not passing the ball as I went down. It was all very orcish, and a further connection with Tolkien was that they were all Old Edwardians, Tolkien's own team. But I knew it was "all in fun". They were trying to cheer me up, and I tried to laugh back. There is a laughter of camaraderie, and it is a considerable psychological resource, not always appreciated. But Tolkien recognised it, even in its orcish mode.

Even after making due allowance for literary traditions known to Tolkien, and for the considerable cultural diversity even in modern society, one may still feel that there are unique elements in Tolkien's humour, and in his many scenes of laughter. Very strongly marked is what one might call mirth, scenes of merriment. The hobbits figure strongly here, they are after all as labelled by Treebeard, "the laughing folk, the little people", and they enjoy mirth as much as they do food and social festivity. In *The Hobbit*, Thorin Oakenshield, dying as he is like a hero of ancient times, nevertheless concedes a kind of superiority to hobbit-attitudes: "If more of us valued food and cheer and song above hoarded gold, it would be a merrier world". Gandalf too, for all his gravity and authority, laughs near the end of *The Lord of the Rings* and Sam recognises in it "the pure sound of merriment".

A pivotal scene of laughter, however, I would suggest, is the one on the Stairs of Cirith Ungol. Sam and Frodo have been discussing their own story and how it will be told in the future, and Sam says someone will then say – in an example of verbal humour – that Frodo was "the famousest of the hobbits". At this Frodo laughs, "a long clear laugh from his heart" – very unlike Brynhild's laugh from her heart, one might note. And at this "it seemed as if all the stones were listening and the tall rocks leaning over them". This seems to me almost a moment of exorcism, breaking the mood of fear and discouragement. Yet the hobbits are laughing at themselves. And while they are laughing, they both insist they are being serious. There is an incongruity between their own self-images and the idea of being heroes in a book (which, of course, they are). Is it a comic incongruity? Once again, the emotional complexity of this scene is hard to express. It is certainly a good example (see Jennifer Raimundo) of "victory in mirth".

One final remark is that Tolkien, like Shakespeare's Falstaff, was not only a celebrator of mirth himself, but also the cause of mirth, and creativity, in many others: as demonstrated convincingly by Davide Martini on Tolkien's many illustrators. A scene like Éowyn's artless fishing for information about Aragorn's age and marital situation (in the second Jackson *Lord of the Rings* movie) has no basis in Tolkien's actual words, but seems to me not inappropriate. I would not say this for all the comic turns which Jackson added to his scripts, but then, opinions about what is funny and what is not, as I have been saying, vary greatly, and no-one can legislate for everyone.

Tolkien, however, has surely added more than almost any other writer to what one might call the gaiety of nations: and he did so in circumstances (his own life, his friends' and family's deaths) which were distinctly adverse. Like Gandalf, he had a spring of merriment inside him, which he frequently released, and which deserves to be fully appreciated: as it is in this volume.

Bibliography

Dahl, Roald. *Matilda*. London: Puffin Books, 1990.

Pratchett, Terry. *Guards! Guards!* London: Gollancz, 1989.

Shippey, Tom. "'The Death-Song of Ragnar Lodbrog': A Study in Sensibilities." *Medievalism in the Modern World: Essays in Honour of Leslie Workman*. Eds. Richard Utz and Tom Shippey. Turnhout: Brepols, 1998. 155-172.

Swanwick, Michael. "A Changeling Returns." *Meditations on Middle-earth*. Ed. Karen Haber. New York: St Martin's, 2001. 33-46.

Tolkien, John Ronald Reuel. *The Legend of Sigurd and Gudrún*. Ed. Christopher Tolkien. London: HarperCollins, 2009.

Chris Riddell
The Author Hanging Out With the Wise Wizard Gaiman

Maureen F. Mann

"Certainly not our sense": Tolkien and Nonsense[1]

Abstract

My paper examines Tolkien's uses of nonsense as a concept, as a genre, and as linguistic disruption or silliness, although there is much slippage among those three. I situate these uses within Tolkien's historical contexts of Victorian Nonsense, traditional folk narrative, and nursery rhymes, but also within his own ideas and practices of language invention and literary descent. For Tolkien the sound of language is as important as its communicative value; unintelligible non sense is as valuable as common sense. My focus is on Tolkien's texts themselves but I draw comparisons and analogies to literary theory and scholarly analysis in order to construe readings of the texts. Nonsense is rarely rubbish in Tolkien.

The quotation in my title comes from Tolkien's essay "On 'The Kalevala' or Land of Heroes" in the recent edition of *The Story of Kullervo* edited by Verlyn Flieger (106). At first thought, the story of the hapless boy Kullervo, as Tolkien described him, who under Tolkien's imaginative development eventually becomes the tragic hero Túrin Turambar, may seem an unusual place to begin a discussion of nonsense, but it is the essay on *The Kalevala* that is pertinent to my topic. (It is, however, Turambar's story that tells of the endless laughter of the falls of Eithel Irvin which can heal Túrin.) Tolkien's recognition of the place of incongruity and of words which have no literal communicative meaning is an important aspect of his thinking about nonsense. This paper situates Tolkien's nonsense within its historical context as well as within his own particular attitude towards things of no sense. For methodology I will refer mainly to Roderick McGillis's chapter "Nonsense" in *A Companion to Victorian Poetry*, with a nod or two to other theorists such as Marnie Parsons in *Touch*

---

[1] An early draft of this paper was delivered to the *Return of the Ring Conference* sponsored by the Tolkien Society at Loughborough University, July 2012, and which has appeared in the Proceedings of the Conference.

Monkeys: Nonsense Strategies for Reading Twentieth-Century Poetry, and a word or several from writers such as George Orwell and G.K. Chesterton.

To begin, I would like to consider a few of Tolkien's comments in which he uses the word nonsense, in both his fiction and non-fiction, as preliminary to a deduction about his use of this kind of humour.

First some words from Bilbo as he contemplates the possibility he has overslept the dwarves.

> 'Don't be a fool, Bilbo Baggins!' he said to himself, 'thinking of dragons and all that outlandish nonsense at your age.' (*H* 43-44)

This is the "Baggins" side of Bilbo speaking, placing dragons, the element of Tolkien's greatest desire in fairy, in the context of things which are foolish or extravagant conduct, or absurd, senseless or worthless stuff (*OED*) in contrast to propriety, banality, and common sense. Bilbo's thoughts come with the assumption that nonsense belongs to children and is something we grow out of. This might seem to be a commonplace use of the word, but its association with dragons and fairy will prove important.

My next quotation comes from a letter written to Edith Bratt in 1916 while Tolkien was in training during World War I, a very early example of Tolkien conflating nonsense specifically with fairy.

> This miserable drizzling afternoon I have been reading up old military lecture-notes again: – and getting bored with them after an hour and a half. I have done some touches to my nonsense fairy language – to its improvement.
>
> I often long to work at it and don't let myself 'cause though I love it so it does seem such a mad hobby! (*L* 8)

It is difficult to determine tone and intent of what is a short public excerpt from a longer private letter, but this passage appears to employ the same slightly breezy tone from other excerpted letters to Edith – at least, it is possible to read "mad hobby" as not entirely a serious questioning of the activity, but a cheeky self-mocking of the hobby.² However, the topically relevant word here is "nonsense". All talk of free adjectives aside, "fairy" and "nonsense" are, I suggest, quite definitely cumulative adjectives; they could not be inverted to "fairy nonsense language". Tolkien is describing his "fairy language" as nonsense; Humphrey Carpenter's note to the letter identifies this as "an early form of the Elvish language Quenya" (*L* 434). More pertinent to the topic, Tolkien is not alone in thinking of nonsense with fairy language. G.K. Chesterton also remarked on the strange effect of Edward Lear's nonsense in an essay from 1902. "But Edward Lear, with more subtle and placid effrontery, is always introducing scraps of his own elvish dialect into the middle of simple and rational statements, until we are almost stunned into admitting that we know what they mean" ("Defense" n.p.). (Of course, Chesterton is not speaking of actual Elvish languages.) Shortly we shall see what exactly nonsense has to do with elves and with words lacking no immediate communicative effect.

One more example of a comment using the word nonsense, this in the *Letters*, written in 1937 in response to Stanley Unwin's reaction on first reading material of the Legendarium.

> My chief joy comes from learning that the Silmarillion is not rejected with scorn. I have suffered a sense of fear and bereavement, quite ridiculous, since I let this private and beloved nonsense out; and I think if it had seemed to you to be nonsense I should have felt really crushed. (*L* 26)

Dimitra Fimi (77) has described this as an expression of Tolkien's embarrassment over his private pass time but the use of "nonsense" again in conjunction with the Legendarium shows how close ideas of the concept were to his thought.³ Once again, he expresses his personal emotions of desire, tension, and loss concerning his "beloved nonsense"; McGillis argues these are important aspects of the genre of Nonsense itself. What is also intriguing about this statement is the fact that Tolkien uses two different meanings of the word nonsense in one sentence. The first is probably closer to "silliness" while the latter use is likely closer to "worthless" or "rubbish" – or perhaps simply "unintelligible", a non-

---

2 It would not be remiss to point out that, while "mad" began its philological life in the *OED* as an Old English word meaning "mentally deranged or foolish, unwise", that dictionary also records a subsequent meaning as "wildly desirous to do something", leading to the rare Modern English usage of phrases such as "music-mad [...] poetry-mad." Tolkien may not have been as self-deprecating as the statement might initially appear.
3 Later in this letter Tolkien agrees that Celtic and Welsh tales are mad but that he is not.

judgmental meaning Tolkien gives to the word nonsense in the "Preface" to *The Adventures of Tom Bombadil* – a meaning absent from the *OED* (ATB 169). (A difference which should not surprise us, given what Tom Shippey says about the mordant omission of medieval writers from the entry on literature in the *OED* (Shippey 7).) Once again, "nonsense" is intimately related through Tolkien's emotional involvement to the mythology which grew out of his invented languages. This involvement may have developed more strongly over time but there are hints the relationship was present even in his early inspiration for writing.

These choices of the word nonsense suggest a particular attitude which is unique to Tolkien's thought. While his use of nonsense does display similarities to contemporary scholarship on the uses of the comic impulse, as represented by Roderick McGillis's chapter "Nonsense" in *A Companion to Victorian Poetry*, Tolkien hints at something else as well. His attitude, in some uses, has more affinity to critics of this humour such as George Orwell and G. K. Chesterton and to his own philological studies of early narrative. In fact, if we can take a work by a fellow Inkling as an example, discussion of early narrative was possibly a topic amongst the Inklings.[4]

Tolkien was familiar with Nonsense as a literary genre and not only as a notion or concept. This familiarity is shown particularly in his essay known as "A Secret Vice" – that title given by Christopher Tolkien, from Tolkien's own phrase and use; the original title was "A Hobby for the Home" (*ASV* 4). The example of *animalic* (the first invented language that Tolkien admits he was involved with) is full of ludic fun and a giddy enjoyment of pricking the pomposity of polite decorum: "*dog nightingale woodpecker forty*" means "you are an ass", he says, the word for "*forty*" being "donkey" but acquiring the "converse meaning" as Tolkien delicately calls it. It shows a typical adolescent willingness to challenge pomposity but this is a quality common to much literary nonsense. More significant is what Tolkien called "one idiotic connected fragment" (*ASV* 12) of his second invented language, *Nevbosh* or "the New Nonsense" (*ASV* 11).

> There was an old man who said "How
> Can I possibly carry my cow?
> For if I were to ask it

---

4 See for instance Adam Fox, who Tolkien and Lewis nominated for Professor of Poetry at Oxford.

To get in my basket
It would make such a terrible row!" (*Biography* 36)[5]

Cows appear to be very prominent in nonsense. Carpenter's translation makes clear the rhythm and rhyme scheme of a limerick (although Carpenter mistranslates *bocte* –i.e. pocket – as 'baskets'). Clearly, the Nevboshites wrote a traditional five-line *aabba*-rhyming limerick that begins with a specific person (if not a specific place), as Carolyn Wells has observed of limericks (Wells xvii). We might wish we had explicit allusions to Edward Lear's limericks, but the Nevboshites could have picked up the form from the habit of their Latin lessons (Wells xxii). Tolkien claims that *Nevbosh* represented a new level of language invention where the speakers were attempting to "*invent* 'new words' (groups of sounds) to represent familiar notions" (*ASV* 13). This is the delight in neologisms which McGillis ascribes to nonsense (159); it demonstrates that the Nevboshites were using language with delight in sound and play and with less concern for being serious about meaning or communication. It was a creative act of artistic play. This seems very similar to what Tolkien in 1914 said was part of the attraction of *The Kalevala*, "meaningless syllables and even meaningless words" (*SK* 116), not quite reduced to "nonsense rhymes with flickers of sense" (*SK* 117).

"A Secret Vice" shows other intriguing affinities with theorising about nonsense. For instance, the title fits nicely with Tolkien's claims about desire and pleasure in the invention of language – "vice" contrasts well with, for example, the "They" of Lear's limericks, who Orwell describes as "sober citizens in bowler hats who are always anxious to stop you doing anything worth doing" ("Nonsense" n.p.). Tolkien's essay is replete with statements about the pleasure of language. Tolkien claims that the *animalic*-speakers delighted less in the secrecy of the language and more in the fun of "using the linguistic faculty [...] purely for amusement and pleasure" (*ASV* 10). For instance, they adopted the word *lint*, meaning "quick, clever, nimble" (*ASV* 15)

---

5 The original Nevbosh is as follows:
 Dar fýs ma vel gom co palt 'hoc
 Pys go iskili far maino woc?
 Pro si go fys do roc de
 Do cat ym maino bocte
 De volt fac soc ma taimful gyróc!' (*ASV* 12)

> because the relations between the sounds *lint* and the ideas proposed for association with them gave *pleasure* [...] The instinct for 'linguistic invention' – the fitting of notion to oral symbol, and *pleasure in contemplating the new relation established* is rational, and not perverted [...] Certainly it is the *contemplation* of the relation between sound and notion which is a main source of pleasure. (*ASV* 15-16 *passim*)

Tolkien reiterates that this pleasure lies less with the "*communicative* aspect of language" and is more keenly "pleasure in articulate sound, and in the symbolic use of it" (*ASV* 18). He highlights pleasure in his definition of his language invention as "the construction of imaginary languages in full or outline for amusement, for the pleasure of the constructor or even conceivably of any critic that might occur" (*ASV* 11). He repeats the point of "phonetic pleasure" again as he concludes his essay; this hobby produces "an attenuated emotion, but may be very piercing – this construction of sound to give pleasure" (*ASV* 32).[6]

Such prioritising of sound over meaning was also the profound attraction of nursery rhymes for the Welsh poet Dylan Thomas. Marnie Parsons, in her study of nonsense strategies for reading his poetry, quotes Thomas's own statement about how he revelled in the delight of the sounds of nursery rhymes as a child.

> The first poems I knew were nursery rhymes, and before I could read them for myself I had come to love just the words of them, the words alone. What the words stood for, symbolised, or meant, was of very secondary importance. What mattered was the *sound* of them as I heard them for the first time on the lips of the remote and incomprehensible grown-ups who seemed, for some reason, to be living in my world. And these words were, to me, as the notes of bells, the sounds of musical instruments, the noises of wind, sea, and rain, the rattle of milkcarts, the clopping of hooves on cobbles, the fingering of branches on a window pane, might be to someone, deaf from birth, who has miraculously found his hearing. I did not care what the words said, overmuch, nor what happened to Jack and Jill and the Mother Goose rest of them; I cared for the shapes of sound that their names, and the words describing their actions, made in my ears [...] Out of them came the gusts and grunts and hiccups and heehaws of the common fun of the earth; and though what the words meant was, in its own way, often deliciously funny enough, so much funnier seemed to me, at that almost forgotten time, the shape and shade and size and noise of the words as they hummed, strummed, jugged and galloped along. (Parsons 76, quoting Thomas)

---

6 See Ross Smith's monograph for an in-depth study of this aspect of Tolkien's imaginary languages.

Younger than Tolkien's Nevboshites, Thomas in his childhood delight addresses the same point of pleasure which Tolkien enjoyed. This is perhaps less a delight in the actual creation of new sounds, the originality of which whetted the adolescent Tolkien's enjoyment, and more a primal delight in simply the human creation of sound and its place in the world. The musical elements of nursery rhymes are an important part of the bag of tricks of Nonsense, to paraphrase Parsons (76), as well as delight.

Chesterton expressed the importance of delight in nonsense by describing its lack in a review of the modernist literature he so disliked. This by no means relates to any of Tolkien's nonsense – joy is central to his concept of eucastrophe in fairy – but the expression is worthy enough to stand beside those Tolkien provides to enforce the importance of real delight. Chesterton's point is telling and the adjective he borrows here has an ominous suggestion for Tolkien's use of the word.

> This new frivolity is inadequate because there is in it no strong sense of an unuttered joy. The men and women who exchange the repartees may not only be hating each other, but hating even themselves. Any one of them might be bankrupt that day, or sentenced to be shot the next. They are joking, not because they are merry, but because they are not; out of the emptiness of the heart the mouth speaketh. Even when they talk pure nonsense it is a careful nonsense – a nonsense of which they are economical, or, to use the perfect expression of Mr. W. S. Gilbert in "Patience", it is such "precious nonsense". ("Smart Novelists" n.p.)

The prominence of delight is significant in contemporary theory as well. Roderick McGillis makes the argument that "desire is perhaps the secret of nonsense" and refers to Maureen Duffy's argument in *The Erotic World of Faery* to "express the unspeakable" as well as themes of fear and loss (159). In his particular examples, McGillis examines secret codes for sexual desire in Victorian nonsense. However, Tolkien's desire is closer to Roland Barthes' explorations of what we enjoy when reading, which Barthes presents in *The Pleasure of the Text*. Tolkien's inventor of language, who sidesteps the limitations of a given language for the delights of creating new relations, is close to Barthes' anti-hero, the reader of the text, who finds bliss in cohabitation with language (Barthes 3). Tolkien's concluding remarks on the free adjective, which he claims no language has yet attained, where one may say "green sun" or "dead life", are logical contradictions which would possibly also have pleased Barthes' anti-hero.

Tolkien prioritises this delight in sound over the communicative function of language. In comparison, McGillis argues that the intense focus of nonsense upon its own noise and sound is a parody of the desire to communicate, as well as a strategy for dealing with the unpleasant realities of Victorian life. Nonsense, says McGillis, is "a way of ironizing from a distance" (155). In Tolkien, the invention of language is clearly a distancing from boredom or unpleasantness that might involve irony. The first person Tolkien identifies as a devotee is a fellow soldier who revealed himself "in a moment of extreme ennui" (*ASV* 6):[7]

> We were listening to somebody lecturing on map-reading, or camp-hygiene, or the art of sticking a fellow through without (in defense of Kipling) bothering who God sent the bill to; rather we were trying to avoid listening, though the Guard's English, and voice, is penetrating. The man next to me said suddenly in a dreamy voice: "Yes, I think I shall express the accusative case by a prefix!" (*ASV* 7)

The last we hear of this fellow is that "probably he was blown to bits in the very moment of deciding upon some ravishing method of indicating the subjunctive" (*ASV* 8). What is also interesting about this passage is the sudden jump into the present tense with "is penetrating" amidst the past tenses of the recollection. Perhaps more evidence of Tolkien's responsiveness to the sound of language rather than its communicative function.

McGillis attributes many subversive traits to Victorian nonsense but perhaps the most predominant one is its ridicule of the "high seriousness of canonised poetry" (158). With Tolkien, that would be canonised criticism. The preeminent example of this ridicule involves Lewis Carroll's "Jabberwocky". I am hunting neither sources nor Snarks here, but simply wish to indicate that Tolkien was familiar with the specific characteristics and traits of Nonsense as a genre. Tolkien had to have been familiar with Carroll's poem because he used it in his essay "Beowulf: The Monster and the Critics" to chastise shortsighted literary scholars.

---

7   Dimitra Fimi, in the new edition of *A Secret Vice*, introduces this recollection in a footnote which begins, "If this is a real encounter […]" (*ASV* 39).

> For it is of their nature that the jabberwocks of historical and antiquarian research burble in the tulgy wood of conjecture, flitting from one tum-tum tree to another. (BMC 9)

The allusion is all the more powerful because "Jabberwocky", in the words of Roderick McGillis, "is a poem about the power of poetry to cut through evasion, bluster and huffery-puffery in language" (168) and here Tolkien is ridiculing the short-sightedness of those who claim to understand language well. More evidence that Tolkien was quite well aware of the tendency of nonsense to challenge humbug.

McGillis mentions several other traits of the genre which we will see in Tolkien's own nonsense, such as its mix of the comic and the morbid, its tendency to lampoon, its speaking to a dual audience. I will focus on only a few of McGillis' traits. There are two significant differences between his theorizing and Tolkien's imaginative writing, amidst the similarities. One is that Tolkien works within a tradition which McGillis does not directly address (it is not, after all, Victorian): the folk tradition of nonsense, particularly as found in nursery rhymes. The other is Tolkien's own conception of ancient texts and their descent. The link between Tolkien's ideas about language creation and nonsense lies in the nature of both to push the boundaries of normal or banal communication. Both challenge a sense of reality that is itself too restrictive or mundane. The clue lies in Tolkien's concept of "unintelligible".

When we turn to *Farmer Giles of Ham*, we learn that Bilbo Baggins is not the only character who associates legends, dragons, nonsense, and childhood delight; so too does the narrator of *Farmer Giles*, who talks about Giles' fondness as a child, before he learnt sense, for tales about dragon slaying (FGH 125). Here again, delight, childhood, and escape are connected. For G.K. Chesterton, this is an essential element in nonsense: "[…] the idea of *escape*, of escape into a world where things are not fixed horribly in an eternal appropriateness, where apples grow on pear-trees, and any odd man you meet may have three legs" ("Defense" n.p.). Giles' story is often regarded as a parody of Arthurian legend[8] and of critics who quarry literature for historical and anthropological data (Scull and Hammond 60, 294),[9] but there is a great deal in this story which

---

8   See Vincent Ferré's paper on this topic.
9   In writing to Stanley Unwin in 1950, Tolkien said that the Silmarillion "was kept out of Farmer Giles with effort" (*L* 136), so it is not part of the Legendarium.

pertains to characteristics of nonsense as well, not the least of which are two allusions to nursery rhymes. The first is an historical reference to the time of King Coel in the "Foreword", who has come down to us as that "merry old soul who called for his pipe and his bowl and his fiddlers three."[10] The second occurs when the dragon taunts the King with the refrain from the Humpty Dumpty nursery rhyme, "All the king's horses and all the King's men" (159). (In this case, the line becomes a threat to kill them all.)

Like much nonsense, *Farmer Giles* has a mixed readership. Tolkien first told the story as "an impromptu tale" (Scull and Hammond 289) to his children. It went through several expansions to satisfy the editor's wish for length. Tolkien himself said that its revision "has taken on a rather more adult and satiric flavour" (*L* 39) although he also noted that children still enjoyed it (*L* 44). As Scull and Hammond have reported, C.A. Furth, the editor, complained that the tale was a selling problem because it was neither a children's story nor a novel (Scull and Hammond 291). Eventually it was published with Pauline Bayne's illustrations to flesh out its length, but critical reviews commented that it was not quite a children's book (Scull and Hammond 291). McGillis points out that Lear's and Carroll's works were also written for children, yet have found enduring appeal with adults. He argues that

> nonsense speaks to a dual audience […] [its] appeal to […] both adult and child, is part of its subversive appeal. Nonsense thus breaks the barriers of high art, art that through sophistication and complexity speaks only to a learned and urbane audience […] the adult and child reader share a laugh at pretention and high seriousness. (McGillis 163)

We might here recall Tolkien's comment on the attractiveness of *The Kalevala*: "We are taking a holiday from the whole course of progress of the last three Milleniums: and going to be wildly unhellenic and barbarous for a time, like the boy who hoped the future life would provide for half holidays in Hell, away from Eton collars and hymns" (*SK* 72). The parody of the four wise clerks of Oxenford with their definition of blunderbuss of course does exactly this, sug-

---

10 A point related to Tolkien's work on folk narrative – the Inkling Adam Fox wrote a "tale in four books" using rhymed couplets, *Old King Coel*, published in 1937. Tolkien alludes to the book, although not by name, in his letter to Stanley Unwin. In his "Preface" to *Old King Coel*, Fox states that his purpose is to please (shades of Philip Sidney!) and to follow his impression of modern pictures. "They look at first gaze to be childish stuff. But they are not, and the pleasure in them grows and lasts" (vi). Two Inklings sussing out childish stuff.

gesting the failure of the kind of scholarship which Tolkien had castigated so humourously in "*Beowulf*: The Monsters and the Critics" with his "Jabberwocky" allusion. One could argue that all Tolkien's narratives are devoted to breaking down this barrier, but the quality is particularly strong in his nonsense.

The definition of "blunderbuss" (to say nothing of its anachronistic presence) exemplifies how nonsense challenges conventional communication. The definition was apparently first included in response to a query from one of the children, but its survival through revisions satisfies another purpose. Nonsense, says McGillis, "draws attention to the inevitable slippage between signifier and signified" (156) – that is, slippage between a name and the thing it names; if one word has such slippage, how much more the attempt to completely explain one word with several words. Chesterton talks about how the shapes of things defy our "trivial definitions" in his "Defense of Nonsense" (n.p.). Marnie Parsons argues that "When Lewis Carroll and Edward Lear take definitions and classifications literally, Nonsense is the 'predictable' result" (12). Tolkien himself gave an opinion on definitions in a letter to his Aunt Jane Neave.

> As for *plenilune* and *argent*, they are beautiful words *before* they are understood – I wish I could have the pleasure of meeting them for the first time again! – and how is one to know them till one does meet them? And surely the first meeting should be in a living context, and not in a dictionary, like dried flowers in a hortus siccus! (*L* 310)

Definitions are ripe for ridicule in nonsense. The reality of Farmer Giles' blunderbuss defies the definition offered by the Oxenford Clerks, judging by all the 'nots' in the passage which follows the definition. And if there were any more nonsensical result of its use, it is that the giant goes home thinking he's been stung by a fierce insect and only at the end of the tale does he learn otherwise from the dragon. The giant can no more recognise reality than the definition can reflect it.

Nonsense "delights in things of the body, including food and drink" says McGillis (163) and he suggests that the riot in the pleasures of bodily existence in nonsense is almost carnivalesque. Whether that specific quality fits *Farmer Giles* may be argued, but the tale does contain many comic depictions of bodies, physical contortions, and ungainly movements; it delights in frailty and deformity and humiliation (of the dragon and the King, at least, both of whom are characters with inflated opinions of themselves). The giant is almost totally described by his body and its calamitous effects: he is near-sighted and rather deaf, while his head has often "left his feet to look after themselves" (FGH 105); he doesn't just kill the cow Galatea; he flattens her. Giles's assault on the giant is full of hilarious physicality, for the giant's "large, ugly face" appears incongruously over the top of a hill and so Giles takes a startled shot with the fully loaded blunderbuss and hits the giant in the eye and nose. The dragon is prone to making bad jokes about the taste of the people he's eaten, while satiation is often his downfall. Giles's wife Agatha is said to become "a queen of great size and majesty [...] There was no getting around Queen Agatha – at least it was a long walk" (FGH 162). There is a great deal of drink spilt down throats in the village, particularly Giles': "Next market day he got enough free drink to float a boat: that is to say, he nearly had his fill" (FGH 112). It takes several days of ale-quaffing for Giles to find his courage to go dragon hunting and he nearly gives up the hunt to return for his dinner before coming upon the dragon unexpectedly (FGH 130). At court there's a good bit of feasting on Dragon's Tail, not the real dragon's tail, but a culinary concoction. Giles' armour is a regaling of details related to the condition of things, which mostly are old, dusty, rusty, second-hand, and the butt of the dragon's jokes. The retreat between Giles and the dragon emphasises puffing and blowing, bawling and shouting, as if Giles were watching a mere horse race (FGH 134). Giles's tribute to the king is "six oxtails and a pint of bitter" (FGH 161) – a comedown from the real dragon's tail of historical legend. And Garm repeatedly contends with the dragon's actual tail. There are a great many tangible things of the body in the world of Ham.

McGillis argues that names are important in Nonsense and lists some of them that have become household names in our time: Jumlies, Jabberwocky, Snark. To his list can be added Lear's Pobbles. In Tolkien's *Farmer Giles* tale, names are foregrounded and usually a humorous incongruity between characters and their names prevails – a prominence which does not pertain to *The Hobbit*, as Tom Shippey has pointed out (Shippey 96). The narrator quickly dispenses with Giles's Latin name, suggesting that the current age has less time for the leisurely pursuit of naming. Then we are told there is both book-Latin and dog-Latin, although of course Garm speaks only the Vulgar tongue and not dog-Latin (a particular joke about the two, since dog-Latin usually involves the translating, very poorly, of the Vulgar tongue into Latin, that is, a mongrel Latin). As McGillis notes parenthetically, "Latin has proved a useful vehicle for nonsense" (165). When the dragon and Giles first meet, each warily refuses to provide his name. When the townspeople encourage Giles to go a-dragon hunting, they invent a plethora of majestically-sounding names for him and for his sword; after his victory and crowning, Giles is given multiple titles and more names. The dragon has a preposterously mixed Greek and Latin name; the cow is named for a sea nymph from Greek mythology whose name means "she who is milk-white". (Or, as Tolkien himself suggests jokingly, "Goddess of milk" (*L* 423)). Giles' wife's name is Agatha, but she is more the nagging shrew than a godly woman or wife. (Her command to "drown that dog in the morning" has all the arbitrary silliness of the Red Queen's "Off with her head" as Garm never deserves the slurs and threats flung at him). The blacksmith, the conversely named Sunny Sam, gloomily foretells a bad fate for the meeting on the feast day of two canonised popes: "Hilarious and Felix! I don't like the sound of them" (138). The giant has no name while "Garmr" is a ferocious watchdog at the gate of Hell in Norse mythology. The concluding analysis of place names lampoons philology. "*Must* a name mean something?" asks Alice of Humpty Dumpty (Carroll 182). Much of the fun in *Farmer Giles* asks just what meaning belongs in the possible incongruities of a name. If Tolkien's adolescent language inventions brought pleasure in contemplating the relationship of new sound to meaning, what can at least be said of *Farmer Giles of Ham* is that it gives pleasure in contemplating the incongruity of sound to concept in the naming of names.

Throughout his essay McGillis argues that parody is a strong element in nonsense, whether parody of overwrought seriousness in the traditional love lyric, or of nature poetry, or of canonical poets such as Wordsworth, Tennyson, Coleridge, Byron, even the pre-Raphaelites. He argues, through a complex argument which I won't rehearse here, that "Jabberwocky" revisions the heroic world of *Beowulf*. (The first stanza of the poem was first published with the title "Stanza of Anglo-Saxon Poetry".) Whether Tolkien knew of this stanza (which is printed in mock Old English script) in the periodical *Mish-Mash* and Carroll's accompanying parody of critical interpretation and poetic communication, I cannot say.[11] What does seem plausible is that *Farmer Giles* is a parody of heroic dragon hunting stories.[12] (It was, after all, written roughly in the same years as *The Hobbit*.) The absurd dialogues of Giles and Chrysophylax defeat any expectations of violence and turn their encounters into battles of wits. They lack the riddling perplexities of Alice's conversation with Humpty-Dumpty and the Red Queen – Tolkien was a linguist, not a mathematician – but they play with knightly behaviour and courtly civility. They begin with the completely unexpected greetings of "Good morning" (131) and the Dragon's "Then we meet by good luck […] The pleasure is mine" is ironically reiterated on their second meeting by Giles (148). On both occasions neither characters' words truthfully represent their motivations and the essence of game which surrounds their conversation seems to be one each recognises; the narrator tells us that Chrysophylax licks his lips as "a sign of amusement" (131) rather than gustatory expectation. And of course the challenge is made all the more ludicrous by the paradox of his challenger – not a knight but "a bold farmer" and a ginger to boot (133). Both eagerly proclaim their desire not to kill each other, a reversal of the expected situation. Giles even taunts Chrysophylax's bargaining with the word "nonsense" (135) – an exclamation of disbelief rather than "absurd" – but the incongruity is identified and extends to much of their relationship. The two do manage to communicate, but find a conclusion completely at odds with dragon hunting adventures. This is not quite as serious as McGillis's claim that nonsense through parody targets the privilege of canonised works (156). It is rather, simply, fun, possibly an asterisk version of dragon tales in the same way that Tom Shippey has described Tolkien's philological work with poems and nursery rhymes.

Farmer Giles of Ham is not the only work of Tolkien to open with a playful preface. *The Adventures of Tom Bombadil* also has a preface which imitates scholarly style, although it is pseudo-serious rather than sarcastic. It explicitly identifies the contents of its book as nonsense or "nonsense rhyme" (ATB 169) – and this is not *Farmer Giles'* nonsense. Of the Red Book we are told that many of

---

11 "This is an obscure, but yet deeply-affecting relic of ancient Poetry"(Carroll, *Annotated Alice* 149). To this point should be added Carroll's use of the obsolete and archaic Old English term "fit" (or fytt) for the eight parts of "The Hunting of the Snark". Tolkien's beloved *Sir Gawain and the Green Knight* has but four fits, with Tolkien's extensive discussion focussing on the important third fit.
12 See Schneidewind and Honegger ("Good Dragon" 49-53).

the carelessly written verses "are nonsense, now often unintelligible even when legible, or half-remembered fragments" (169). This attitude towards nonsense sounds similar not to McGillis's study of Victorian nonsense but to comments about Nonsense made by George Orwell in 1945; the idea had possibly become quite common by then. For Orwell, the bulk of English folk nonsense lies

> in nursery rhymes and scraps of folk poetry, some of which may not have been strictly nonsensical at the start, but have become so because their original application has been forgotten. (Orwell n.p.)

Orwell suggests that when Edgar in *King Lear*, disguised as Mad Tom – there's that name again – quotes "Pillicock sat on Pillicock hill" and other refrains, Edgar is uttering nonsense, that is, fragments coming from largely forgotten ballads. Tom Shippey (36) has suggested that Tolkien "tried his hand" at two versions of "The Man in the Moon" in order to "provide a narrative and semi-rational frame for the string of totally irrational non sequiturs which we now call 'nursery rhymes'." For Shippey, the Man in the Moon Poems are possible reconstructions of a primary text that has been lost; his term is "asterisk" poems. They are an attempt to make meaningful what now appears irrational or incongruous. It is, however, also a sign of "nonsense's polyphony" (McGillis, 157, referring to the theorist Lecercle) that Tolkien can produce two different ur-texts.

Thomas Honegger has also examined this motif in a comprehensive account of both western European and Middle-earth literature in which he presents three ways in which Tolkien developed the motif. Honegger shows that "the complex and often contradictory depiction of the Man in the Moon in the real world is matched by a likewise intricately woven (and often contradictory) tradition of the Man-in-the-moon figure in Tolkien's universe" ("Man in the Moon" 57-58); this suggests a studied and deliberate rather than random development in Tolkien's work on nursery rhymes. Honegger also shows how Tolkien was "familiar with and interested in the theory that postulated a descent or dwindling of myth into legend and then into folk-tales, märchen and nursery tales" ("Man in the Moon" 47) – evidence which reinforces the validity of Tolkien's own comments about nursery rhymes. And, thirdly, Honegger argues that Tolkien is not simply filling out an asterisk: "[Tolkien] thus makes it not merely an 'asterisk' link between the 'real' world nursery rhyme and an allegedly lost late medieval and early modern Man-in-the-Moon folk-poem tradition, but the descendant of an independent Middle-earth tradition" ("Man in the Moon" 47). In other words, Tolkien applies not only philological theories of language development in his creative writing; he uses close study of narrative structure as well; the narratological structures he observed in medieval literature he applied to his own stories.

What is particularly intriguing is how early in Tolkien's ideas on nonsense this thought about unintelligible fragments appears. And here I return to where I opened this essay, for in his college talk (as Flieger describes it, *SK* xi) on *The Kalevala* in 1914 Tolkien describes his undergraduate ideas about how tales and legends have come down to us. Tolkien draws a distinction between the Finnish tales and the Welsh tales of the Mabinogion. Of the latter, he says, "there is in many places a thick dust of a no longer understood tradition lying on them; strings of names and allusions that no longer have any meanings, that were already nonsense for the bards who related them" (*SK* 107). Tolkien had recourse to this idea later for his 1953 W.P. Ker Memorial Lecture on *Sir Gawain and the Green Knight* at the University of Glasgow. At the risk of too long a quotation, I will copy the thoughts which are relevant to his concept of nonsense.

> For [the poem] belongs to that literary kind which has deep roots in the past, deeper even than its author was aware. It is made of tales often told before and elsewhere, and of elements that derive from remote times [...]
>
> It is an interesting question: what is this flavour, this atmosphere, this virtue that such *rooted* works have, and which compensates for the inevitable flaws and imperfect adjustments that must appear, when plots, motives, symbols are rehandled and pressed into service of the changed minds of a later time [...] Behind our poem stalk the figures of elder myths, and through the lines are heard echoes of ancient cults, beliefs and symbols remote from the consciousness of an educated moralist of the late fourteenth century. His story is not *about* those old thing, but it receives part of its life, its vividness, its tension from them. (SGGK 72-73 *passim*)

I hope my argument will not be considered a piece of nonsense if I suggest that Tom, Goldberry and the House of Bombadil might well be seen to function similarly to this kind of reused ancient tale. While *their* author was no doubt aware of what he was doing, the Bombadil characters can be seen to echo the early versions of his own fay creatures in the Legendarium.

As is well-known, Tom and Goldberry first appeared in a poem in the *Oxford Magazine* in 1934, a poem reproduced later in *The Adventures of Tom Bombadil*, and showing traces of inspiration from the sad tale of Aino and Väinämöinen in cantos 3, 4, and 5 of volume one of *The Kalevala*. Yet it is their similarity to characters in very early versions of the Legendarium that I wish to refer to. As Christopher Tolkien pointed out[13] the "lesser spirits" in this early version of "The Coming of the Valar" did not survive into *The Silmarillion*.

> About them [i.e. Aulë and Palúrien] fared a great host who are the sprites of trees and woods, of dale and forest and mountain-side, or those that sing amid the grass at morning and chant among the standing corn at eve. These are the Nermir and the Tavari, Nandini and Orossi, brownies, fays, pixies, leprawns [ie, leprechauns] and what else are they not called, for their number is very great: yet must they not be confused with the Eldar, for they were born before the world and are older than its oldest, and are not of it, but laugh at it much, for had they not somewhat to do with its making, so that it is for the most part a play for them; but the Eldar are of the world and love it with a great and burning love, and are wistful in all their happiness for that reason. (*LT I* 66)

Tom and Goldberry are not pixies; nor are they winged or antennaed creatures from "Goblin Feet"; nor are they Maiar or Valar or Eru, or Yavanna and Aulë. However, it is difficult not to consider that these "sprites of trees and woods", "who are older than the world's oldest" and who laugh much, have come down to us in *The Lord of the Rings* in the enigmatic characters of Tom and Goldberry, about whom many legions of fans and scholars have created many theories, because they are so seemingly strange and incompatible with other elements in the story. For comparison, here is the well-known passage from *The Lord of the Rings* where Tom explains who he is to his hobbit guests.

> Eldest, that's what I am. Mark my words, my friends: Tom remembers the first raindrop and the first acorn. He made paths before the Big People, and saw the little People arriving. He was here before the Kings and the graves and the Barrow-wights. When the Elves passed westward, Tom was here already,

---

13 "In the later work [the Silmarillion] there is no trace of any such explanation of the 'pixie' element in the world's population: the Maiar are little referred to, and certainly not said to include such beings as 'sing amid the grass at morning and chant among the standing corn at eve'." (*LT I* 80)

before the seas were bent. He knew the dark under the stars when it was fearless – before the Dark Lord came from Outside. (*LotR* 129)

As well, Tom's singing bears some euphonious resemblance to songs of Tinfang Warble, at least in the earliest version of the eponymous song in "The Chaining of Melkor" chapter of *The Book of Lost Tales*: "Oh the hoot! O the hoot! / How he trillups on his flute! O the hoot of Tinfang Warble!" (*LT I* 108). Tom as well in *The Lord of the Rings* is said to be singing possibly "an ancient language" (143). Doubtless Tolkien is using Tom as an opportunity to hint at the long ages of the mythology before the Great Years of the Third Age. However, it is not inconceivable that Tolkien could have incorporated in his later writing rejected characters or ideas of the early versions of his own mythology, in a clever imitation of the folk narratives that have come down to us as nonsense because of unintelligible or inconsistent contexts, consistent with his knowledge of the descent of great mythic tales, as Honegger has argued. This would of course have been a personal, private satisfaction, as the construction of private languages was. As Tolkien said about his doubts over publishing the Silmarillion, part of the attraction of *The Lord of the Rings* is "the glimpses of a large history in the background" (*L* 333). It is not by chance that the first two volumes of *The History of Middle-earth* are called *The Book of Lost Tales* and not by chance that Tolkien drew upon his early tales as the author of *Sir Gawain and the Green Knight* did with the early tale of magic and fairy that came down him. Tom and Goldberry echo those very early tales without fitting seamlessly into the later tale.

To return to less speculative thought and to more characteristics of Nonsense as a genre: McGillis observes that "much nonsense comes with a visual aid" (160). For him, illustrations such as those accompanying Lear's limericks complicate the decoding of the limericks. *Alice in Wonderland* is renowned for Tenniel's original illustrations as well as for the great variety of illustrators coming after him who have tried their hand at depicting Wonderland. Pauline Baynes was asked to illustrate the Bombadil book specifically because Tolkien had been so satisfied with her illustrations for *Farmer Giles of Ham*.

> If I dare say so, the things sent to you [...] were conceived as a series of very definite, clear and precise pictures – fantastical, or nonsensical perhaps, but not dreamlike! And I thought of you, because you seem able to produce wonder-

ful pictures with a touch of 'fantasy', but primarily bright and clear visions of things that one might really see. (*L* 312)

Tolkien clearly had a definite sense of what he was doing with these poems, and that sense included a particular notion of nonsense as something dealing very tangibly with the thingness of things, a quality McGillis also argues in his study of nonsense (164). Parsons calls this quality "the 'thisness' of a thing" in discussing Gerard Manley Hopkins' "nonsensicality" (Parsons 72).

The "Preface" to the Bombadil book also identifies another quality of nonsense, one which returns us to "A Secret Vice". The stanza of Bilbo's "When winter first begins to bite" is clearly offered as a fragment of nonsense (ATB 171) which delights in pleasing, harmonious sound; this quality is identified specifically as Hobbit taste. The poem "Errantry" is described as "another kind which seems to have amused Hobbits: a rhyme or story which returns to its own beginning, and so may be recited until the hearers revolt" (ATB 170). We are told, as well, that Hobbits

> are fond of strange words, and of rhyming and metrical tricks – in their simplicity Hobbits evidently regarded such things as virtues or graces, though they were, no doubt, mere imitations of Elvish practices. They are also, at least on the surface, lighthearted or frivolous, though sometimes one may uneasily suspect that more is meant than meets the ear. (ATB 174)

Note the word "ear". "Errantry" is replete with rhythm, euphonious sounds, assonance – the kind of qualities that Tolkien enjoined especially in the lecture "A Secret Vice". These points suggest that this "Preface" plays with an important part of Tolkien's concept of nonsense – a kind that McGillis does not consider because he accepts Noel Malcolm's argument that "nonsense existed only in a literary culture [...] [because it is a genre] deeply self-conscious about form [which] foregrounds such features of language as onomastics, rhythm, rhyme, stanza shapes and rhetorical devices – especially paradox, prosopoeia, repetition, alliteration, and paronomasia" (McGillis 155-156 *passim*). Yet rhetorical features of language can be found in children's nursery rhyme as well as satisfy hobbits' taste in literature. One need not know the formal rhetorical terms to intuit the music of words. Chesterton again is relevant here.

> Now the old nursery rhymes were honestly directed to give children pleasure. Many of them have genuine elements of poetry, but they are not primarily

meant to be poetry, because they are simply meant to be pleasure. The imagery of it is exactly what is wanted for the first movements of imagination when it experiments in incongruity. For it is full of familiar objects in fantastic conjunction. ("Child Psychology" n.p.)

Here again is the idea of pleasure in language play, something that for Tolkien can belong to any and all, not only the literary elite. It is particularly appropriate for Hobbits to favour such nonsense, because a taste for incongruity in rhyme is a way to avoid incongruity in real life, a trait most Hobbits display, except the Tooks. McGillis argues that "The Victorians' delight in nonsense [...] fits with their delight in things simple and straightforward" (168). True enough of hobbits too.

Orwell addresses another point which very clearly suggests how extensive the landscapes of nonsense can be and how Tolkien can be seen working within that terrain.

> Lear was one of the first writers to deal in pure fantasy, with imaginary countries and made-up words, without any satirical purpose. His poems are not all of them equally nonsensical; some of them get their effect by a perversion of logic, but they are all alike in that their underlying feeling is sad and not bitter. They express a kind of amiable lunacy, a natural sympathy with whatever is weak and absurd. (Orwell n.p.)

"Fantasy," "imaginary countries," "made-up words" are all eminently applicable also to Tolkien's works while "amiable lunacy" suits Tom Bombadil as well as "Errantry" and the two Men in the Moon poems. The final three – "The Hoard", "The Sea-Bell", and "The Last Ship" – are far less ludic but their strongest characteristic is a deeply sad undertone of loss. These are not lighthearted poems about nothing, yet they hint at a world beyond the mundane and banal one we all know. Tolkien and Orwell share a similar understanding of nonsense.

Other characteristics of McGillis' study of nonsense can be found in *The Hobbit*, and not merely the euphony of the elves' Tra la la lally song. That is exactly what the narrator calls it: "So they laughed and sang in the trees; and pretty fair nonsense I daresay you think it. Not that they would care; they would only laugh all the more if you told them so" (*H* 68). Yet there is another similarity as well. The song operates similarly to the function of nonsense to provide escape from the confines of reality into something less predictably constraining, something related to "ironizing at a distance", for the elves are attempting to lighten the spirits of the travellers by making fun of their travails. So also is the lullaby nonsense that the elves sing to Bilbo in the final chapter, with its incongruous blossoming stars, flowering moon, and bright windows of Night (*H* 358); its gentle cadences are a release into the realm of sleep. Nonsense, not simply humour, is a strong feature of *The Hobbit*.

First, the story is consistent with other works in the nonsense tradition in having a dual audience of child and adult. Second, a constant theme is to play with meaning. Gandalf's first greeting with Bilbo and the jokes about what "Good Morning!" means can stand beside any of Alice's absurd dialogues in Wonderland and the conversation of Farmer Giles and Crysophylax (*H* 14-16 *passim*): "'What a lot of things you do use *Good morning* for!' said Gandalf. 'Now you mean that you want to get rid of me'" (*H* 16). The greeting involves as well joking about names – "I am Gandalf and Gandalf means me" (*H* 16). It is no mistake that Gandalf searches for a thief in the Took family and the extensive explication of the mark on the door provides another bit of zaniness about meaning – in fact, there is quite a bit of meaning given for a single mark. Third, the story of Golfimbul's defeat and the genesis of the game of golf combines a common theme of dismemberment with another joke about a name – and it's about a rabbit hole as well. A fourth example: the dwarves' washing-up song lampoons Bilbo's fuss and bother about domestic decorum (*H* 24) – another example of nonsense deflating high seriousness shown to mundane matters (McGillis 158).

Interestingly, nothing in the depiction of the trolls is nonsense – slapstick, I would argue; nor is there any nonsense in the queer lodgings of Beorn, nor in the Laketown events, nor in the scenes with the goblins inside the mountain. The riddle game with Gollum is too sacred to deserve nonsense; it forms the basis for Bilbo's heroism, where word replaces sword – not quite a vorpal sword; it is an intensely profound game of survival without any pomposity to it; the riddling with Smaug does not rise to the level of absurdity, although again we have play with names, a strategy for which the narrator praises Bilbo. Nor is the goblins' song of taunting and ridicule in "Out of the Frying-Pan into the Fire" quite nonsense: it is too uncomfortably close to what likely is to happen;

there is nothing incongruously pretentious about the situation. This absence is consistent with McGillis's argument that Victorian nonsense "avoids the overtly serious" (163).

Yet for all its focus on tangible things and physicality, nonsense, McGillis suggests, "reminds us that the world we know is perhaps less tangible than we might like to believe" (165). Perhaps this is one reason why Bilbo's loss of reputation does not matter. This characteristic is argued slightly differently by Chesterton:

> So long as we regard a tree as an obvious thing, naturally and reasonably created for a giraffe to eat, we cannot properly wonder at it. It is when we consider it as a prodigious wave of the living soil sprawling up to the skies for no reason in particular that we take off our hats [...] Everything has in fact another side to it, like the moon, the patroness of nonsense. ("Defense" n.p.)

(It is, by the way, in this essay that Chesterton claims Carroll "would cheerfully call the sun green".) This wonder is also what happens when trees become Ents. Again, Tolkien's nonsense challenges a common sense approach to the world.

This quality of wonder might also explain Tom Bombadil's lack of seriousness. Tom Bombadil's hat is clearly a runcible hat. His verse obviously reflects the pure pleasure of sound without communicative effect, to say nothing of their simple rhymes and refrains and euphonious sounds.[14] His mere words have the power to heal or resolve, as is shown in his defeats of Old Man Willow and the Barrow Wight. Even Tom's prose is rhythmic.[15] McGillis argues that a similar quality is a feature of Victorian nonsense, particularly the style of George MacDonald in *At the Back of the North Wind*, where "language aspir[es] to the condition of pure sound" (166) and develops an "incantatory force" such as is found in nursery rhymes (167). This might be an appropriate time to point out that "absurd" comes from the Latin, meaning "out of tune, jarring, inharmonious" as well as "out of harmony with reason or propriety" (*OED*). Tolkien referred to "word music" at both the beginning of his academic career and later. In discussing *The Kalevala* he noted the jolly sound created when

---

14 Parsons discusses David Sonstroem's claim of the primacy of rhyme in nonsense when analyzing Hopkin's "musical subtext": "the nonsense poet's practice is first to make rhyme and have it come out to the embarrassment of sense" (71).
15 Verlyn Flieger points to the similarity of Tom's "rhythmic, chanted speech" to the style of *The Kalevala* (*SK* 141).

meaningless words are inserted to echo communicative words (pankerelle and Penkerelle, Ihvenia and ahvenia, Tuimenia and taimeania) (*SK* 77). He returns to discuss this "merry freedom" in his essay on language creation when he refers to the "unsophisticated days when even Homer could pervert a word to suit sound music" and again mentions these Finnish echoes as "notes in a phonetic rune struck to harmonize" (*ASV* 33). Dimitra Fimi's footnote points out that Tolkien is "quoting nearly verbatim" from C.N.E. Eliot's *A Finnish Grammar* (*ASV* 58-59). The idea may have been Eliot's originally, but Tolkien made it his standard.

The word "nonsense" is used on two occasions to describe Tom and both involve sound. Frodo first hears Tom when he has been calling desperately for help as Merry and Pippin are trapped and swallowed by Old Man Willow:

> He turned around and listened, and soon there could be no doubt: someone was singing a song; a deep glad voice was singing carelessly and happily, but it was singing nonsense:
>
> *Hey dol! Merry dol! Ring a dong dillo* […]
>
> Half hopeful and half afraid of some new danger, Frodo and Sam now both stood still. Suddenly out of a long string of nonsense-words (or so they seemed) the voice rose up […] (*LotR* 116)

This is quite obviously ironizing from a distance. The second use occurs as Tom leads them away from the Barrow and on towards their journey to Bree:

> Tom sang most of the time, but it was chiefly nonsense, or else perhaps a strange language unknown to hobbits, an ancient language whose words were mainly those of wonder and delight. (*LotR* 143)

This is Tolkien's specific point about language, the communication of thought through sound even when "unintelligible". This is, after all, the effect on the hobbits of Gildor singing "O Elbereth": "It was singing in the fair elven-tongue, of which Frodo knew only a little, and the others knew nothing. Yet the sound blending with the melody seemed to shape itself in their thought into words which they only partly understood" (*LotR* 77-78). So Tom Bombadil not only qualifies as a nonsense figure because of the possibility that he was included to add an incongruous or unintelligible story from earlier times (a private narratological satisfaction for Tolkien), but also because he represents so many of the attractions of oral language for Tolkien. Nonsensical Tom does not communicate meaning, not for all our desire to determine what he signifies. Tom simply is.

Both Frodo and Sam have recourse to nonsense verse shortly after leaving Tom. Frodo's reciting of the "Man in the Moon" has calamitous consequences, but nonetheless it provides a clear example of the social context that Tolkien likely thought surrounded the nonsense of nursery rhymes in their ancient form: delight in incongruity. Sam himself, when invited to sing to cheer the group after the terrifying conflict with the Black Riders on Weathertop, recites a rhyme apparently of his own invention which he specifically calls "nonsense" rather than "proper poetry" (*LotR* 201), the Stone Troll song, which first saw the light of creation in Tolkien's "Songs for the Philologists".[16] Whether this was something Sam recalls, or something we are to understand he invents after the influence of Tom, is not clear, but Frodo says it shows a quality in Sam that Frodo has never seen before; Sam is the hobbit most intrigued by Tom. The Stone Troll song features all the traditional characteristics of nonsense, mixing the morbid with the comic, delighting in rhyme and repetition of lines, and retelling an absurd encounter over family bones. In the version of the song which Tolkien sings in a You Tube video, the names are different; in Sam's version, Tom challenges the troll, in Tolkien's, John. Then again, when Sam, Frodo and Gollum are wrapped in fear of the Black Riders outside Cirith Ungol, and ever more horrifying warriors march into Mordor, Sam responds by thinking of Oliphaunts and recites the Oliphaunt song. The Black Riders on two occasions motivate Sam to recite nonsense verse. When finished, he adds "that's a rhyme we have in the Shire. Nonsense maybe, and maybe not" (*LotR* 633). Significant also is Frodo's response: "He had laughed in the midst of all his cares when Sam trotted out the old fireside rhyme of *Oliphaunt*, and the laugh had released him from hesitation" (*LotR* 632); Frodo then makes the ominous decision to follow Gollum. Sam's recital of what amounts to folk nonsense verse in these contexts clearly suggests the value of nonsense which McGillis (168-69) claims:

---

16 Thanks to Jessica Yates for reminding me of the "Songs for the Philologists".

> Nonsense for the Victorians was, paradoxically, a means of staying grounded, of returning to the shore after sailing the dark, broad seas [...] this eminently loony genre of poetry kept the Victorians sane.

When Sam Gamgee hears from Robin Smallbarrow that the pubs have been closed as part of the new regime in the Shire, he calls such closure "nonsense", and here the word most definitely does mean "rubbish" (*LotR* 979).

I have followed a meandering route around Tolkien's many uses of the word and the concept, from unique definitions to narrative theory and linguistic thought, which demonstrate the close relationship between language and nonsense in Tolkien's corpus. If only Frodo had been able to enjoy nonsense after his return to the Shire … but as Tolkien noted in *A Secret Vice*, "Wars are not favourable to delicate pleasures" (8). Tolkien's nonsense shares a great many qualities with Nonsense in his cultural context, both Victorian Nonsense and inherited folk nonsense. However, Tolkien also developed a unique understanding about the significance of beauty and pleasure in language, separate from the communicative aspect of language, and delighting in the unintelligible and the incongruous. I close with Tolkien's observation to his Aunt Jane Neave, that "adults [...] have stopped listening to the sound [of words] because they think they know the meaning" (*L* 310).

About the Author

MAUREEN F. MANN holds a PhD in English literature from the University of Toronto and has taught at Wilfrid Laurier University, York University, and the University of Toronto; she is now retired. Her interests include Victorian and medieval literature, fantasy, and conspiracy and detective fiction, in addition to Tolkien.

List of Abbreviations

ASV: see Tolkien, *A Secret Vice*.

ATB: see Tolkien, "The Adventures of Tom Bombadil"

BMC: see Tolkien, "Beowulf: The Monsters and the Critics"

FGH: see Tolkien, "Farmer Giles of Ham"

H: see Tolkien, *The Hobbit*

L: see Tolkien, *Letters by J.R.R. Tolkien*

LotR: see Tolkien, *The Lord of the Rings*

LT I: see Tolkien, *The Book of Lost Tales I*

SK: see Tolkien, *The Story of Kullervo*

Bibliography

BARTHES, Roland. *The Pleasure of the Text*. Trans. Richard Miller. New York: Hill & Wang, 1975.

CARROLL, Lewis. *The Annotated Alice: The Definitive Edition Alice's Adventures in Wonderland & Through the Looking Glass*. New York: Norton, 2000.

Alice's Adventures in Wonderland and Through the Looking-Glass. London: Penguin, 1980.

CARPENTER, Humphrey. *J.R.R. Tolkien: A Biography*. London: Allen & Unwin, 1977.

CHESTERTON, G.K. "Child Psychology and Nonsense." (1921) http://www.chesterton.org/child-psychology-and-nonsense/

"A Defense of Nonsense." *The Defendant*. Project Gutenberg. http://www.gutenberg.org/files/12245/12245-h/12245- h.htm#A_DEFENCE_OF_NONSENSE.

"On Smart Novelists and the Smart Set." http://www.gutenberg.org/files/470/470-h/470-h.htm#chap14

FERRÉ, Vincent. "The Rout of the King: Tolkien's Reading on Arthurian Kingship – *Farmer Giles of Ham* and *The Homecoming of Beorhtnoth*." *Tolkien's Shorter Works*. Ed. Margaret HILEY and Frank WEINREICH. Zurich and Jena: Walking Tree Publishers, 2008. 59-76.

FIMI, Dimitra. *Tolkien, Race and Cultural History: From Fairies to Hobbits*. Basingstoke, Hampshire UK: Palgrave MacMillan, 2010.

Fox, Adam. *Old King Coel: A Rhymed Tale in Four Books*. London: Oxford University Press, 1937.

Honegger, Thomas. "The Man in the Moon: Structural Depth in Tolkien." *Root and Branch: Approaches Towards Understanding Tolkien*. 2nd ed. Eds. Peter Buchs and Thomas Honegger. Zurich and Berne: Walking Tree Publishers, 2005. 9-70.

"A good dragon is hard to find or, from *draconitas* to *draco*." *Good Dragons are Rare. An Inquiry into Literary Dragons East and West*. Eds. Fanfan Chen and Thomas Honegger. Frankfurt a.M.: Peter Lang, 2009. 27-59.

McGillis, Roderick. "Nonsense." *A Companion to Victorian Poetry*. Eds. Richard Cronin, Alison Chapman and Anthony H. Harrison. Oxford: Blackwell, 2002.

Orwell, George. "Nonsense Poetry (1945)." *Fifty Orwell Essays*. Project Gutenberg Australia. http://gutenberg.net.au/ebooks03/0300011h.html#part29 .

Parsons, Marnie. *Touch Monkeys: Nonsense Strategies for Reading Twentieth-Century Poetry*. Toronto: University of Toronto Press, 1994.

Schneidewind, Friedhelm. "*Farmer Giles of Ham*: the Prototype of a Humorous Dragon Story." *Tolkien's Shorter Works*. Eds. Margaret Hiley and Frank Weinreich. Zurich and Jena: Walking Tree Publishers, 2008. 77-100.

Scull, Christina & Wayne G. Hammond. *The J.R.R. Tolkien Companion and Guide: Reader's Guide*. Boston: Houghton Mifflin, 2006.

Shippey, Tom. *The Road to Middle-earth*. Revised and expanded edition. Boston: Houghton Mifflin, 2003.

Smith, Ross. *Inside Language. Linguistic and Aesthetic Theory in Tolkien*. Zurich and Jena: Walking Tree Publishers, 2011.

Tolkien, J.R.R. "The Adventures of Tom Bombadil." *Tales From the Perilous Realm*. London: Harper Collins, 2008. 167-242.

"Beowulf: The Monsters and the Critics". *The Monsters and the Critics and Other Essays*. Ed. Christopher Tolkien. London: Harper Collins, 2006. 5-48.

The Book of Lost Tales I. Ed. Christopher Tolkien. London: HarperCollins, 2002.

"Farmer Giles of Ham." *Tales From the Perilous Realm*. London: HarperCollins, 2008. 99-165.

The Hobbit or There and Back Again. London: HarperCollins, 1998.

The Letters of J.R.R. Tolkien. 1981. Ed. Humphrey Carpenter. London: HarperCollins, 2006.

The Lord of the Rings. London: HarperCollins, 1995.

A Secret Vice. Ed. Dimitra FIMI and Andrew HIGGINS. London: HarperCollins, 2016.

"Sir Gawain and the Green Knight." *The Monsters and the Critics and Other Essays*. Ed. Christopher TOLKIEN. London: HarperCollins, 2006. 72-108.

The Story of Kullervo. Ed. Verlyn FLIEGER. London: HarperCollins, 2015.

WELLS, Carolyn. "Introduction." *A Nonsense Anthology*. New York: Scribner's, 1905.

Jef Murray
The Balrog Hanging Up His Wings

Alastair Whyte

A Fountain of Mirth: Laughter in Arda

Abstract

The relationship between laughter and critical thinking is an expanding area of investigation for the understanding of human behaviour. To this point, however, insufficient attention has been afforded to understanding laughter when reading texts as both a narrative event and a signifier. This paper will investigate how laughter informs both the construction of the "Fairy-Story" and the representation of its themes. In the works of J.R.R. Tolkien, including *The Silmarillion* and *The Lord of the Rings*, despite differences of race, gender and moral standing, characters consistently laugh: humans and non-humans, heroes and villains, in joy and in contempt. With reference to Robert Provine's scientific investigation into laughter as well as traditional laughter theories, this paper will examine how Tolkien uses laughter in his texts in relation to themes of morality, power and the inevitability of change. This paper will therefore argue that Tolkien takes a flexible approach to the role of laughter in the dynamics of morality and history and places them within his broader theodicy as explored in *Morgoth's Ring*. The paper aims as such to provide a greater depth of understanding to the place of laughter in Tolkien's work and how this deepens his understanding of the questions and themes which are so integral to the narratives of Arda as well as enhancing the appreciation of Tolkien's work as a corpus of interconnected texts.

Characters in the narratives of J.R.R. Tolkien consistently laugh. This is one feature which occurs throughout the entire length of the history of Arda, Tolkien's mythic, prehistoric Earth, despite this grand narrative featuring an enormous cast of characters of numerous "races" from Hobbits to angelic Ainur. It can be identified in examples from the beginning of Tolkien's mythic history[1] to its end at the conclusion of *The Lord of the Rings*. If any activity in Tolkien's works is universal among characters, it is certainly laughter. In *The Lord of the Rings* alone, forms of the verb "to laugh" including "laughed" and "laughter" are used on at least two hundred and forty-one occasions. It is similarly, if not equally, proliferate in *The Silmarillion* and *The Hobbit*, and none of these

---

[1] The term, if not the concept, of 'mythic Prehistory' goes back to John D. Rateliff (see his paper "'And All the Days of Her Life Are Forgotten' *The Lord of the Rings* as Mythic Prehistory").

instances account for further references to mockery, jest and mirth. Laughter is often a casual occurrence, commonly found in the facetious conversations of hobbits, but it is also dwelt upon at various times, such as when Sauron laughs three times in mockery of the deluded venture of Ar-Pharazôn from his throne in the Temple of Melkor in Armenelos. It is surprising, then, that so little attention, which is to say almost none, has been paid to the prominent status of laughter in the works of Tolkien.

This is not as surprising, however, when considering the fact that laughter has generally been overlooked in the study of human behaviour. In the fundamental work *Laughter: A Scientific Investigation*, Robert Provine (9) observes that laughter "has been overlooked because of the human tendency to neglect and undervalue the commonplace." This phenomenon must, therefore, extend to Tolkien's work, where laughter is widespread, yet it has thus far almost entirely gone unnoticed and unstudied. This chapter will therefore endeavour to establish a working understanding of what laughter actually is and its relevance to Tolkien's theory of fantasy proposed in "On Fairy-Stories", and then proceed to apply that understanding to a reading of Tolkien's narratives of Arda. The main argument of this chapter, as a result, is that laughter fundamentally functions as a signifier in Tolkien's narratives of his primary thematic concerns, these being spiritual or moral conflict, the limitations of worldly power and, most importantly, Tolkien's central theme, the inevitability of change. It will be observed that laughter is an applicable response to these thematic concerns, but also that Tolkien does not necessarily use them in immediate or obvious ways. Tolkien's characters certainly do react with laughter to certain situations with thematic relevance to his arguments, but laughter is also used to indicate the presence of a thematic concern. This is to say that characters do not always laugh because they themselves recognise, for instance, the inevitability of change, but rather that certain characters' laughter also indicates on a more abstract level instances of thematic relevance.

Laughter can be understood on a fundamental level as a human instinct. Provine establishes it as related to the evolution of respiration and a psychological relationship between enjoyment and breath: "the sound of labored breathing came to symbolize the playful state that produced it" (97). Laughter is a primal action ingrained in the human psyche. In this way, its prevalence in Tolkien's narratives serves to humanise better the disparate peoples which cannot be classified, or wholly classified, as "Men": Elves, Dwarves, Hobbits, Orcs and the Ainur. In that way alone laughter serves a valuable purpose in ensuring that the behaviour of Tolkien's characters is credible and realistic and that his themes therefore have relevance through their supernatural and fantastic content. This has bearing to the concept of "Enchantment" in Fantasy, as proposed by Tolkien in "On Fairy-Stories", in which it is defined as "the hard recognition that things are so in the world as it appears under the sun" (OFS 144). Laughter is a mechanism which portrays the function of the Secondary World, which is to say that there are behaviours which are consistent and identifiable despite the non-real setting and supernatural contents. That being said, laughter has a substantially greater role in the texts beyond humanising the characters. In this way laughter is not purely some instinct over which individuals have no conscious control or utter in simplistic circumstances.

In *Studies of Laughter in Interaction*, Alexa Hepburn and Scott Varney note that laughter is "something which is closely interactionally coordinated and used to accomplish specific interactional tasks" (26). In *The Linguistics of Laughter* Alan Partington (22) perceives similarly that "laughter can express aggression, ridicule and embarrassment but also courage and defiance and a sense of achievement." In this way "laughter and humour, though connected, are not entirely one and the same" (Partington 22). Laughter cannot be understood simply as a response to humour, and it occurs in a variety of scenarios. This is of course fairly appropriate when dealing with Tolkien's works, which vary in tone from the whimsical and humorous narration of *The Hobbit* to the lofty mode of *The Silmarillion*, in which probably the only instance of observable humour is the Vala Aulë's blithe remark to his spouse Yavanna regarding how the existence of the Ents will not in any way eliminate the Dwarves' need of wood. It is necessary, therefore, to consider laughter in a more complex fashion.

The traditional theories of laughter, which are discussed by both Provine in *Laughter: A Scientific Investigation* and Michael Billig in *Laughter and Ridicule*, are narrow and reductive in modern terms, although they may have elements of applicability to the occurrence of laughter in Tolkien's work. These traditional theories are summarised by Billig (38) as such: "the superiority theories, the incongruity theories and the release theories." The superiority theory argues that "laughter results from disparaging or degrading others" (Billig 39). The incongruity theory is described by Provine as "the effect of the unexpected in triggering laughter" (14) while the relief theory can be understood from Partington's (97) summary that its supporters traditionally believed that "laughter often accompanies a release from constraint." Laughter is, of course, all of these things and more. Each of these theoretical understandings of laughter applies to certain characters and situations in Tolkien's narratives. Just as people do not laugh for one reason alone, characters in the works of Tolkien laugh for a variety of reasons, and laughter in Tolkien's works contributes to each of the aforementioned themes.

The first way in which laughter functions as a signifier of the thematic concerns of Tolkien's narratives is in how it is uttered in moral conflict by Good and Evil characters. Tolkien's antagonists utilise laughter as a weapon and as an instrument of deception, while their enemies utilise laughter as a way of acknowledging the inevitable victory of good. This can be observed at the earliest point in the history of Arda by contrasting the ancient foes Melkor and Tulkas. Tolkien states that when Tulkas arrives in Arda, "Melkor fled before his wrath and his laughter, and forsook Arda, and there was peace for a long age." A connection is therefore formed here between laughter and confidence, strength and righteous anger. The anger of Tulkas "passes like a mighty wind" (*S* 35). Tulkas "laughs ever," a characteristic which is contrasted to Oromë, who is "dreadful in anger" (*S* 29). It is the laughter of Tulkas, foremost, which represents his strength of personality and conviction: "even in the face of Melkor he laughed" (*S* 29). Here Tolkien uses laughter as an expression of the futility of evil, for though less mighty than Melkor, Tulkas has right on his side. As such the laughter of Tulkas is, ultimately, a more fitting response to evil than the "dreadful" anger of Oromë. In the essay "Melkor Morgoth" published in *Morgoth's Ring* Tolkien observes that

> Tulkas represents the good side of 'violence' in the war against evil. This is an absence of compromise which will even face apparent evils (such as war) rather than parley; and does not (in any kind of pride) think that any one less than Eru can redress this, or rewrite the tale of Arda. (*MR* 392)

Observable in Tulkas' laughter are elements of both the superiority theory and the relief theory: relief from Melkor's evil, and indulgence of the ultimate superiority of Eru over Melkor. This is heavily associated with the concept of consolation proposed by Tolkien in "On Fairy-Stories" which perceives the final victory of good in the face of adversity: "it denies (in the face of much evidence, if you will) universal final defeat and in so far is *evangelium*, giving a fleeting glimpse of Joy" (OFS 153). Laughter in this way is presented by Tolkien as an act of repudiating the seeming might of evil and the inevitability of disaster. If Tulkas embodies the notion of openly confronting evil, and one of his primary characteristics, as observed, is laughter, then laughter can be seen to represent an act of consolation which defies the final victory of evil. This defiant quality of laughter can be observed through less demiurgic examples elsewhere. When Saruman is exerting his efforts of persuasion at their uttermost in the final interview in the ruins of Isengard, for instance, and the Men of Rohan are convinced, the narrative abruptly alters trajectory with the remark "[t]hen Gandalf laughed. The fantasy vanished like a puff of smoke" (*LotR* 568). Here again it can be observed that laughter is used as a form of public confrontation of deception and evil, and one with a particular propensity for changing perceptions. It is an act of "dispelling" which cuts through and eliminates plots and devices.

The role of laughter in moral conflict can also, however, be explored from the opposite side. Understanding Tolkien's use of laughter is increased by seeing laughter as a signifier of evil and its relationship to good. This is the point at which laughter's signifying quality emerges, in reference to the circumstances in which it is uttered by antagonists. To Tulkas must be opposed, of course, the laughter of Melkor, which embodies evil in despite, or perhaps in wilful ignorance, of its ultimate failure. Melkor's laughter is associated with deception. Tolkien writes that in Valinor Melkor "laughed in secrecy" (*S* 68) as Fëanor begins to believe the lies he has been spreading. Melkor also "laughed in his heart" (*S* 74) upon convincing Ungoliant to assist his plan to destroy the Two Trees with the false promise of jewels to consume. In contrast Tolkien observes that Melkor "laughed aloud" as he "leapt swiftly down the mountain slopes" but it is essential to observe that "Ungoliant was at his side, and her darkness covered them" (*S* 74). Melkor's laughter is again dissembled and hidden. Tolkien reiterates this theme when Melkor laughs a second time in *The Silmarillion* when, safe in Angband and now referred to as Morgoth, "seeing the division of his foes he laughed" and he "caused vast smokes and vapours to be made [...] staining the bright airs in the first mornings of the world. A wind came out of the east, and bore them over Hithlum, darkening the new Sun" (*S* 109). Here Morgoth's laughter is again associated with hiding, deception, confusion and the rendering of truth obscure. Morgoth next laughs when the increasing fame of Túrin brings him to his attention: "Then Morgoth laughed, for now by the Dragon-helm was Húrin's son revealed to him again; and ere long Amon Rûdh was ringed with spies" (*S* 205). Here a failure of his enemy's secrecy brings him mirth. Morgoth laughs a final time after the fall of Gondolin when the Elves are pressed to their last haven at the Sirion: "in his black thought he laughed, regretting not the one Silmaril that he had lost, for by it as he deemed the last shred of the people of the Eldar should vanish from Middle-earth and trouble it no more" (*S* 244). Careful examination of the language in this passage reveals the depth of Morgoth's deceit, which here verges on self-deception. By this point in the narrative Tolkien has already revealed Morgoth's "great wrath" at the loss of the Silmaril to Beren and Lúthien, given cataclysmic shape as "thunder rolled, lightnings leaped upward, and the mountains quaked. Fire and smoke belched forth from Thangorodrim, and flaming bolts were hurled far abroad, falling ruinous upon the lands; and the Noldor in Hithlum trembled" (*S* 182). Morgoth's reaction belies his true regret for the absent Silmaril at the time. The narration of Morgorth's thoughts presents his desire that "the Eldar should vanish from Middle-earth and trouble it no more." This is to say that Morgoth perceives the Elves troubling Middle-earth, not troubling him. He portrays his enemies, as such, as the villains of the piece in the depths of his evil. Morgoth's laughter in this way is consistently associated with deception: of his enemies, of his allies, and ultimately of himself. Morgoth never laughs again; in the succeeding chapter the Host of the West comes to the succour of the people of Beleriand and his power is destroyed.

Laughter is, however, utilised elsewhere in deceptive moments beyond the defeat of Morgoth. When the Mouth of Sauron is striving to convince the Captains of the West that their plan, the nature of which is actually still unknown to Sauron, has failed, the Mouth of Sauron "laughed" (*LotR* 870), "laughed aloud" and "laughed again" (*LotR* 871). The latter examples in particular occur when his enemies have failed to dissemble their intentions: first when Pippin springs forward "with a cry of grief" from behind Imrahil, and later when the "faces grey with fear and the horror in their eyes" reveal to him that the captured hobbit, whom they know to be Frodo, is "dear" to them. All this laughter is, of course, in itself an elaborate deception. Frodo has escaped, the Ring has not been found, and Sauron is in fact ignorant both of Frodo's identity and his purpose in Mordor. The Mouth of Sauron accidentally gives this away in his repeated mockery, having described Pippin as an "imp": "What use you find in them I cannot guess; but to send them as spies into Mordor is beyond even your accustomed folly" (*LotR* 871). Sauron is, in fact, as blind as his enemies as to Frodo's fate, and knows less still about the Ring. The laughter of his herald, therefore, is an act of bravado, and a signifier of deception. Sauron has "a mind first to play these mice cruelly" (*LotR* 870) with no better motive for his mockery. The deception is elaborated upon in the Mouth of Sauron's effortlessly unreasonable terms for the surrender of the West. His brazen attitude is challenged by Gandalf, but after a brief struggle "swiftly he laughed again" (*LotR* 872). It might be said of the Mouth of Sauron that, in his deceptive habits, he cannot refrain from laughing, but this is plainly contradicted when Gandalf's light shines forth and he condemns Sauron as "faithless and accursed." As Provine (14) observes, "earnestness kills jesting." After this it is noted that "the Messenger of Mordor laughed no more." He immediately flees the scene. It is, of course, Gandalf who has the last laugh once the Ring is destroyed. The "white light" (*LotR* 872) of Gandalf, which reveals the truth, cuts through the laughter of lies, and thus the elimination of laughter here corresponds with the recognition of the necessity at times of forsaking laughter when it has become unnecessary. The time for laughter will be later, but the laughter of the Mouth of Sauron looks towards his master's defeat. It is significant that antagonists so regularly laugh in acts of deception, only revealed through interpretation from later parts of the text, as it in fact places focus on the deception and directs attention towards its falsehood.

In the article "Paulo Freire's Last Laugh" Tyson Lewis (642) argues that "[t]he laugh is a threshold between sound and signification, between animal *phone* and human *logos*." This encapsulates the concept present in Tolkien of laughter as a signifier. It is an instinctive behaviour, but one which serves complex purposes. These purposes can be observed to exist on a level of the text removed from the narrative action. Morgoth, the Mouth of Sauron, and other antagonists laugh in satisfaction at their deceptions and confidence of their enemy's failures, but these in fact signify to the reader ultimately that their confidence is misplaced. Tolkien uses laughter to indicate the folly and self-destructive capacity of evil.

Laughter is a prominent device for propounding the theme of moral conflict. Tulkas and Morgoth are the only two among the Valar whom Tolkien presents as laughing, yet their opposition is emphasised in their laughter. Tulkas, sent specifically as a threat to Melkor, laughs in confidence and open confrontation, while Melkor laughs in secrecy and deceit. The context of their laughter, in effect, summarises Tolkien's entire philosophy of good and evil. The laughter of evil is laughter in opposition to truth and the particular truth of the ultimate failure of evil. The laughter of good is open and exists in response to evil, taking it into itself and transforming that evil into a positive emotion. It can be associated closely with the concept of "Arda Healed" from the essay "Notes on motives in the Silmarillion" which is also to be found in *Morgoth's Ring*: "'Arda Healed' is thus both the completion of the 'Tale of Arda' which has taken up all the deeds of Melkor, but must according to the promise of Ilúvatar be seen to be good; and also a state of redress and bliss beyond the 'circles of the world'" (*MR* 405). Tulkas' laughter takes the evil of Melkor and finds in it joy in the ultimate triumph of good, and so it presents Tolkien's entire theodicy. Jacqueline Bussie argues in *The Laughter of the Oppressed* that a "theology of laughter [...] asks us to take up [...] a position of antitheodicy that acknowledges the incomprehensibility of suffering yet encourages us to continue the fight of resistance" (192). Tolkien's theodicy, however, is quite clear: evil is comprehensible, but there exists consolation for evil. The consolation renders evil absurd, and as a result laughter signifies the failure of evil. When Morgoth laughs in deception the narrative foreshadows his own defeat. It can be observed from this analysis, therefore, that laughter functions as a signifier of Tolkien's main themes in addition to being an element of characterisation. This is consistent with the understanding of laughter as a social instrument with multiple functions.

In a manner which is consequent upon the ultimate victory of good, laughter similarly occurs in Tolkien's narratives as a means by which false forms of power are resisted and dismissed. It serves, as elsewhere, as a signifier of the failure of oppressive power and totalitarian rule. Traditionally, laughter has been seen as an instrument of oppression, which is termed the "superiority theory of laughter" and described by Michael Billig in *Laughter and Ridicule* as such: "The superiority theory is basically a theory of mockery, for it suggests that laughter results from disparaging or degrading others" (39). In this manner laughter is used as a social tool which keeps potentially dangerous elements in their place by ridiculing and humiliating them. Morgoth, for instance, laughs upon chaining Húrin upon Thangorodrim (*UT* 86). However, the laughter of oppressors is similarly subverted by the laughter of those inferior in power. Imrahil "laughed aloud" when considering the attack on the Morannon, claiming it to be "the greatest jest in all the history of Gondor." Aragorn responds that the occasion is "too bitter for laughter" (*LotR* 864) but nonetheless the expedition succeeds. Imrahil's laughter on this occasion is a response to the seeming absurdity of their situation, but it functions as an acknowledgement in the text of the limitations of great power as represented by Sauron. Laughter functions as a form of resistance to the schemes and machinations of the powerful. Against Sauron, the Captains of the West are in themselves powerless, but Imrahil's laughter, sardonically uttered as it is, signifies externally that absolute power in the scenario does not rest with Sauron. In this way laughter is used by Tolkien to indicate that there are limits to the power of worldly individuals and that there are other, greater powers beyond their control. During the Scouring of the Shire, the hobbits are "not quite sure whether laughing was allowed" (*LotR* 980) but this decree has already been subverted by the laughter of the protagonists. Frodo, Sam, Merry, and Pippin "roared with laughter" (*LotR* 978) when the Shirriffs try to coerce them into obedience of the new rules. Here the situation is reversed to that of the attack on the Morannon. The hobbits are experienced, well-equipped and confident compared to the oppressors of the Shire, but their laughter instead signifies the falsity of the power which the ruffians believe themselves to have.

Bussie (13) theorises this kind of laughter in the following fashion: "when the 'weak' and oppressed laugh, their laughter *also* affirms autonomy and power, and thereby struggles to be heard over the laughter of the hegemony. The competing laughter of the oppressed serves as counterpoint to the dominant laughter and destabilizes the oppressor's assertion of dominance." This can be understood in Tolkien's narratives in reference to the laughter of people who are not dominant or who do not represent the authority with the advantage. It is laughter which refuses to give respect or acknowledgement to totalitarian forces, even, as in the case of Imrahil, as a signifier. In any event it treats the schemes of the powerful as nothing more than frivolous games. Laughter attacks power. It reduces the seemingly serious affairs of the world to trivialities and minor absurdities which must simply be accepted with an amused resignation, as displayed by Frodo when the Shirriffs insist that he is under arrest. Laughter does not destroy power, but it questions how meaningful it is. This is observably connected to Tolkien's theodicy as it reflects the entire power structure of his narratives. In Tolkien's works, true power lies ultimately and singularly with god, Eru, alone. In any event, absolute power exists only externally to the narrative of the world, beyond the grasp of any individual, even very mighty beings like Morgoth and Sauron who are still nonetheless finite in their potency. Therefore the schemes of those seeking to usurp this power or perform acts of evil in general are tiny and insignificant in comparison. Laughter embodies this triviality. In the final lines of *The Hobbit*, Gandalf reminds Bilbo that he is "only quite a little fellow in the wide world after all", and he receives the reply, "'Thank goodness!' said Bilbo laughing" (*H* 280). Bilbo's laughter of relief at being only "little" in respect to wider events is crucial to the notion that all individuals are only components in sequences of events and do not have the power or even the particular metaphysical or cosmic importance to exercise absolute control or influence over them. Even Morgoth cannot be said to wield so much might; each individual is ultimately only one of numerous players in the music. For Tolkien, the correct response can only be laughter which serves as a reminder of this fact.

As such laughter subverts power. It is in Tyson Lewis' (637) words "an experiential democracy of the flesh." This concept is best embodied in the character of Bombadil, who laughs regularly and is "his own master" (*LotR* 259). Bombadil "laughed" and "laughed again" (*LotR* 130) upon toying with the Ring, which according to Gandalf "has no power over him" (*LotR* 259). Frodo finds himself "perhaps a trifle annoyed with Tom for seeming to make so light of what even Gandalf thought so perilously important" (*LotR* 131). Frodo's resentment may derive from the Ring itself and its own corruptions. The Ring may insist that it is taken seriously. Bombadil's refusal to do so places him outside the power structures embodied in the Ring. In *The Alchemy of Laughter* Glen Cavaliero argues that it "is tempting to see in [Tom Bombadil] a figure analogous to the celebratory function of comedy in a world riven by good and evil, whether these be accorded a metaphysical dimension or not," that he is "outside the dualistic conflict which is the subject of Tolkien's story" (Cavaliero 195-96). Yet Bombadil's separation from the nature of the Ring does not necessarily separate him from the conflict. Bombadil is undeniably a good character, but also a passive character in a world which is almost entirely directed towards conflict. His laughter at the Ring in this way is a further signifier of the ultimately limited nature of the struggle. As Tolkien himself observes, "[t]he power of the Ring over all concerned, even the Wizards or Emissaries, is not a delusion – but it is not the whole picture, even of the then state and content of that part of the Universe" (*L* 192). This perspective on reality is one outlined in the Last Debate by Gandalf, who reminds that "Other evils there are that may come; for Sauron is himself but a servant or emissary" (*LotR* 861). As a laughing character, therefore, Bombadil signifies the concept of the breadth of the narrative of history, which cannot be reductively attributed to a handful of key incidents or participants. Bombadil perceives the Ring as only one part of a far greater whole, and indeed the narrative of *The Lord of the Rings* as only part of a greater whole. Tolkien represents him, perhaps, in an advantageous position of being undisputed Master of his own small country, but his laughter exemplifies why this is so: he is abstracted and distanced from immediate events into a more general perception of time and nature, a conception of reality embodied in his stories. Bombadil "knew the dark under the starts when it was fearless – before the Dark Lord came from Outside" (*LotR* 129). Judging by the description this is a reference, seemingly, to Morgoth rather than Sauron, and this indication of the vast scope of history and deep time embodied in the perception of Bombadil coupled with his laughter demands a sense of perspective. The powers and affairs of individuals, while individually important, simultaneously cannot be attributed too great a metaphysical weight or significance.

Laughter is the response to the seriousness of the world. Tolkien's narratives deal, generally speaking, with serious themes. The recurrence of laughter exemplified in this way, however, emphasises that as serious as they are, there are limits to seriousness. Bombadil perceives the world beyond individual items of history and for that reason he laughs. This relates to Tolkien's arguments regarding the Fairy-Story achievement of recovery, which is crucial for bringing the world into perspective. Recovery is the "regaining of a clear view […] so that the things seen clearly may be freed from the drab blur of triteness or familiarity" (OFS 146). Laughter in this capacity maintains and promotes this sense of clarity, one which must particularly serve to prevent evil gaining the upper hand, being seen as inevitable or unalterable. This is clearly related also to the earlier example of Gandalf's laughter dissipating the persuasiveness of the voice of Saruman. Laughter alters the dynamics of power and as such transforms the perspective of those who laugh into fresh conceptions of reality and history. It can be observed that as a signifier, then, laughter has two functions: firstly to signify the absurdity of power structures, and secondly to recognise the vastness of history and reality. The conclusion to draw from these two representations of laughter is that laughter expresses the limitations of human power, even that which Tolkien embodies in non-human characters, and to take consolation in the nature of existence as outside individual control.

What is arguably the most essential characteristic of laughter in Tolkien, however, is its relationship to the overriding theme of all of his texts about the inevitability of change. If Tolkien's narratives have a central message, it is that change must be accepted, not resisted, and that new events will always come to pass. This of course can be observed through Tolkien's own account of *The Lord of the Rings* in particular: that "it is about Death and the desire for deathlessness" (*L* 203), and the "hideous peril of confusing true 'immortality' with limitless serial longevity" (*L* 267), when in actual fact "Death is not an enemy" (*L* 267). *The Lord of the Rings* is of course replete with examples of the corruptive nature of artificial eternity and endlessness embodied in Gollum, the Rings and the Nazgûl. *The Silmarillion* too represents this in the Jewels themselves, in which the light of the Trees of the Valar is "preserved imperishable" (*S* 67). The lust for these of course consequently motivates enormous bloodshed and disaster. Things must be allowed to change if disaster is to be averted. The desire for permanence is associated with terror and violence, while change is accounted for with laughter. Change can be characterised in the narratives, particularly *The Lord of the Rings*, as the unexpected and the unprecedented. This is consistently borne out in studies of laughter. Partington establishes a theory of laughter which is highly effective at explaining the quality of laughter in Tolkien's narratives, observing that "much laughter-talk involves the sudden shift from one narrative to another" (57). Tolkien incorporates this concept within his narrative in situations in which laughter signifies an unexpected change in narrative direction. This is an established concept with origins in the aforementioned "incongruity theory" of laughter, where laughter is caused by the unexpected. Provine (15) observes that "[o]ur success at incongruity detection is celebrated with laughter." Tolkien's narratives may be read as such. Incongruities and the unexpected represent the inevitability of change, and the response to this is laughter, and this is a reaction borne out in both simple and complex ways in Tolkien's narratives. More simply speaking, laughter is used as an expression of the achievement of new events. Upon finally giving up the One Ring, Bilbo Baggins' anger, evidence of the Ring's control over him, gives way to a "look of relief and a laugh" (*LotR* 34). Similarly, Pippin observes of Gandalf after the fall of Sauron that he "laughs now more than he talks" (*LotR* 934). In both cases these are related to major instances of change. The voluntary passing on of the Ring is unique to "Bilbo alone in history" (*LotR* 54). Gandalf himself acknowledges with the fall of Sauron, the source of his great mirth, that "though much has been saved, much must now pass away" (*LotR* 949). In each case laughter accompanies the release of a great burden through the mutability of the future. Laughter in this context embodies Tolkien's argument that nothing lasts forever. This argument furthers the notion that good will ultimately triumph. As stated in the "Ainulindalë", "in every age there come forth things that are new and have no foretelling, for they do not proceed from the past" (*S* 18). Laughter is crucial to understanding this notion. There can be no definite knowledge about the future, but there can be definite knowledge that elements of the future will be surprising and unexpected, and that good will occur out of evil.

Laughter here also clearly associates closely with "Arda Healed", as Arda Healed is the successful redemption of evil, specifically the evil of Melkor, into history such that the future will be "a third thing and a greater, and yet the same" (*MR* 318). Laughter anticipates this situation because in these instances it is associated with the idea of change and growth, and the expectation of the future. This is consistent with Partington's theory: "One interesting and effective type of narrative shift is evaluation reversal, whereby something which is normally expected to be appraised as good or bad is suddenly re-presented as the opposite" (73). In Tolkien this is almost universally when an evil situation is revealed to contain hidden good. Laughter is an expressive act which occurs numerous times for this reason throughout *The Lord of the Rings*. Aragorn laughs when he discovers Frodo relatively unharmed by the orc-chieftain who attacks him in the tomb of Balin in Moria. Galadriel utters a "sudden clear laugh" (*LotR* 356) when Frodo offers her the One Ring, but she laughs again upon rejecting it. It is observed that Frodo "actually laughed" (*LotR* 397) when Sam refuses to let him continue the journey to Mordor alone. Quickbeam regularly laughs at the unexpected: "if the sun came out from behind a cloud […] if they came upon a stream or spring […] sometimes at some sound or whisper in the trees" (*LotR* 471). The recently-resurrected Gandalf laughs "long and softly" (*LotR* 483) when Aragorn, fearing him to be Saruman, asks him his name. Sam laughs "for heart's ease, not for jest" upon the discovery of the "sweet odours" of Ithilien (*LotR* 636). Laughter is also associated with the good which can be maintained from the past. Eating lembas reminds Merry and Pippin "of fair faces, and laughter, and wholesome food in quiet days now far away" (*LotR* 447). One of the most powerful qualities of laughter in Tolkien's work is that it reminds of the enduring nature of good in the presence of evil. Along the desolate pass of Cirith Ungol, Frodo's laughter is unprecedented: "Such a sound had not been heard in those places since Sauron came to Middle-earth" (*LotR* 697). This occurs when Sam is relating their journey to that of the ancient heroes of *The Silmarillion* such as Beren and Eärendil and musing upon their narrative becoming such a tale. As such he is situating their lives in the past, but projecting a narrative into the future. Laughter is both an emblem of the inevitability of change and the survivability of good, and is itself in this case a new thing which brings a positive feeling to an evil place. Frodo's laughter signifies in this way the continuation of good throughout time. It is both a new event and already signalling what is to come in the future as a reflection of the past. Tolkien as such emphasises that the foretelling of future evil is not absolute and that good is not purely the purview of the past. Laughter is motion and progresses forward, reminding that there will be good in the future also. In these cases, laughter is hope.

Tolkien also uses laughter, however, in a more complex fashion, in which the laughter of characters in the supposed certainty of the future is subverted. Laughter is in this way a signifier of change even when the characters who are laughing are unaware. Denethor, for example, laughs three times in his despair. He argues that "against the Power that now arises there is no victory. [...] even now the wind of thy hope cheats thee and wafts up Anduin a fleet with black sails." Gandalf's response is that "Such counsels will make the Enemy's victory certain indeed," to which he receives the reply: "'Hope on then!' laughed Denethor" (*LotR* 835). Denethor's laughter here is misplaced. His language is that of absolute conviction, as Gandalf observes. Denethor has no doubt that Sauron is on the very brink of an inevitable and unalterable victory. His laughter, however, belies this certainty. The black sails of the corsair fleet from Umbar of course in fact deliver Aragorn's reinforcements and victory on the Pelennor. Denethor's laughter does not foreshadow a certainty but in fact denotes the arrival of a change, one already known to the reader. As such, the laughter again comes after the surprise. Thus Gandalf observes to Denethor's attendants: "so pass also the days of Gondor that you have known; for good or evil they are ended" (*LotR* 836-37). In this way laughter is regularly associated with change, and particularly the arrival of the unexpected and of hope in the face of apparent disaster, despite the character who laughs uttering laughter in hopelessness and despair.

As an expression, therefore, laughter does not need to be uttered in a particular mood. The character is not even always significant. It nonetheless signifies a sense of relief and the capacity of realising that evil is never absolute and that unexpected events, particularly good events, will occur in spite of evil. As Bussie (14) observes, "tragedy and oppression also involves incongruity, and therefore it too could evoke laughter." Laughter is not just linked to the actions of characters. It functions as Tolkien's device for placing focus upon and reflecting things unexpected, mutable, and surprising. Even in the most evil moments, laughter is attached to change. Sauron's threefold laughter in the Temple of Melkor in Armenelos is ill-timed, as it correlates with the Changing of the World. This event signifies the spiritual estrangement of the Valar and the Eldar from Men, but it also heralds the great weakening of Sauron and the establishment of vital events in the Third Age which will bring about his eventual downfall. In terms of the signification of laughter in Tolkien's narratives, Sauron is in fact giving voice to his own inevitable defeat when he laughs in the temple. This is comparable to the case of Denethor's laughter, as it occurs in an assumption of absolutes when in fact uncertainties exist. Sauron believes that he is "rid of the Edain for ever" (*S* 280) and in this delusion he is thwarted as Elendil and his sons escape. In this way, of course, Sauron is living up to his reputation as "a shadow of Morgoth and a ghost of his malice" (*S* 32) as this laughter is strongly evocative of Morgoth's aforementioned laughter in his erroneous conviction that the Eldar will trouble Middle-earth "no more." When characters perceive certainty, their laughter signifies that it is unjustified. Sauron's inheritance of Morgoth's behaviour establishes that those who deal in certainty will inevitably be proved wrong in time. It can be observed once again when the Lord of the Nazgûl enters the broken gate of Minas Tirith and declares that "This is my hour" following the utterance of "a deadly laughter" (*LotR* 811). Immediately afterwards his confidence is seen to be misplaced as the horns of Rohan signal the succour of Gondor. Each time a character uses laughter to revel in surety about the future, it in fact signals the opposite. When evil characters laugh the joke is, in fact, on them. To continue with the Lord of the Nazgûl, laughter is in fact fatal as an abolition of certainty: Éowyn laughs when revealing her true identity to the Ringwraith, in opposition to his prophetic delusions of invincibility. Her laughter is "of all sounds in that hour the strangest. It seemed that Dernhelm laughed, and the clear voice was like the ring of steel" (*LotR* 823). Indeed the laughter of Éowyn at this moment captures all three aspects of laughter: it openly exposes the weakness of evil, it negates its power and it obliterates certainty as a new, unexpected, incongruous thing. It is no wonder that in that moment the Lord of the Nazgûl is "silent, as if in sudden doubt" (*LotR* 823).

Laughter repeatedly subverts absolute language and absolute modes of thought, even in the case of the individuals using that language and having those thoughts. Laughter is linked to the unexpected. Tolkien's argument is that change itself is not evil but ultimately redemptive, and as such laughter represents this notion. Laughter in positive mood represents hope; in negative or evil mode it is self-deception about the assuredness of the future. In either case, laughter occurs when unforeseen events arise in the face of certainty or lack of precedent, and functions as a signifier of change. This is evoked by the "theology of laughter" described by Bussie, who argues that "[f]aith and hope are paradoxical and proleptic" (183). In this way hope is associated with the laughter of incongruity, as a "theology of hope must be the counterpart of a theology of laughter" (184). In Tolkien's work, laughter is even hope when it is being uttered by those in the business of destroying hope and propagating despair, although they themselves do not realise it.

There is no single theory of laughter which is sufficient to account for everything in Tolkien, or indeed anywhere else, especially in fiction. As Cavaliero (6) observes, "a novel tends to evade the solicitations of a monolithic point of view." While Tolkien's works, more correctly speaking, are romances rather than novels, the point is the same: the text functions as an assembly of complex signifiers. Nonetheless, it can be observed from the examples given above that laughter can serve an extremely valuable function in Tolkien's work if it is given the attention and notice that laughter so rarely receives. Laughter has observable correlations to Tolkien's own theories of "Fairy-Stories" and the themes he proposes most substantially in *The Silmarillion* and *The Lord of the Rings*. Laughter is an instrument by which the Secondary World is internally consistent and functional. Moreover, laughter is a signifier of those core arguments of the grand history of the narrative of Arda as a whole: that power is limited, that evil is subordinate to good despite appearances, and that in the fullness of time change will bring about the victory of good. Laughter does not have to be uttered by a good or even a powerful character to function in this way. Rather it has a textual significance which indicates the continuing relevance of hope and the nonexistence of absolutes and certainties in a changing world. Like almost everything in Arda, laughter is to some degree "fallen", but evil cannot create. The utterance of laughter by the evil only serves as a reminder of its intrinsic grounding in goodness. The use of this signifier is emblematic of the need to interpret Tolkien on his choice of language and representation in addition to the narrative presentation of themes and ideas. As a textual operation on a level above or outside the narrative, the use of such signifiers contributes a layer of complexity to the interpretation of Tolkien's work which is vital for understanding how his narratives express crucial thematic concerns. Tolkien himself has argued for the need for consistency in the "Fairy-Story", but this must be observed to go beyond the construction of an imaginary world or extraordinary characters. As a character action and a signifier laughter establishes a textual continuum of character, narrative, language and theme which provides a broader consistency to the texts. This concept is particularly important for considering the vast amount of posthumously published material contributing to the corpus of texts of Tolkien's work and how "finished" components like *The Lord of the Rings* and *The Hobbit* correlate with the remainder. As can be observed when comparing the thematic content of both *The Lord of the Rings* and *The Silmarillion* with reference to laughter, it is noteworthy that this consistency of theme can be identified. Laughter is commonly overlooked, but it is altogether useful for understanding human nature and behaviour. In the same way, laughter is proliferate throughout the works of Tolkien, and must be appreciated as a valuable thread of investigation for understanding and interpreting these texts and perceiving their themes, particularly the inevitability of change and the consequent irrationality of despair.

About the Author

ALASTAIR WHYTE is a PhD graduate from the English Department of the University of Sydney, with his thesis, "Utopian Intersections in the Works of J.R.R. Tolkien", exploring the conversation between Middle-earth and the canonical utopias and dystopias. He is interested in the parallels of literary and speculative fiction in the nineteenth and twentieth centuries.

Abbreviations

L: *The Letters of J.R.R. Tolkien*

LotR: *The Lord of the Rings*

OFS: "On Fairy-Stories"

S: *The Silmarillion*

Bibliography

BILLIG, Michael. *Laughter and Ridicule: Towards a Social Critique of Humour.* London: SAGE Publications, 2005.

BUSSIE, Jacqueline A. *The Laughter of the Oppressed: Ethical and Theological Resistance in Wiesel, Morrison and Endo.* New York: T&T Clark, 2007.

CAVALIERO, Glen. *The Alchemy of Laughter: Comedy in English Fiction.* London: Macmillan, 2000.

HEPBURN, Alexa, and Scott VARNEY. "Beyond ((Laughter)): Some Notes on Transcription." *Studies of Laughter in Interaction.* Ed. Phillip GLENN and Elizabeth HOLT. London: Bloomsbury, 2013. 25-38.

LEWIS, Tyson Edward. "Paulo Freire's Last Laugh: Rethinking critical pedagogy's funny bone through Jacques Rancière." *Educational Philosophy and Theory* 42 (2010): 645-648.

PARTINGTON, Alan. *The Linguistics of Laughter: A corpus-assisted study of laughter-talk.* New York: Routledge, 2006.

PROVINE, Robert R. *Laughter: A Scientific Investigation.* London: Faber and Faber, 2000.

RATELIFF, John D. "'And All the Days of Her Life Are Forgotten.' *The Lord of the Rings* as Mythic Prehistory." *The Lord of the Rings 1954-2004. Scholarship in Honor of Richard E. Blackwelder.* Ed. Wayne G. HAMMOND and Christina SCULL. Milwaukee: Marquette University Press, 2006. 67-100.

TOLKIEN, J.R.R. *The Hobbit.* London: HarperCollins, 2000.

The Letters of J.R.R. Tolkien. Ed. Humphrey CARPENTER with the assistance of Christopher TOLKIEN. New York: Houghton Mifflin, 2000.

The Lord of the Rings. London: HarperCollins, 1997.

Morgoth's Ring. (The History of Middle-earth 10). Ed. Christopher TOLKIEN. London: HarperCollins, 1994.

"On Fairy-Stories." In *The Monsters and the Critics and Other Essays.* Ed. Christopher TOLKIEN. London: HarperCollins, 1997. 109-161. (The original essay was first delivered as a lecture in 1939, and first published, somewhat enlarged, in 1947.)

The Silmarillion. Ed. Christopher TOLKIEN. London: HarperCollins, 1999.

Unfinished Tales of Númenor and Middle-earth. Ed. Christopher TOLKIEN. London: HarperCollins, 1998.

Ulla Thynell
Tom Bombadil

Jennifer Raimundo

Mirth's Might: The Tenacity of Humour in the Works of J.R.R. Tolkien

Abstract

A study of humour's appearances in the works of J.R.R. Tolkien reveals that for this author humour should be taken very seriously. "Mirth's Might" seeks out these instances of humour in Tolkien's legendarium and delves into how and why various forms of laughter and mirth act upon the characters in his stories. Going from Sam Gamgee to Túrin Turambar and travelling all the way from Niggle's Parish to Wootton Major, this essay discovers that humour holds many strengths each of which contributes to escape, recovery and consolation. In the pages of Tolkien, readers learn that humour is essential to the art of story-making and to life itself.

The Playful Philosopher and the Pranking Poet

J.R.R. Tolkien was at heart a hopelessly funny man. Behind Melkor, Sauron, the fall of Númenor, and the destruction of an enticing golden ring there lies a mind that took delight in switching old teeth for coins and composing clerihews to parody close friends. Tolkien's sense of fun was so memorable it led his biographer Humphrey Carpenter to write, "He could laugh at anybody, but most of all at himself, and his complete lack of any sense of dignity could and often did make him behave like a riotous schoolboy" (*Biography* 134). This is the simple, childlike humour Tolkien embraced. Yet Carpenter's vision of a laughing-eyed prankster might prove rather jarring to those who think of Tolkien primarily as a philologist turned legendary mythopoet. The two images, one of a professor and one of a playful schoolboy, do not seem to fit.

However, they do. From a careful reading of Tolkien's legendarium and his other works, a striking picture of mighty mirth forms. All of the battered conquerors and unlikely heroes of Tolkien's stories are marked, almost eccentrically so, by a profound appreciation for and exhibition of humour. Indeed, beneath every blow in good's defence, behind every step taken towards a goal after hope has glimmered away, there rests a stength sprung from a hearty laugh, a penchant for irony, and a knack for genuine, wholesome play. In Tolkien, mirth marks the mighty.

Of course, as with everything he touched, Tolkien's treatment of mirth's might is deep and complex. Preceding many of today's psychiatrists and physiologists (see Roy et al., and Wilkins and Eisenbraun), Tolkien noted the intricate causes and effects of humour, but rather than analyse them he put them into story, much to his readers' benefit. Humour in Tolkien is not merely what happens during a clever joke nor is laughter simply a sound that follows something amusing or glad. Rather, the circumstances surrounding humour and the characters experiencing it reveal that Tolkien understood the startling effects of humour for good or ill, that he grasped both its power and its mystery as it plays a fundamental role in human life. While no psychologist will find controlled test results and no physiologist will find conclusive neurological evidence in Tolkien, this author provides his readers with people, people like ourselves who share similar humour and hardships. Through that display, Tolkien reminds us that our tears and our laughter are strong, in more ways than we would imagine.

From all the individual instances of humour appearing within Middle-earth and beyond, three areas of strength in particular come forth. First, Tolkien suggests that a certain protection arises from cultivating a clean sense of humour and honing a talent for laughing cheerfully at the ironic. Even a little mischief seems encouraged. However, this general jollity soon matures into the second area of strength, namely, the ability to laugh at oneself. Here the serious services humour can perform start to shine, beckoning all heroic hopefuls to humour's strength. Finally, Tolkien welcomes his readers onto serious grounds indeed when his blood-smattered soldiers find strength to fight in a good laugh and a resilient smile, suggesting that Tolkien's humour was not so boyish after all. No, humour lives in honey-clovered gardens as well as death's gruesome field, and mirth can reach into the darkest night to open our eyes to day's dawning.

However, the benefits of humour do not end with those three strengths. Rather, within them we discover the very ideas Tolkien hoped Fantasy would express.

Those virtues he could only describe in "On Fairy-Stories" come to life in the characters populating Middle-earth, Niggle's Parish, Wootton Major, and Ham, as they display, through their laughter or lack thereof, the important role that humour plays in "Escape", "Recovery", and "Consolation". Humour can release us from the prison of this world's ills, help us regain a clear view of what life is really about, and open to us the possibility of a happy, unexpected ending. Yes, even wry commentary and childish giggles can contribute to the greater purposes of grand narrative. Even laughter can "rend indeed the very web of story, and let a gleam come through" (OFS 176). In short, humour is neither for the silly nor the weak. Humour, I believe Tolkien says, lives for those who engage in the battle of Good versus Evil and emerge victorious to a recovery of Tolkien's "Great Escape" and find a "fleeting glimpse of Joy, Joy beyond the walls of this world, poignant as grief" (OFS 175).[1]

Protection in Mirth

> "I keep a treasure or two near my skin, as precious as Rings to me. Here's one: my old wooden pipe." (Pippin at the foot of Orthanc in *The Two Towers*)

"In the hole in a ground there lived a hobbit." So begins *The Hobbit* by J.R.R. Tolkien. When one alights upon these words, one has no idea of the twisted dragons lurking under deep mountains in the east, no inkling of dark goblins secretly spreading in mines, no clue of the bloody battle about to take place between five armies, and certainly no thought of a Necromancer preparing to resurrect as the evil menace of the age. The funny thing is that, if the reader does not know of these evils, neither does our hole-dwelling hobbit. Bilbo Baggins and all his folk of the Shire have absolutely no idea of the great dangers storming around their sunny garden land, and they will remain shockingly unperturbed for the rest of the story, except for some uproar by a Baggins-gone-Took. What makes these half-pint hobbits so impenetrable? Is it possible for us the readers to enjoy the same protection they experience? Although we may not have wizards watching over us nor elves in mountains and forests taking the brunt of the world's evil wrath, a survey of hobbit traits unlocks a wealth of protective wisdom. Were we more like hobbits, perhaps we too could laugh at the evil in our midst.

Our survey begins with a lesson in cheer, learnt from some of the most carefree people on Middle-earth. The world was first introduced to hobbits on September 21, 1937, and their creator considered these the chief characteristics anyone need know about them:

> There is no magic about [hobbits], except the ordinary everyday sort which helps them to disappear quietly and quickly when large stupid folk like you and me come blundering along, making a noise like elephants which they can hear a mile off. They are inclined to be fat in the stomach; they dress in bright colours (chiefly green and yellow); wear no shoes, because their feet grow natural leathery soles and thick warm brown hair like the stuff on their heads (which is curly); have long clever brown fingers, good-natured faces, and laugh deep fruity laughs (especially after dinner, which they have twice a day when they can get it). Now you know enough to go on with (*H* 12).

We certainly do. Notice what "enough" entails: hobbits are earthy, sprightly, jolly little people whose everyday magic consists in the ability to be left alone. This magic has more to do with the nature of hobbits in general than any sort of conjuring in particular. However, is that all Tolkien tells us in this paragraph? I think not, for nestled in this description of hobbits rests a description of their sharp minds. Tolkien contrasts hobbits against us "large stupid folk" and applauds them as clever with their fingers, an adroitness that rarely ends with handiwork. My aim in drawing our attention to this detail before embarking on our discussion of hobbit humour is to point out that Tolkienian mirth never belongs to simpletons. It is often simple, yes, but not for simpletons.

As well hobbits are a simple people who fully appreciate simple pleasures, wherein I believe lies their protective strength. They seem the sort of people who prefer delicious second meals to decadent second banqueting rooms and feel more comfortable bustling around in gay frocks than gorgeous gowns. They would rather be carefree and happy than cosmopolitan and concerned, at liberty to laugh at a humble joke than be the talk of the town. When they say something they honestly mean it, just as Bilbo genuinely meant his airy "Good morning!" to a grey old man on that fateful day. In other words, no guile lurks about a hobbit, and living as cozily and un-worriedly as possible proves their chief end. Since hobbits actively avoid anxiety, Gandalf's charge to Frodo to keep the Ring secret and safe could not have been better placed. Hobbits simply do not go looking for, nor do they attract, trouble. Their very own lifestyle keeps them protected from the desire to bother or be bothered. They are by nature safe.

Of course, Tolkien would never blandly tell us this. Instead, he depicts a hobbit's good-natured delight in life. The Shire sparkles as a sort of paradise, where all that matters is to relish food, gardening, village chatter, and the humdrum beauty of daily life. Right in the midst of this paradise there flashes a droll sense of humour, a taste for comedy which causes danger to slide off hobbit backs as if it were nothing more than the passing rain. Throughout *The Hobbit*, Bilbo grows more and more into a jokester until we find him laughing about the downsides of magical rings when they make one too invisible for warm beds (*H* 242). He slips out of Gollum's clutches by playing with riddles and later speaks to Smaug as though their conversation were a game of hide-and-seek! By the end of his adventure, Bilbo feels perfectly confident jesting with elves about how their lullabies would wake up drunken goblins and jokes with the elvenking that "even a burglar has his feelings" about stealing an admittedly large quantity of food (*H* 251, 247). Indeed, the very last act Bilbo performs in *The Hobbit* is to laugh in gratitude for how small he is in this wide world, even after having watched many of its perils befall his little frame. That humble playfulness is a strength rare and difficult to match.

This playfulness makes perfect sense in the Shire. Just like the simple pleasures in their down-to-earth quality of life, the slightly saucy, pranking, childlike humour of hobbits protects them by the power of innocence and a conscious insistence on maintaining that innocence. Take, for example, the tense exchange between the Gaffer and Sandyman the Miller at the very beginning of *The Fellowship of the Ring*. Here we note the sensitivity hobbits have to the difference between clean chuckles and malicious gossip. The Gaffer begins speaking to his heart's (and the surrounding hobbits') content about the oddities of the Bagginses, but as soon as Sandyman turns play into insinuations of murder and shady accumulations of wealth, the hobbits turn on the miller, just as they will eventually turn on Sandyman's son, Ted, when his corrupt mockery sets him on an evil path. For hobbits, that sort of talk is simply neither funny nor pleasant.

Pleasantness ranks so high in hobbitish esteem that when relational problems do arise – an occurrence even in the Shire – a bit of lighthearted gesturing is all they require to settle their disputes. After all, how else did Bilbo bid his relatives goodbye than by leaving them with a few well-chosen presents? Bilbo's pointed sporting is hilariously evident in his gift "*for the collection of* HUGO BRACEGIRDLE, *from a contributor*; on an (empty) book-case. Hugo was a great borrower of books, and worse than usual at returning them" (*FR* 37). This "borrowing" habit could lead to serious family feuds in our world, but instead hobbits choose to sort it out through a proper joke. At least most hobbits. The Sackville-Bagginses seem determined to miss the humour in their gift of silver spoons (Lobelia, too, was a great borrower), but is it then a coincidence that these unfunny hobbits come very near to going bad before their story is over? In Tolkien, those who cannot take a joke tend to find themselves in morally precarious situations.

Still, Lobelia and Sandyman are, again, anomalies in the Shire's culture. Most hobbits, like Farmer Maggot and Fatty Bolger and Pippin Took and Bilbo himself "joke about serious things" and they come out perfectly unscathed in the end (*FR* 35). Perhaps this seems counterintuitive to the reader, but I believe Tolkien shows that the hobbits' knack for making light of the weight of the world is what keeps them, personally, safe in the end. Their childlike humour reflects an innate desire to give and take no trouble that oversteps their satisfied life, and this protects them from the critical crookedness of a Saruman, the cynical despair of a Denethor, and the bullying, belittling malignancy of a Sauron. These gross and evil humours strike hobbits as profoundly unfunny, for just as the Shire-folk still relish the inhalation of good green air, they still find contentment in the sweet hilarities of a good life.

In the midst of this paradisiacal encounter with halflings, however, Tolkien inserts a note of caution. The hobbits are individually protected from the dangers of ambition through their contented humour, but this protection is of the retreating sort, a kind of sanctuary from an evil world lurking just beyond their doors. Rangers are still required to watch over the Shire, and the hobbits' time of personal protection is running out in the light of global warfare. While we must not overlook this troublesome reality, we also must realise the happy humour of hobbits is, according to Tolkien and Aragorn and Gandalf, worth protecting. It is worth the adventurers, bounders, and wizards. It is worth the long rides across Middle-earth and the late-night searches in dark, dank Gondorian libraries. Tolkien at the beginning of his story has therefore introduced a tension of humour and harm that will only be strengthened throughout his chronicle until they meet a final resolution at the end of his tale. But a hobbit's unambitious peace through his unambitious humour is a good, noble trait, even if something more, something we shall see in a moment, is requisite to keep that peace from devolving into denial and isolation. For now, let us continue with the knowledge that both protections – humour's integral protection from evil's unsatisfied hunger and external protection from evil's otherwise unchecked consumption – are real and good in Tolkien's mythology.

Although the protective quality of humour is most fully characterised in hobbits, there are a few correlating instances worth mentioning. The first resides dangerously near Old Man Willow and frightfully close to the Barrow-downs. I mean, of course, Tom Bombadil, that merry fellow with a face "creased into a hundred wrinkles of laughter" (*FR* 117). There breathes no one in Middle-earth so confident and safe, so caught within his own world of comfortable and changeless security, as Tom Bombadil. And what sets this bonnie man in a bright blue jacket with yellow boots above and apart from the rest? Why, his cry of "Merry dol! Derry dol! My darling!" (*FR* 117). Where Bombadil roams there follows laughter and gaiety and a sudden attack of fearlessness, such an attack that Sam sleeps like a log safe under the eaves of his jolly host's house. Although Sam does not understand the cause of his safe and sound sleep, Tolkien reveals that the mysterious power prevailing in Bombadil's sanctuary happens to be the same vigour supporting the Shire. Goldberry explains it best when she describes Bombadil's identity with, "He is, as you have seen him," and then reassures her new guests to "have peace now […] until the morning! Heed no nightly noises! For nothing passes door and window here save moonlight and starlight and the wind off the hill-top. Goodnight!" (*FR* 122-123). Bombadil simply is as he is. Because he seeks nothing more, he need not fear rotten-hearted trees or bitter Barrow-wights. Thus Bombadil is Master, and he can laugh, laugh all the day. In fact, all he has to say regarding Old Man Willow is, "What? […] Old Man Willow? Naught worse than that, eh? That can soon be mended. I know a tune for him" (*FR* 117). Bombadil's strength expresses itself in a song! This mirth is insurmountable, and it comes from being so himself that he can whistle a tune about it. Just as sweet fragrance dispels a foul stench and light wards off darkness, none can imprison Tom Bombadil. None can imprison the merry heart.

To speak truth, this protective analogy of laughter and light is not original to me. It comes straight from Tolkien in *The Unfinished Tales*, where he uses it to rationalise why the Drúedain could not possibly have been used by Melkor to breed orcs. According to him, "Morgoth, since he can make no living thing, bred Orcs from various kinds of Men, but the Drúedain must have escaped his Shadow; for their laughter and the laughter of Orcs are as different as is the light of Aman from the darkness of Angband" (*UT* 401). Here lies some strong authorial authority on the seriousness of laughter and mirth as certainly an indicative, and potentially a protective force. Tolkien eliminates the Drúedain from the list of potential orc-ancestors without a second glance, simply because of the way the two races laugh. The Drúedain could not have been used to breed Orcs because their laughter is light. But Tolkien's nonchalant confidence in the laughter of the Drúedain ought not surprise careful readers, for similar power is given to elvish merriment in *The Fellowship of the Ring*. Frodo, marching steadily toward Buckland away from pursuant Black Riders, cannot help but feel an urge to put on the Ring, "so strong that, almost before he realised what he was doing, his hand was groping in his pocket. But at that moment there came a sound like mingled song and laughter. Clear voices rose and fell in the starlit air. The black shadow straightened up and retreated" (*FR* 77). Far from causing vulnerability, the laughing light of Gildor and his frolicsome companions banishes any presence of darkness in their midst, and so long as the hobbits remain with the elves, they only gain insight and security. An uncanny strength resides in elvish laughter and light.

The elves continue to emphasise this strength, for our last supporting illustration of mirth's protective nature dwells in Rivendell, the Last Homely House at the very edge of the Wilds, secure under the shadow of the Misty Mountains. Despite its precarious surroundings, this happy vale shall ever speak to our minds of comfort and rest. Tolkien's descriptions of Rivendell in *The Hobbit* intensify these qualities. After a few pages of preparation for the coziness about to come their way, a weary Bilbo and his tired companions stumble upon a troop of very merry elves. If we were at all wondering what makes the elves who dwell here different from the treacherous lands around them, a glance at their culture proves sufficient to allay our curiosity. They laugh. They sing. They are, in fact, ridiculous, and we often forget that Tolkienian elves made their debut in *The Hobbit* warbling:

> O! Will you be staying,
> Or will you be flying?
> Your ponies are straying!
> The daylight is dying!
> To fly would be folly,
> To stay would be jolly
>   And listen and hark
>   Till the end of the dark
>   to our tune
>   ha! ha!

This gleeful melody is quickly followed by quite the elvish introduction: "So they laughed and sang in the trees; and pretty fair nonsense I daresay you think it. Not that they would care; they would only laugh all the more if you told them so. They were elves of course" (*H* 49).

Surprised? But herein lies the very homeliness of Rivendell; this is precisely what heartens Bilbo and sets Gandalf at his ease. Remember my previous suggestion that Tolkien makes a clear connection between mirth and wisdom? Well, the people of wise, judicious Elrond are one of the merriest of them all, and they continue to be so even as readers enter the more mature version of Rivendell in *The Lord of the Rings*. The number of times the elves are described as merry is astonishing, and mentions of laughter in Elrond's halls tumble one after another. Frodo laughs, Bilbo laughs, Aragorn laughs, and so do Elrond and Gandalf. Sam does well to exclaim, "Elves here, and Elves there! Some like kings, terrible and splendid; and some as merry as children" (*FR* 219), while an exchange between Pippin and Frodo summarises the mirth abounding in Rivendell: "'It seems impossible, somehow, to feel gloomy or depressed in this place. I feel I could sing, if I knew the right song for the occasion.' 'I feel like singing myself,' laughed Frodo" (*FR* 220). While this may not strike one as any great revelation, we must keep in mind that Frodo has just been stabbed with a Morgul blade by the Ringwraith on Weathertop. Yet now he, along with his older and wiser friends, are busy merrymaking! And that is the nature of The Last Homely House. "Merely to be there was a cure for weariness, fear, and sadness" (*FR* 219). If laughter is contagious, Rivendell's cheer heals the deepest wounds. It stands as a beautiful escape.

In fact, escape is precisely what Tolkien puts on display through his buoyant depictions of shelters along a terrible road. In true "On Fairy-Stories" fashion, the laughter of the Shire offers hobbits an escape from the "whims of evanescent fashion," whims which would otherwise draw the folk of the Four Farthings to lusts that would destroy them, to lusts that had already destroyed so many other men (OFS 169). In the same manner, the laughter of Tom Bombadil and the elves in Rivendell opens to characters of Middle-earth the chance to escape from a terrible prison, even if for just a short while. But if just a short while enables heroes to continue on their journey, it is enough. What would have happened to Frodo and the Ring without Tom's merry dols or the merry feasts of the Last Homely House? The possibilities chill our hearts, but they should also charge our hearts with the importance of escape – good, noble, dignified escape from the prisons of envy and bitterness and fear – through laughter. Mirth's first strength is the sheltering of our souls.

Discovery in Mirth

> "'I see,' laughed Strider. 'I look foul and feel fair. Is that it? All that is gold does not glitter, not all those who wander are lost.'" (Aragorn to some very frightened hobbits in *The Fellowship of the Ring*)

Thus for the shelter and protection of simple pleasures and simple laughs. But sheltering can only last for a time, and escape does not equal victory. Indeed, within the three examples of mirth's escape – the hobbits, Tom Bombadil, and Rivendell – Tolkien quietly advances the idea that it would be very ill for us to rest contented in sanctuary. After all, Bilbo needs an adventure, Tom Bombadil is unanimously rejected as an option to guard the Ring because he would "most likely throw it away. Such things have no hold upon his mind," and The Last Homely House must either answer the call to war or steadily repair to the Grey Havens (*FR* 259). Escape does not achieve the final goal. Ultimately, danger must be contested. Tolkien teaches us how to contest it by portraying a certain quality in each of those characters who do not merely avoid harm, but consciously skirmish with the source of evil in their own lives. It is a subtle portrayal, to be sure, but one which upon discovery proves difficult to ignore. It is the picture of a man laughing at himself.

You see, there is such a thing as the danger of taking oneself too seriously, and Tolkien knew it well. Thus, through "Leaf by Niggle", "Smith of Wootton Major", "Farmer Giles of Ham", hobbits, dwarves, and elves Tolkien encourages us to laugh at ourselves, as if just what we need were a mirror in which to better behold our foibles and correct them. Indeed, an opportunity for introspection might be precisely what we lack, and that is what the mirror of humour offers us. While sometimes our mirrors must take sombre and grave and even dangerous forms, such as Frodo's strange dreams throughout *The Lord of the Rings* and Galadriel's pool in Lothlórien, oftentimes correction can just as well be found in merrier looking glasses. In fact, the graver introspections often become needful simply because we neglect to make use of the frolicsome ones. In his works, therefore, Tolkien presents us with the utility and enjoyment of comic self-encounters. He offers us the power of laughing at ourselves.

This image of the man who laughs, nestled though it is within pages of beauty and grandeur and pain, slowly makes itself conspicuous both through positive and negative example. Here we see Gandalf contentedly smoking his pipe whilst snickering between puffs; there we note Saruman who cannot make fun without mockery. Here we find Pippin cracking jokes about himself in blissful abandon; there we encounter the Witch-king who cannot abide wisecracks in any form. And as the multi-storied picture unfolds, we gradually come to realise the virtue of a self-induced chuckle. For, far deeper than a moment's relief from the weightiness of life, these laughing moments provide an open door to recovery, a clear vision which hopefully leads to a little miracle of growth.

All of Tolkien's above mentioned works, as well as *The Hobbit* and *The Lord of the Rings*, begin with an opportunity for recovery. Their opening lines describe a place and people not our own but very like our own, imperfections included and perhaps writ rather large. As soon as we discover that Farmer Giles "was a slow sort of fellow, rather set in his ways, and taken up with his own affairs" who "had his hands full (he said) keeping the wolf from his door: that is, keeping himself as fat and comfortable as his father before him," we instantly feel at home and comfortable, too (FGH 71). Certainly, we may chuckle at Farmer Giles' long, officious-sounding name, and at Garm his dog who fears Giles mainly because "he could bully and brag better than [Garm] could," but were we honest we would admit our chuckles bubble up mostly because in the farmer and his dog we see ourselves (FGH 70). The loveable, lazy yet clever Farmer Giles and his desire for respect touches us right at our funny bones, mainly because we share the same desires and idiosyncrasies. We see ourselves also in the protagonist of "Leaf by Niggle", who has a nuisance of a kind heart, a propensity to be idle, and a knack for starting projects he does not finish because they are "too large and ambitious for his skill" (LN 195). The way Niggle curses in his heart the visitors whom he himself invited, and the fact that most of his accomplishments are the "many things that he had not the face to say *no* to," are unfortunate realities in our own lives that we would never admit to were they not set forth before us in a congenial, smirk-inducing manner (LN 197). When it comes to neighbours, Tolkien proves positively hobbit-like in using humour to unmask the petty nature of our squabbles. Instead of a sermon, we smile our way to the conclusion that we really just ought to look after our potatoes, and that maybe not all canvas and paint should be used for house-repairs. The stories sting us with their clarity, but there could not exist a more enjoyable way to be stung.

"Smith of Wootton Major" proffers a sadder outlook on the importance of laughing at ourselves through the negative example of Master Cook Nokes. Whereas the Queen of Faery delights in laughter and dance and play, Nokes cannot stand the tiniest bit of humour at his expense. Actually, Nokes laughs all the time, but, as with most anything else good in life, he reserves that right to himself alone. Granting nobody permission to question his dignity, authority, or expertise, Nokes meets his downfall instead. First, he takes himself so seriously that the truly serious things in life, like the world of Faery, to him appear laughable by comparison. Second, by denying insight to others, Nokes denies insight to himself and thus remains blind to truths regarding his character. The end of the tale leaves him a gaunt fool, oblivious to art, beauty, wisdom, and the proper use of sugar.

On the other hand, the Faery world that ought not to be laughed at oddly enough inspires laughter. The Faery Queen's gaiety has already been mentioned, but everyone else who enters Faery also imbibes the gift of laughing and being laughed with. The first Master Cook returns from his long holiday to Faery a wiser man, and the narrator explains, "Now he was merrier, and often said and did most laughable things; and at feasts he would himself sing gay songs, which was not expected of Master Cooks" (SWM 247). For Smith Smithson, an encounter with Faery leads to a life full of song, including a merry dance with the Faery Queen herself and the humility to be graced with the sound of her laughter. And Smith learns, and he grows, and his works are beautiful. Finally, when a clumsy, silent little boy named Tim comes across the Even-star, he is suddenly changed, "and he laughed and became merry, and sang softly to himself. Then he got up and began to dance all alone with an odd grace that he had never shown before. The children all laughed and clapped" (SWM 280). That last sentence is easily overlooked in the joy of Tim's transformation, but it is key. Tim can now be laughed with because Faery's wisdom and joy have granted him Faery's humility and humour. So the wise laugh and the humble are wise, for they have met the clear view.

This also we find in *The Unfinished Tales*, where even members of the White Council benefit from play. Although Tolkien does not use this version of the White Council in *The Lord of the Rings*, it still bears study, for here Tolkien offers us an unmistakable display of humour's clear-sighted abilities through Saruman and Gandalf's contrary approaches to laughter. The former walks as one clothed in lofty wisdom far above merry hobbits and their silly pipe-weed, whereas the latter sees strength in their jolly ways and mirth in general. If only, for Saruman's sake, their differences stopped at pipe-weed! But they do not. Saruman, like Master Cook Nokes, takes himself much too seriously and therefore envies Gandalf to the point of distraction, secretly imitating him by taking up pipe-weed while openly scoffing at him for "playing with his toys of fire and smoke, while others are in earnest speech" (*UT* 366). Of course, Saruman "hated mockery, however gentle" (*UT* 366). Gandalf, however, shows a completely opposite attitude to laughter. He chuckles at Saruman's exaggerated sensibilities but, instead of shaming him, gently prompts Saruman to a better understanding of himself by playfully suggesting that "smoke blown out [clears the] mind from shadows within" (*UT* 366). Nobody notices the crooked path Saruman is walking; that is, nobody but lighthearted, puffing Gandalf. He suddenly grows keen on Saruman's relationship to the rings, and we get the point that laughing grey wizards might have a clearer view of things than grave white wizards do.

Their different perspectives to merriment follow these wizards to the very end. Saruman, the one who cannot laugh unless it be to mock another, hides his wicked, self-deceived heart until he is back-stabbed by a servant. But the back-stabbing only takes place after Saruman has sold his soul to destroy the joyful culture of the hobbits, that "childish folk" unworthy of any serious attention (*UT* 366). On the contrary, Gandalf, who does not deem himself too wise to laugh and play with fireworks, reaches startling discernment about the Ring, the wizard, and his own role in the greater story of the Third Age. He observes in *The Fellowship of the Ring* that "it would be a grievous blow to the world [...] if all your kind, jolly, stupid Bolgers, Hornblowers, Boffins, Bracegirldles, and the rest, not to mention the ridiculous Bagginses, became enslaved," and thus is content to remain a laughable and strange old man to the hobbits until he gives his life to protect them (*FR* 48). Gandalf sees clearly and conquers because he knows how to laugh.

Now, it is all well and good for readers to appreciate self-laughter when it is safely tucked away in a story not of this world, when we are not the ones doing the laughing. It is quite another matter to reenact that mode of self-discovery in our own lives. But Tolkien anticipates this recalcitrance on our part and therefore goads us to join in the fun by simply browsing through any one of his short stories. It proves quite impossible to pick up a copy of "Smith of Wootton Major" or "Farmer Giles of Ham", or, most telling, "Leaf by Niggle", and get through the tale without chuckling about the way our neighbour reminds us of Ham's pessimistic blacksmith or how Nokes's self-importance brings to mind that one college professor we had twenty years ago. Tolkien was an artist and, fantasy writer or no, his favourite subject was us, a truth inescapable as you see the eccentricities of our world come to life in his narratives.

However, Tolkien does not stop with merely presenting a funny picture of our world. The point of laughing at ourselves is not to make us laughable. That would be useless and cruel, like the mockery which took place before the Black Gates of Mordor. Rather, Tolkien takes his readers a step further into that almost cathartic power of humour he showcases in his legendarium. Of course, Tolkien would prefer "recovery" and "escape" to "catharsis", but they all point to the healing nature of humour he wants us to embrace. Instead of cornering us into a silly depiction of ourselves, he gifts us with a clear view of what we are like, thereby enabling us to escape from the prison of our current foibles into the pastures of what we could, and should, become. In other words, Tolkien shows us how the world is grey, and then gives us the tools to paint it green. And though he often hands us these paintbrushes through tears, he just as often does so through laughter. His hope, I believe, was for all his readers to end like Niggle and Parish who after a difficult process of self-discovery "both laughed. Laughed – the Mountains rang with it!" (LN 220).

Victory in Mirth

> "First he was a conspirator, now he's a jester. He'll end up by becoming a wizard – or a warrior!" (Frodo about Sam in *The Fellowship of the Ring*)

We have so far seen that in Tolkien those who are wise laugh the hardest and those who are good laugh the most. Now we shall discover that those who are great laugh the strongest. Mirth and might sing together in all of Tolkien's writings, whether in Middle-earth or Wootton Major or Ham or Niggle's Parish. Shocking is the number of times laughter rings out on the battlefield and perilous are the situations occasioning the silliest jokes and most playful banter. But it is the good mirth that prevails. In this third area of humour's strength, then, we reach a fuller understanding of the way merriment fits into the cosmic battle of good versus evil, and we finally cross from escape and recovery into consolation.

Tolkien's legendarium features at least three facets to the fighting power mirth can bring to this cosmic battle. The first facet of power is the Power to Decide. Although we might not immediately link laughter with decision, Tolkien forges this link in a variety of ways. For one, before many a terrible determination or dreadful leap in Tolkien's works there echoes an eery laugh. In that horrid Kinslaying in *The Silmarillion*, Fëanor "laughed as one fey" before crying "What I have left behind I count no loss; needless baggage on the road it has proved. [...] Let the ships burn!" (S 90). This must be the most sickening moment in *The Silmarillion*, but it is not the only time sickening glee accompanies sickening deeds. Túrin, too, laughs as one fey before taking his own life, essentially calling his existence nothing but "a bitter jest, indeed" (S 225). Leaving *The Silmarillion* for *The Lord of the Rings*, we watch helplessly as Denethor, on the brink of choosing good or ill, laughs towards his conclusion: a fiery death on the pyre of his reason, sanity, and hope. These terrible decisions were each sped by a fiendish cackle.

Most of the laughing resolutions in Tolkien's works, though, are made by merrier people in brighter times, even if they do not always lead toward brighter courses. Hobbits choose most clearly under mirth's influence than anything else, as Bilbo so neatly shows in his Long-Expected Party and elaborate farewell joke. The prank Bilbo plays on all his dearest friends enables him to do something grand, something difficult: leave the Shire. Even if his vanishing act was rather "spoiled" by Gandalf's additional flash of light, and even if Bilbo managed to "alarm or offend most of [his] relations" for his private enjoyment, one realises that just such a merry farewell was about the only way he could ever leave his dear old home, and indeed "was the only point [Gandalf] ever saw in the affair" (*FR* 31-32, 34). Frodo, as usual, follows in his uncle's footsteps, for it takes not one but two merry feasts plus a jolly good conspiracy to get him away from the Shire. The first "very cheerful" party, which involves wine and a few witty pleasantries at the Sackville-Bagginses' expense, occurs before Frodo leaves for his house in Crickhollow, while the second happy dinner entails some very merry mushrooms and the unmasking of an equally merry conspiracy of friends, which leaves Frodo laughing and feeling "happy; happier than I have felt for a long time" despite himself (*FR* 67, 103). Only after these parties and pranks is Frodo truly ready to leave his homeland. Mirth provides both Bilbo and Frodo the might to decide to leave.

And long after Frodo has left Hobbiton behind, the same sort of humble humour helps him make much darker decisions. How else than by laughing do Frodo and Sam in *The Fellowship of the Ring* seal their decision to break from the Fellowship? In the middle of a tense and tearful debate, Sam declares, "I'm coming too, or neither of us isn't going. I'll knock holes in all the boats first" (*FR* 397). Here lie two hobbits staring at a dreadful choice between friendship and hell, but look at Frodo's response: "Frodo actually laughed. A sudden warmth and gladness touched his heart. 'Leave one!' he said. 'We'll need it'" (*FR* 397). Frodo laughs, and the chasm of decision is crossed. This hobbit-like cheer and companionship see Sam and Frodo to the very end, even to the pass of Cirith Ungol. This also was a path chosen with laughter. Indeed, Tolkien explicitly states the case as if to make it easier for us to understand what mirth can do. As wave upon wave of evil men enter the Black Gate of Mordor, oliphaunts pop into Sam's mind and he cites a sweet, sunny poem about these legendary beasts – right in front of the Black Gate, with Gollum pawing at their heels, and in the midst of Frodo's tortuous choice between one terrifying unknown and another! Despite the seeming inappropriateness of Sam's childlike bit of verse, Tolkien explains, "Frodo stood up. He had laughed in the midst of all his cares when Sam trotted out the old fireside rhyme of *Oliphaunt*, and the laugh had released him from hesitation" (*TT* 633). Frodo's choice is hard, but after voicing a wry wish for a thousand oliphaunts to break into Mordor, he makes his decision: they go to Cirith Ungol. For hobbits, mirth gives might not just to leave, but also to go.

While this usage of laughter is fun to observe, humour's decision-making power makes more startling appearances in Tolkien's ring narratives, those soliloquies preceding a character's final decision regarding his or her relationship to the Ring. Everyone but Frodo and Sam, who are each doomed to carry the Ring for a time, employs laughter in their process of deciding against donning Sauron's baneful trinket. As Gandalf deftly retrieves the Ring from a clawing Bilbo, "a spasm of anger passed swiftly over the hobbit's face again. Suddenly it gave way to a look of relief and a laugh. 'Well, that's that,' he said" (*FR* 34). Bilbo's spastic look of wrath followed by sudden laughter reoccurs when Bilbo encounters the Ring in the Hall of Fire, and again he overcomes temptation by aid of "the light and music of of Rivendell" until he "smiled and laughed happily" once more (*FR* 226). Bilbo laughs to let go of the Ring.

Though this outburst of laughter might be an odd coincidence, it characterises every one of the Ring's defeats in *The Lord of the Rings*. Gandalf requires light streaming in from a Shire window to settle his rejection of Frodo's pleading offer. Later Tom Bombadil, quite possibly the merriest soul alive, laughingly toys with the Ring before putting it on his finger as though it were child's play. And Tom does not vanish. Instead, the Ring vanishes in a sparkle until "Tom leaned forward and handed it back to [Frodo] with a smile" (*FR* 130). Tolkien was right to describe this scene as "both comical and alarming," but it is also telling (*FR* 130). Tom's excessive jubilation acts as a shield against the wiles of the Ring. And lest we say this power belongs to Tom Bombadil alone, the interplay of mirth and the Ring continues when Aragorn confronts the golden band. Alone with Frodo, Sam, and Pippin, he points out the frighteningly obvious danger: "If I was after the Ring, I could have it – NOW!" (*FR* 168). But Strider embraces who he is, Aragorn son of Arathorn, the gold that does not glitter and the wanderer who is not lost, and his face softens into "a sudden smile" as he laughs heartily (*FR* 168). Aragorn passes his test, and the Ring passes into safety once more.

A more beautiful and terrible ring narrative awaits in the person of Galadriel. In her we also find more beautiful and terrible laughter. Her temptation begins with "a sudden clear laugh," and then escalates into that horrifying line, "All shall love me and despair!" only to melt away as "suddenly she laughed again, and lo! she was shrunken: a slender elf-woman, clad in simple white, whose gentle voice was soft and sad. "I pass the test […]. I will diminish, and go into the West, and remain Galadriel" (*FR* 356-357). Like Aragorn, Galadriel needs to laugh. She at last grasps a clear view of herself through laughter, and through laughter she gathers strength to embrace her perfect consolation.

However, this strength does not belong to kings and queens only, for Boromir and Faramir demonstrate the same melancholy mirth in their decisions to overcome the Ring. After all, "Boromir smiled" are the last words describing his life, a life he gave defending the four hobbits who made his mastery of the Ring impossible (*TT* 404). When Faramir later stumbles upon the Ring, his stern and glinting grey eyes seem anything but impervious to its call. Then he "sat down in his chair and began to laugh quietly," and the tension recedes into ripples of calm (*TT* 665). Faramir's laughter with the Ring lurking so near appears strange only if we forget the might of mirth to do hard things. Ring narratives simply provide stronger examples of the laughter which released Frodo from hesitation, and the mirth accompanying a hard task done well.

Laughter and hardship are invariable companions in the story of Middle-earth, as shown by the second facet of humour's power, the Power to Battle. In fact, the partnership between mirth and might takes us back to the Ainur themselves, where Tulkas greets us with abounding laughter and fearful warfare. He "laughs ever, in sport or in war, and even in the face of Melkor he laughed in battles" (*S* 29). This war god may laugh, but he is no joking matter, for his "spirit of great strength and hardihood" saves the Valar: "and Arda was filled with the sound of his laughter. So came Tulkas the Strong, whose anger passes like a mighty wind, scattering cloud and darkness before it; and Melkor fled before his wrath and his laughter" (*S* 35). Strong, hardy Tulkas laughs, and that laughter dispels the strongest malice. If we ever had any doubts about mirth's might, this truly epic scene must surely bid them flee, just as Melkor cowers before the joyous shouts of Tulkas.

Moving from Valar to Maiar, we find Gandalf's jollity likewise grows into battle-strength. Unwittingly echoing characteristics of Tulkas, Frodo commemorates Gandalf as "swift in anger, quick to laugh" as though he realised both mirth and might joined to mark Gandalf's life (*FR* 351). Frodo remembers well, for Gandalf was swift to laugh "long and merrily" with a sound "warm and kindly like a gleam of sunshine" (*TT* 485, 530). But when Gandalf's sunshine strives with Saruman, the Witchking, or the Mouth of Sauron, it only blazes with victory. In fact, Gandalf's struggle with Saruman before Isengard in *The Two Towers* conclusively ends with Gandalf indulging in a hearty fit of laughter. And although Gandalf had previously warned Merry and Pippin that jesting would make one susceptible to Saruman's subtle words, Tolkien makes clear that Gandalf's laughter made Saruman's "fantasy [vanish] like a puff of smoke" (*TT* 568). I highly doubt we should not be thinking of *The Unfinished Tales* account, where laughter, clear vision, and smoke also make an appearance. Whatever the case, Gandalf's mirth wins him many a battle before his work is done and his consolation arrives.

Much the same proves true of Aragorn, rightful King of Gondor, and Éomer his royal ally. Although some picture Aragorn as grim, Tolkien's depiction of his character differs drastically. We find the Ranger laughing with hobbit friends as they await Black Riders in Bree, and again they laugh while undergoing recovery in the Houses of Healing. However, for the most moving picture of wartime laughter we must look to the Pelennor Fields, where not only recovery but also consolation greet the merry heart: "'Now for wrath, now for ruin and a red nightfall!' These staves [Éomer] spoke, yet he laughed as he said them" (*RK* 829). What an incongruous image! In the face of despair, Éomer laughs. No help has come, but he sings. While this is undoubtedly Tolkienian homage to Northern courage – laughter in the face of despair – Tolkien does not allow the despair to win. Certainly, he makes us walk through the despair with Éomer, but he does not let the despair set his story's, or our story's, boundaries. Tolkien acknowledges the hopelessness, but in a distinct variation from Northernness, he does not let the hopelessness prevail. For then Éomer meets his consolation, his greatest eucatastrophe. A few moments into his future the despair he despised crumbles before the Return of the King, "and the mirth of the Rohirrim was a torrent of laughter and a flashing of swords" (*RK* 829). Yet again, Tolkien here specifically draws a connection between mirth and battle power. The flashing of the Rohirrim's swords ringing with the sound of their laughter is no coincidence. Rather, their mirth was their flashing of swords. The warrior's valour and gaiety flow from the same source and express themselves together, each weaving into the other, to give strength to both. While Tolkien sets up this picture of Northern bravery mainly to jar our expectations with a eucatastrophe, a reason behind the singing slaying, Tolkien does cause Éomer to walk through shadow and Éomer does persevere under the darkness, showing us that we can persevere even when we think we cannot win. And humour is the expression of that seeming incongruity – until the eucatastrophe comes. Just what the source of strength is that gives laughter and song to swords we shall discover in a moment, but for the present let us never forget that Éomer laughed before the King arrived. His laughter prepared him for a good battle, and the battle's good turn led to a joyous consolation.

Before I address eucatastrophe, I should provide some final samples of mirth's Power to Battle that beg for our attention. After all, how can a discussion of humour in Tolkien exclude the overtly funny battleground scenes in *The Lord of the Rings*? The swaggering competition between Gimli and Legolas for highest death toll exemplifies the perseverance a game can give. Beginning with the hopeless siege on Helm's Deep and continuing all the way to a desperate struggle on Pelennor Fields, the killing contest between this dwarf and elf enables them to combat evil until eighty-three orcs lie dead between them. On a less gruesome note, Tolkien shows how a competition of banter can also breathe perseverance into struggle. When Merry and Pippin find themselves caught by a ruthless gang of orcs, witty play helps them devise a way out of their captors' clutches and into Fangorn Forest. Though their position is dark and dangerous, we laugh as Merry first congratulates Pippin on his "good work" of "playing up to [...]that hairy little villain" but hastily asserts that "Cousin Brandybuck is going in front now" with his unsurpassable knowledge of the lay of the land (*TT* 448). Their humour mingles with cleverness to produce a courage only a funny hobbit could display. Together the merry companions reach safety, leaving us to marvel at the power hobbits have to joke and at the power hobbits gain by joking. Yes, humour can help dawrves, elves, and even halflings win battles.

Not surprisingly, Merry and Pippin continue to play starring roles in the last area of mirth's victory, the Power to Hope and Heal. During the siege of Minas Tirith, both hobbits draw near to death's door, with Merry suffering the poison of the Witchking himself. Thankfully, Merry and Pippin find hope to heal through shared merriment, something Éowyn lacks until Faramir's warmth revives her. Similar to Faramir's warmth, Pippin's decision "to sound cheerful" as he escorts his friend to the Houses of Healing, is successful and his cheerful medicine stops Merry's descent into shadow (*RK* 841). Merry remains open to merriment, regardless of any recent altercations with witch wraiths, and this coupled with Pippin's pleasantries brings him to full healing. In fact, as Aragorn plainly states, "He is weary now, and grieved [...]. But these evils can be amended, so strong and gay a spirit is in him. His grief he will not forget; but it will not darken his heart, it will teach him wisdom" (*RK* 850-851). Not only does the king with healing hands put "strong" and "gay" together, and not only does he ascribe Merry's recovery to that strong and gay spirit, but he also states Merry's light heart will grant the hobbit hope to overcome his grief and teach him wisdom. Many are those who would benefit from just such a light heart, one that does not darken with sorrow but becomes purer, brighter, fairer through it. Little wonder does the Warden deem hobbits "a very remarkable race" and "very tough in fibre" (*RK* 852). His understanding is correct, as mirth gives Merry and Pippin the courage and victory for which they hoped.

It is well the Warden had a chance to see this remarkable recovery, because back in the Shire hope is steadily being beaten out of the hobbits, one by one, laugh by laugh. By the time Merry, Pippin, Frodo, and Sam return to their homeland, Saruman – that wizard who will not be mocked – has wrought ruin on the hobbits by snatching away their hope so effectively that the good people of the Four Farthings "did not seem quite sure whether laughing was allowed" (*RK* 980). Here we learn through negative example that hope and humour go together. Only the very incorruptible hobbits, the ones with the highest propensity for jollification, such as Farmer Maggot (great friend of Tom Bombadil that he is) and the Cottons (who never give up on Sam for a certain lively, lovely reason), do not lose their humour and hope during Sharkey's siege. They alone are ready to fight against and heal from Sharkey's pessimistic rule. The rest of the hobbits have forgotten how to laugh.

In contrast to this sorry picture of sad hobbits, Merry, Pippin, Frodo, and Sam return as heroes, sitting "at their ease laughing and talking and singing" (*RK* 980). They bring a hope covered in laughter, full of healing, and crowned with victory, as the Scouring of the Shire proves well. From this scouring, we realise that their comedy has matured in spirit and grown wiser, much like Merry and Pippin have grown taller in body. If their laughter made them strong, now their strength emboldens their laughter. Far from anomalous, Tolkien paints this lightheartedness as normal for weathered conquerors. In *The Two Towers*, Gandalf who conquered the Balrog "can be both kinder and more alarming, merrier and more solemn than before," while in the last chapters of *The Return of the King* a victorious Gandalf the White becomes "not so close as he used to be, though he laughs now more than he talks" (*RK* 576, 934). If Gandalf returns merrier from his long, dark night, should we be astonished when Tolkien says of Merry and Pippin, "if they were now large and magnificent, they were unchanged otherwise, unless they were indeed more fairspoken and more jovial and full of merriment than ever before" (*RK* 1002)? What happened to Gandalf in all his wars likewise happened to these hobbits in all their struggles: they learned to laugh. And their laughter brought hope and healing.

Indeed, they learned to laugh through their tears. This picture of mourning and mirth remains to complete our study of humour in Tolkien, to expose the full sting of laughter's power to hope and heal. And where best to find mourning than in *The Silmarillion's* most tragic character, Túrin Turambar? The man who laughed as one fey may yet teach us about mirth's power to mend, for if ever one were without hope of recovery and consolation, it was Túrin. His murder of Beleg Strongbow, truest of friends, drives Túrin so mad that his life evaporates into a horrifying, aimless hush. Could there exist a cure for such sorrow, a hope ready to heal the deepest of wounds? Yes. Awaiting Túrin's madness there sparkles a strangely simple remedy: a draught of water from the lake of "endless laughter" which is "fed from crystal fountains unfading, and guarded from defilement" (*S* 209). Túrin kneels to drink from these pure springs, and then he suddenly begins to weep only to arise "healed of his madness" (*S* 209). It is a moving scene, but do we grasp what we see? A madman is healed by weeping before a laughing lake. A murderer comes back to life through sorrow mingled with joy. Laughter and tears work together towards the strength of consolation, just as Nienna, the Vala of mourning, embodies. Tolkien describes her as mighty, "and those who hearken to her learn […] endurance in hope" (*S* 28). These words sound familiar, linking might and hope and endurance all together. Why? Because Tolkien describes humour in exactly the same manner! The endurance Nienna teaches corresponds to the perseverance Tulkas shows, and her release of tears mingles with his release of laughter. By inspiring hope as well as strength, mirth and mourning will eventually lead us to consolation.

And thus the most glorious occasions require both laughter and tears, as Sam discovers when he awakes from Mount Doom's nightmare to the bliss of beholding Gandalf in the land of Ithilien. The darkness ended, the eagles come, and Gandalf alive once more – what could be more glorious than this? The joy surpasses Sam's expression and he is left speechless, but then Gandalf teaches him, and us, how to rejoice. After uttering that breathtaking sentence, "A great Shadow has departed," the Wizard laughs, "and the sound was like music, or like water in a parched land; and as he listened the thought came to Sam that he had not heard laughter, the pure sound of merriment, for days upon days without count" (*RK* 930-31). Here is Sam's lake of laughter, where the madness of Mordor melts before the purity of merriment which that madness had, for a time, dispelled. Pure laughter heals him, just as Túrin encounters Eithel Ivrin to allay his evil. And, like Túrin, Sam's immediate response to the overpowering purity of Gandalf's gladness is to weep. However, while each walk through a recovery of laughing tears, there awaits for Sam a greater release to a greater consolation than Túrin's experience affords. His tears accomplish more than conquering an illness; they bring him to that joy which comes in the morning, described by Tolkien in natural hobbit terms: "Then, as a sweet rain will pass down a wind of spring and the sun will shine out the clearer, his tears ceased, and his laughter welled up, and laughing he sprang from his bed" (*RK* 931). From pure joy that awakens tears, Sam soars into life-giving laughter, and glimpses the consolation belonging to that great eucatastrophe of which Tolkien believes every fantasy should whisper. Sam becomes well again, to "feel like spring after winter, and sun on the leaves; and like trumpets and harps and all the songs [he has] ever heard" (*RK* 931). Here is a taste of heaven; here is laughter's resurrection. Here dwells a joy as poignant as grief and the glory of a great consolation.

Melkor Laughed, Too: The Fount of Mirth's Might and the Assurance of Consolation

Although I have gone on at length to show the high regard Tolkien pays to humour, and the noble role it can play in our lives, I cannot leave the subject as it has so far been presented. Especially in the previous section I alluded to the notion that the side on which humour sits might be just as important to its power as the humour itself. Now comes the time to make the point emphatically: humour is not an end in itself. For Tolkien, the friendly grins in a sunny garden and the playful teasing on a dark battlefield either results from something deeper than the grin and the joke, or they are pointless. After all, Melkor laughed, too, and he lost. The secret of victory, then, does not lie in laughter itself. There must lie behind good, strong humour something much better and stronger than humour alone. But what is it? Wise men have said laughter is the best medicine, yet I believe Tolkien suggests an even wiser statement of the case might be "a merry heart maketh a cheerful countenance" and "doeth good like a medicine" (Prov. 15.13, 17.22). Did you catch the difference? Laughter is not the best medicine; the merry heart, the joyful soul that does the laughing, is. Mirth proves but a stepping stone, a tool whose potency depends entirely on the springs from which it sprung. And that spring is goodness itself.

Goodness, that essential quality derived from a perspective larger than selfish gain and a realisation of a higher story greater than our own, is the fount from which mirth's might flows. It is Sam Gamgee looking up through a black sky and cherishing the white star still blazing. It is Túrin finding respite in pure waters. It is Éomer smiling at the black ships with the banner of the White Horse rippling in the wind behind him. It is Parish and Niggle, after much toil and labour, laughing so that the mountains ring with their glee. They see the greater story, the bigger battle, the completed Parish, and it gives them the right hope and the right fears and the right purpose. This good brings them joy, even in the pitch of pain, because this good causes them to trust there really is a "Joy beyond the walls of this world, poignant as grief" that yet endures (OFS 175). Gandalf knows this good joy well, as we see through the eyes of our merriest hobbit:

> Pippin glanced in some wonder at the face now close to his own, for the sound of that laugh had been gay and merry. Yet in the wizard's face he saw at first only lines of care and sorrow; though as he looked more intently he perceived that under all there was a great joy: a fountain of mirth enough to set a kingdom laughing, were it to gush forth (*RK* 742).

Gandalf's joyful heart is what causes uproarious laughter. Mirth is the expression of joy's confidence, and joy's confidence is bigger than oneself. It is the assurance that right will win, which was why Tolkien wrote, why his characters press on, why Bombadil tosses the Ring and Nienna weeps and Tulkas laughs and Rohan's swords sang as they slew. Humour works only when we embrace the source of its strength, when we grasp history's fuller story of consolation, that great eucatastrophe, and we fight for it. When mirth rests in good's might, mirth will make us mighty, and we too will know victory.

Thus we end where we began, at the battle of good versus evil, but hopefully a bit wiser for the laughs. Joy now shines as something very grave indeed, and its mirth the one that leads to good's triumph truly is as poignant as grief. But Tolkien, as usual, says it best through story, and so I conclude with one of his own conclusions, with laughter and tears, with that "piercing glimpse of joy, and heart's desire" from "On Fairy-Stories" (176), and with the beauty of consolation:

> And all the host laughed and wept, and in the midst of their merriment and tears the clear voice of the minstrel rose like silver and gold, and all men were hushed. And he sang to them, now in the Elven-tongue, now in the speech of the West, until their hearts, wounded with sweet words, overflowed, and their joy was like swords, and they passed in thought out to regions where pain and delight flow together and tears are the very wine of blessedness. (*RK* 933)

About the Author

JENNIFER RAIMUNDO has been enchanted by Tolkien ever since her parents first read *The Lord of the Rings* aloud for family time. This enchantment grew into fascination and study as Jenn used her undergraduate program to learn more about Tolkien and his literary friends and then set out on a Master of Arts in Inklings and Medieval Studies with Signum University. Jenn has written several articles and conference papers on the Inklings, and plans to pursue a doctoral degree in the Inklings and Education. In addition to reading and writing about the Inklings, Jenn works at Signum University as the Lead of Institutional Planning. She currently resides in Washington, D.C., where she enjoys to hike and drink too much coffee.

Bibliography

CARPENTER, Humphrey. *J.R.R. Tolkien: A Biography*. Boston: Houghton Mifflin, 2000.

The Holy Bible. King James Version. *Bible Hub*. 2014. Web. 28 June 2014. <http://www.*biblehub.com*/kjv>.

ROY, Durga, et al. "Pathological Laughter and Crying and Psychiatric Comorbidity After Traumatic Brain Injury." *Journal of Neuropsychiatry and Clinical Neurosciences* 27.4: 299-303 (2015). Web. 10 April 2016.

TOLKIEN, John Ronald Reuel. "Farmer Giles of Ham." 1949. In *Tales from the Perilous Realm*. New York: Houghton Mifflin, 2008. 99-166.

—— *The Hobbit: Or, There and Back Again*. London: George Allen & Unwin, 1937. Fourth edition, London: George Allen & Unwin, 1978.

—— "Leaf by Niggle." 1964. In *Poems and Stories*. New York: Houghton Mifflin, 1994. 193-224.

—— *The Lord of the Rings*. 2nd ed. New York: Houghton Mifflin, 2003.

—— "On Fairy-Stories." 1964. In *Poems and Stories*. New York: Houghton Mifflin, 1994. 113-192.

—— *The Silmarillion*. Ed. Christopher TOLKIEN. 2nd ed. New York: Houghton Mifflin, 2001.

—— "Smith of Wootton Major." 1967. In *Tales from the Perilous Realm*. New York: Houghton Mifflin, 2008. 243-282.

—— *Unfinished Tales*. Ed. Christopher Tolkien. New York: Ballantine, 1980.

WILKINS, J. and A.J. EISENBRAUN. "Humour Theories and the Physiological Benefits of Laughter." *Advances in Mind-Body Medicine* 24.2: 8-12 (2009).

Ted Nasmith
Lalaith

Łukasz Neubauer

Plain Ignorance in the Vulgar Form: Tolkien's Onomastic Humour in *Farmer Giles of Ham*

Abstract

As a die-hard philologist, J.R.R. Tolkien was always exceptionally careful in the choice of names for his numerous characters and locations. Whether they be of (originally) Norse, Celtic, Finnish or other provenance, both the anthroponyms and the toponyms he used for the Middle-earth characters give the appearance of having been methodically selected to comply with the rigid contours of his complex linguistic map. Seen in this light, his short and light-hearted medieval fable *Farmer Giles of Ham* makes a notable, if somewhat disregarded, exception where the typically serious author frequently gives vent to his outstanding sense of philological humour. Here Tolkien's comic talent really shines through, as the reluctant hero Giles suddenly finds himself face to face with his not-quite-mortal foe, the greedy but craven dragon by the name of Chrysophylax Dives, and so the story gradually develops into what in all likelihood is a tongue-in-cheek rendering of the dragon episodes in *Beowulf* and the *Vǫlsunga saga*. A noteworthy addition to the witty plotline is the aforementioned philological humour which may not necessarily seem to be of prime importance to its younger readers, but could easily provoke many a smile amongst the more scholarly-minded people (as it doubtlessly did amongst his fellow Inklings). In *Farmer Giles of Ham* Tolkien evidently amused himself (and others) by giving the characters elaborate Latinate names and making up false etymologies. The paper seeks to examine the nature and supposed purpose of these little onomastic bits and pieces (i.e. mostly personal and place-names) with a particular emphasis on the sometimes surprisingly complex (and thus amusing) implications of their cultural roots.

Introduction

There seems to be no unanimity amongst Tolkien's scholars as to the actual genesis and, in particular, the purpose of writing of *Farmer Giles of Ham*. Originally published in 1949, though in all likelihood written at least a decade earlier,[1] around the time of *The Hobbit*'s publication in 1937, this somewhat neglected mock-medieval fable is a charming tale of its own which literally bursts with the writer's immense sense of humour, both situational and linguistic. Hence, in the introduction to its 1999 edition Christina Scull and Wayne G. Hammond argue that Tolkien's tale may have been invented mainly "to entertain his children" (*FGH* iii). His biographer Humphrey Carpenter appears to be a little bit more cautious, suggesting that it was probably written "in part to amuse [the writer's own] children, but chiefly to please himself" (220). Yet another view was once put forth by the author himself. Upon hearing that Allen & Unwin had decided to publish the story as a separate book, Tolkien declared that it "was not written for children; though as in the case of other books that will not necessarily prevent them from being amused by it" (*L* 108).

Perhaps, as is usually the case, the truth lies somewhere in the middle. No doubt, the origins of Farmer Giles and at least one more, unfortunately unfinished, story set in the Little Kingdom are to be found in an unspecified "local family game" (*L* 36) the Tolkiens are reported to have played in Oxfordshire in the 1930s, but its further development is visibly marked by the academic interests of the future author of *The Lord of the Rings*. At the very core of its plot is perhaps Tolkien's lifelong fascination with dragons and dragon-like creatures which stemmed from his vast knowledge of early medieval texts such as *Beowulf* and the *Vǫlsunga saga*. Another vital, perhaps even more intriguing, component of *Farmer Giles of Ham* is the writer's keen interest in the origins and meaning of words, in this case mainly the few but noteworthy names of both places (toponyms) and characters (anthroponyms and zoonyms). For Tolkien, who is known to have possessed "a most unusual sensitivity to the sound and appearance of

---

1 Although different dates have been suggested, the majority of scholars concur that *Farmer Giles* was written in or about 1937. It was certainly in existence by 1938 when Tolkien is believed to have read the story to a group of undergraduate students at Worcester College (Duriez 164). In *The Road to Middle-earth*, Tom Shippey cautiously maintains that *Farmer Giles* was written "in the period 1935-8" (11).

words" (Carpenter 177), the very contact with *nomina propria*, both English and not, appears to have regularly generated curious semantic associations that spurred his uncommonly vivid imagination.[2] Such is in all likelihood the principal *raison d'être* for such characters as Eärendil[3] and Gandalf[4] or places like Mirkwood[5] and Mordor[6] as well as various other names that may be found in the indices to *The Lord of the Rings* or *The Silmarillion*.

The case of *Farmer Giles of Ham* is no exception. While its plot centres on the rather disinclined, and for the most part largely reluctant, hero bearing the proud name of Ægidius Ahenobarbus Julius Agricola de Hammo, or "in the vulgar form […] Farmer Giles of Ham" (*FGH* 9), it is not improbable that perhaps as important as the narrative is the subtle, but nonetheless distinct layer of philological humour which may easily go unnoticed in the eyes of a less-informed reader. Tolkien's witty puns and ingenious wordplays, however, certainly did amuse his fellow Inklings when the earliest drafts and thoughts for the story were presented to them during the regular evening meetings in C.S. Lewis's rooms at Magdalen College or the somewhat less formal lunchtime gatherings at the Eagle and Child. It is not difficult to imagine their understanding nods and smiles or even outbreaks of contagious laughter upon hearing that, for instance, the crucial question of what a blunderbuss is should be settled by the "Four Wise Clerks of Oxenford" (*FGH* 15)[7] or that the scheming dragon Chrysophylax Dives should promise to pay his enormous ransom on the feast of St. Hilarius and St. Felix (*FGH* 48).

It seems rather doubtful that the very character and classification of all the personal and place names that appear in *Farmer Giles of Ham* could have been consciously predetermined prior to its actual composition. While some of them,

---

2 Well known is, for instance, the story of young Tolkien's "excitement" by certain Welsh words (not necessarily proper names) he once saw painted on coal trucks (1971 radio interview for BBC4, quoted in Hooker 243). There is no denying that his professional interest in languages could be traced back to some such incidents in the writer's childhood.
3 Cf. Old English *éarendel* "ray of light, morning star" in Cynewulf's *Crist* (104).
4 Cf. Old Norse *Gandálfr* "Staff-Elf", one of the many dwarves listed in the *Dvergatal* section (9-16) of the eddic poem *Vǫluspá*.
5 Cf. Old Norse *Myrkviðr* "Murky Wood" which originally appears in the eddic poems *Lokasenna* (42) and *Vǫlundarkviða* (1), but was later borrowed (and anglicised into "Mirkwood") by William Morris. Tolkien probably first came across this name in Morris's novel *A Tale of the House of Wolfings* (1888).
6 Cf. Old English *morðor* "mortal sin" (later also "murder, manslaughter").
7 Christina Scull and Wayne G. Hammond believe that the said clerks, whose impoverished prototype is to be found in Chaucer's *Canterbury Tales*, were in fact the editors of the *Oxford English Dictionary*, James A.H. Murray, Henry Bradley, W.A. Craigie and C.T. Onions (111).

such as Worminghall, might have indeed ignited Tolkien with a creative spark for the narrative, it is almost certain that others (e.g. Thame, which is not be found in the earliest manuscript version of the story), only came to him at some later stage, in the course of writing, or during the unusually long – though in his case rather habitually prolonged – ten-year process of revising this relatively short text. Regardless of their debatable origins, though, those names which bear some discernible traces of Tolkien's sense of philological humour could be loosely divided into four (sometimes overlapping) major categories which include: pseudo-classical reframing, replication of reality, semantic reversal and false etymology.

Pseudo-classical reframing

As a rule, the practice of lexical reframing could be defined as a purpose-led redescription or refiguration of the existing concept in a creative way which may – if such be the author's intention – produce the effects of a satirical commentary, ironic imitation or just a plain joke. There are obviously countless ways in which this comic effect may be achieved. Depending on its various linguistic properties, a particular name may invoke a certain degree of conceptual associations: temporal (e.g. medieval), cultural (e.g. Celtic), physical (e.g. tall), or other. The associations may of course be based upon specific stereotypical or arbitrary assumptions whose precision does not need to be so exceptionally high. What is more, the actual character of such associations may sometimes differ quite radically depending on the reader's cultural and/or educational background.

There are numerous instances of pseudo-classical reframing in Tolkien's tale, the first and foremost being of course the very name of its protagonist, Ægidius Ahenobarbus Julius Agricola de Hammo (*FGH* 9). Although unspecified with respect to time, the narrative appears to be set in post-Roman Britain,[8] when people are reported to have been "richly endowed with names" (*FGH* 9). The time frame is of course of lesser significance here. What matters is the somewhat exaggerated accumulation of Latinate names which, instead of

---

8 Its "postness" is naturally a matter of unsolvable debate. The anachronistic inclusion of the blunderbuss (a post-medieval firearm with an interesting etymology) may, for instance, call to mind the cannons which greatly disturb King Arthur in T.H. White's novel *The Once and Future King*.

raising the esteem for the character (as was indubitably the case with many a respected Roman citizen who would customarily have had three or more names), sometimes consciously, sometimes perhaps intuitively, brings a smile to the reader's face (much as it did in the times of Swift, Pope, Carey and other leading parodists of the Augustan age when the influence of classical literature was at its strongest).[9] Unlike the aforesaid Augustans, Tolkien was not much of a satirist, though. His most probable intent was to create a tongue-in-cheek analogy with medieval chronicles where the sense of pluperfectness could be enhanced by the not-always-factual references to the contacts a certain nation is said to have had with the Greek and/or Roman world.[10]

This amusing sense of pseudo-historical formality appears to be even further exercised in the case of the ruler of the Middle Kingdom. In the official letter he sends to Giles in recognition of the farmer's unanticipated heroics, the impressive stock of royal *nomina* is literally stretched out of any reasonable proportion, appearing as "Augustus Bonifacius Ambrosius Aurelianus Antoninus Pius et Magnificus" (*FGH* 20). Perhaps to amplify the effect, the king's names are additionally embellished by the four honorary (and for the most part synonymous) titles of "dux, rex, tyrannus et basileus" (*FGH* 20). Interestingly, this naturally overstressed aura of almost imperial decorum was perfectly captured by the book's illustrator Pauline Baynes who envisioned a serious-looking scribe with an enormous scroll whose third part appears to be covered only by the aforesaid names and titles (*FGH* 21).

Replication of reality

Those readers who possess at least a passing knowledge of Latin should notice that there is much more to these names than just their pseudo-classical look. In

---

9 Cf., for instance, the pseudo-classical names in Henry Carey's satirical play *Chrononhotonthologos* (1734) or the name of an imaginary Bavarian antiquarian Martinus Scriblerus which was originally Alexander Pope's pseudonym, but was subsequently adopted as a mock-patron of the literary group founded in 1714 by a number of London satirists. While these early-eighteenth-century names are not as expanded and elaborate as those of Tolkien's, it seems more than plausible that the very idea behind their use was likewise of comical nature.

10 A good example of this is the fabulous *Chronica Polonorum* which was written at the turn of the twelfth and thirteenth centuries by Master Vincentius of Cracow. Amongst the most intriguing pseudo-classical episodes to be found in its first book are those that relate the Poles' victorious confrontations against Alexander the Great and Julius Caesar.

fact, Tolkien's philological jest becomes all the more funny when the onomastic layer is properly understood. It is only then that the reader becomes fully aware of the writer's efforts to replicate the reality, which is of course hardly surprising in the case of the characters' nicknames,[11] but is not so apparent when it comes to their *pronomina*. To illustrate, those parents who chose to call their son Sigurd (Old Norse *Sigurðr* "protector of victory") may have had in mind a long and, above all, glorious military career for their offspring, but there was at the time absolutely no guarantee that their parental dreams could ever come true. The employment of highly meaningful names in literature, however, appears to be dictated by an entirely different purpose. They may, for instance, serve as useful *aide-mémoires* for the younger readers or provide the author's valuable comment on the actual disposition or character of a given person.[12]

It would not be particularly revealing to say that Tolkien's names are always in some way related to the characters that bear them. Those that appear in *Farmer Giles* are obviously no exception. Here the protagonist's first name (which is only superficially Latin, as its etymology is beyond any doubt Greek) ingeniously reflects the role that, willy-nilly, Giles ultimately plays in the history of the Little Kingdom. The Latin name Ægidius (also spelt "Aegidius") derives from Ancient Greek Αἰγίδιος (Aigidios), meaning "the bearer of the aegis" (i.e. the fearsome shield used, amongst others, by Athena and Zeus), which was one of the many titles borne by the supreme Hellenic god. As such it may thus figuratively allude to Giles' protective, if not perhaps entirely intentional, endeavours against, first, the giant, and then, the dragon, and so his ultimate role as the actual defender of the realm.[13] Worth noting is also Tolkien's use of two other names, *Julius* and *Agricola*. The former is of an indeterminate origin and meaning, but the latter is evidently to be associated with Giles' farming profession. Side by side, however, they appear to recall the character of the famed Roman general, Gnaeus Julius Agricola (AD 40-93) who in the second

---

11 As a rule, nicknames are given as a tribute to someone's traits (e.g. Hákon the Broad-shouldered) and abilities (e.g. Richard the Lionheart), or in recognition of their deeds (e.g. William the Conqueror). As such, they cannot obviously precede the emergence of the agent that generates them.
12 Perhaps nowhere is it better realised than in the works of Charles Dickens, where the characters' whimsical made-up names often speak volumes of their bearers' personality or social position.
13 It cannot be ruled out that the protagonist's name was also indirectly inspired by the name of the street where the Inklings' favourite Oxford pubs are to be found, the Eagle and Child and the Lamb and Flag (respectively 48/49 and 12 St Giles' Street).

half of the first century AD brought under his control most of what would subsequently become the imperial province of *Britannia*. Needless to say, this evidently anticipates the role that Giles later plays in the creation of his small but well-managed realm.[14]

None of this could ever be achieved without the legendary blade *Caudimordax*. Briefly mentioned in the context of the magnificent sword that Giles receives from the King is its once owner by the name of Bellomarius, "the greatest of all dragon-slayers of the realm" (*FGH* 33). Here again, the name appears to speak volumes of the hero's unaccounted, but presumably glorious martial past. Its etymology is not in the least complicated, and so may be easily understood by those who only know a little Latin by way of its various English cognates. The word *bellum* "war", which constitutes the name's first component, may be found in, amongst others, *belligerent* and *bellicose*. It can also be found in the name of *Bellona*, the Roman goddess of war, vividly evoked, for instance, in William Shakespeare's *Macbeth* (I.ii.54). There is some doubt as to the actual origins of *Marius*, the second element in the hero's name, but the most common opinion is that it is derived from, or at least related to, that of the Roman god of war. If such indeed be the case, the divine pair of Bellona and Mars[15] should therefore constitute not only fitting patrons for the famed dragon-slayer, but also an instantly recognisable onomastic pun whose meaning should perfectly recapitulate the very character and military accomplishments of the legendary hero.

Although he is but a minor character in the book, the slothful blacksmith who undertakes to produce Giles' ring-mail also bears a Latinate name whose meaning happens to account for his general disposition towards work and, once again, testifies to Tolkien's keen sense of philological humour. Fabricius Cunctator, better known to the local people as "Sunny Sam", does not seem to be particularly pleased with the prospect of any kind of labour. His visible lack of enthusiasm and inclination to put things off for later is perfectly illustrated by means of the blacksmith's second name which might be translated

---

14 Giles' royal aspirations appear to be further emphasised by means of his highly descriptive nickname *Ahenobarbus* "red beard" which clearly evokes the character of the Holy Roman Emperor Frederick I (1155-90), commonly known under his Italian name *Barbarossa*.
15 The two are sometimes described as siblings, sometimes as spouses.

as "delayer". *Fabricius* has an unclear etymology, but it is even more amusing than the blacksmith's second name, its joke resting upon the fact that the word *fabricator*, whence the name may derive, could in reality mean two closely related, though not entirely synonymous, things. One is that of a "craftsman, artisan" or even "smith" (the last of which is of course perfectly in line with the character's profession). The other, however, carries a far more pejorative meaning, signifying a person who counterfeits or even falsifies things. This way or another, the very nature of Sunny Sam as well as his vocation are once again deliberately revealed by means of highly suggestive *nomina*.

Finally, equally relevant with regard to the character's disposition is the name of Chrysophylax Dives, the not-quite-terrifying dragon that ravages "the midland realm of Augustus Bonifacius" (*FGH* 25). The beast is said to be "of ancient and imperial lineage" (*FGH* 25) which clearly explains why he should be endowed with both a Greek and a Roman name. The former, Chrysophylax, is evidently a compound consisting of χρυσός (*krysos*) "gold" and φύλαξ (*phylax*) "guardian, protector". The dragon is therefore a "protector of gold" whose first name is further semantically intensified by the second one meaning "rich".[16] All this seems to imply that what at first sight appears to be his proper names is in fact no more than a descriptive moniker relating to its owner's most significant attribute. Tolkien's intricate jest does not become apparent, however, until some twenty pages later, when the dragon is forced to dispose of much of his treasure. In doing this, he turns out to be a very poor "protector of gold" who, in addition to the woes he suffers at the hands of Giles, becomes less and less *dives* with every box and bag bound on his back by the victorious farmer. In the end, though, his wheel of fortune seems to be turning back, for we are told that, contrary to what we may have thought, even after he pays the enormous contribution, Chrysophylax is still a *chrysophylax* with "a mort of treasure [hidden] at home in his cave" (*FGH* 78).

---

16 In fact, he even introduces himself as "Chrysophylax the Rich" (*FGH* 43). It looks like for Tolkien this may have seemed to be the proper way of addressing a dragon. This practice can be seen at its fullest in *The Hobbit* where Bilbo clearly does not want to enrage Smaug, and so calls him "Smaug the Tremendous", "Smaug the Chiefest and Greatest of Calamities", "Smaug the Mighty", "Smaug the unassessably wealthy", "Lord Smaug the Impenetrable", and, finally, "Your Magnificence" (278-83).

Semantic reversal

This intriguing swapping of meanings brings us to the third category of Tolkien's philological humour in *Farmer Giles of Ham*, namely that of semantic reversal. There are obviously numerous instances of such alterations to be found in world literature, some being more laudatory, others evidently depreciatory in their nature. One of the best examples is of course that of Little John, Robin Hood's second-in-command, whose descriptive nickname is in stark contrast with the outlaw's enormous stature. The actual reasons for semantic reversal may vary significantly, often depending on the author's intentions and the character of the work in which the name is to be found. On the whole, however, it appears that by giving a character a name that does not quite correspond to his or her physique and/or personality the writer may wish to accentuate certain features (or their lack) which somehow typify the person in question. This by and large humorous effect could be achieved, for instance, by means of tagging the character with a nickname which is not quite consistent with his or her physical dimensions (as is the case with the abovementioned character of Little John). It may also be accomplished by way of "christening" the said individual with an authentic name whose etymology and/or cultural connotations would suggest an entirely different person.

The most evident example of semantic reversal to be found in *Farmer Giles of Ham* is of course that of the overanxious dog called Garm. Upon introducing Giles' faithful companion, Tolkien immediately informs the reader that in those days dogs "had to be content with short names in the vernacular [as] the Book-latin was reserved for their betters [and] Garm could not even talk dog-latin" (*FGH* 9). All this is naturally far from being a serious scholarly explanation, the real point of this jest lying elsewhere, in the cultural heritage of Northern Europe. What is interesting, perhaps, is that the actual meaning of the Old Norse word *garmr*,[17] whence the dog's name could be derived, is of lesser significance here, although it ought to be noted that its literal rendering into English is "rags" or "tatter" (which may be highly indicative of the dog's

---

17 The above form is not a spelling mistake. Several Old Norse nouns end in *-r* in the nominative singular, although the suffix is lost or substituted by another (e.g. the genitive *-s* or *-ar*) in the oblique cases. In Modern Icelandic the word is spelt *garmur*.

appearance). On the more figurative level, it could also be used in the sense of an unfortunate person (which is quite symptomatic of Garm's numerous woes).[18]

As has been observed, though, the most important semantic dimension of the name Tolkien chose for Giles' canine companion is its cultural rather than strictly semantic legacy. After all, in Norse mythology Garmr is the Cerberus-like hellhound that guards the gates of the underworld and forewarns the Æsir of the nearing apocalypse of Ragnarǫkr. Being *æztr viða* […] *hunda* (*Grímnismál* 45) "the finest of all dogs" of course puts the beast in marked contrast with its less distinguished counterpart in Tolkien's book. In fact, it may be concluded that the two hounds somehow epitomise the opposite, though not necessarily extreme, poles of what constitutes man's best friend, from the most alert guardian to the least vigorous lapdog. Tolkien's Garm is probably neither – the author himself is silent on this matter, although Pauline Baynes depicted it as a slim Greyhound – but the disparity is just too striking to be overlooked. The craven Garm frantically yelping about the coming of the giant (*FGH* 13-14) was in all likelihood meant to be a humorous reinterpretation of the eddic Garmr who at the time of imminent doom *geymr* […] *mjǫk fyr Gnipahelli* (*Vǫluspá* 44) "bays loudly before Gnipa cave". This "echoing" sound (the words are repeated chorus-like in stanzas 49 and 58) also indirectly heralds the advance of, amongst others, the roaring giants of Jǫtunheimr (*Vǫluspá* 48), the proper antecedents of Tolkien's famished giant.

A similar approach seems to be employed by Tolkien in the case of Giles' sovereign, the brusque and greedy ruler of the Middle Kingdom. As has been observed, the long list of his Latinate names and titles may have been intended to accentuate his near-imperial status. However, given the king's indecisiveness and overall incompetence, it is far more likely that at least some of the names were in fact meant to express open disapproval of his largely ineffective reign. Indeed, the king may be "richly endowed with names" (*FGH* 9), but, as maintained by the book's editors Christina Scull and Wayne G. Hammond, "they are [actually] an embarrassment of riches" (*FGH* 112). Hence, not counting the king's first name *Augustus* "majestic", which was originally adopted by Gaius

---

18 In their notes on *Farmer Giles of Ham* Christina Scull and Wayne G. Hammond also suggest a Welsh connection, whereby the noun *garm* "shout, cry" should account for the dog's "bullying or bragging or wheedling, or yelping under Giles' window" (*FGH* 109).

Octavius and was henceforth used by Roman emperors as a title, he is plainly criticised in every conceivable way, being ironically referred to as, amongst others, *Bonifacius* "doer of good", *Pius* "dutiful" and *Magnificus* "great, noble". Not surprisingly, given the enormous extent of his political ineffectiveness as well as, it seems, overall indolence, self-importance and greed, it looks as if the monarch lived up to none of his *de facto* superficial and ostentatious *nomina*. In other words, when it comes to semantics, the King is not quite who he is really supposed to be.[19]

Perhaps the least obvious instance of humorous semantic reversal is to be found in the name of Giles' own wife Agatha. Given its relative popularity in the Western world, Tolkien's use of that name may not immediately strike one as particularly unusual and, least of all, amusing. However, a closer look at its etymology allows us to see that it is actually a Hellenic name Ἀγαθή (*Agathé*) derived from the Ancient Greek adjective ἀγαθός (*agathos*), meaning "good, honourable". Needless to say, with all her malevolent suggestions to have the yelping Garm drowned (*FGH* 14) or otherwise killed (*FGH* 55) as well as the furious insinuation that her husband might be a "fool" (*FGH* 14), Agatha is perhaps as far as can be from actually being ἀγαθή. In the end, however, she seems to live up to the semantic properties of her name, at least in the sense of being "honourable" or "noble", for, as Tolkien informs the readers, she "made a queen of great size and majesty [who] kept a tight hand on the household accounts. There was no getting round Queen Agatha – at least it was a long walk" (*FGH* 75).[20]

False etymology

The last category of Tolkien's philological humour in *Farmer Giles of Ham* has to do with the fictionalised etymologies of two Oxfordshire place-names,

---

[19] It is hard to escape the feeling that the name Tolkien assigns to the sword that Augustus Bonifacius bestows on the local hero might also be suggestive of the monarch's incompetence and his practice of double standards. After all, Giles' *Caudimordax* is the real "Tailbiter" (if only in its terrifying potential), while the "tailbiters" invited for the King's Christmas Feast must face the shortage of genuine dragon's tails and content themselves with a substitute, "a Mock Dragon's Tail of cake and almond-paste, with cunning scales of hard icing-sugar" (*FGH* 22-23).

[20] Worth noting here is also the case of Giles' favourite cow Galathea who is trampled to death by the probably unaware giant. Being now "as flat as a doormat", she is probably no longer as γαλάτεια "milk-white" as she used to be.

namely those of the old parish village of Worminghall and the slightly younger town of Thame (respectively 4.5 and 9 miles east of Oxford). In serious linguistics the term "false etymology" (or "paraetymology") is typically used to embrace all sorts of fallacious explanations of the origins of words (including proper names) as well as their later historical development and meaning. While the term itself is an obvious oxymoron,[21] it is perhaps a little bit broader than the oft-used phrase "folk etymology" which cannot really be employed in the case of Tolkien's deliberate reinterpretations of the existing toponyms that appear in the book. However, the explanations he gives are clearly modelled after the principles of *Volksetymologie*, whereby similar sounding words are generally suggested as lexical items of formative nature. Their meaning might be at a considerable variance with the words which actually formed the said toponyms, but it is of course of little significance to the people with no etymological apparatus, or, as was surely the case with the author of *Farmer Giles*, those writers whose intention is to give a philological wink to the better-informed readers.

The case of Worminghall is a perfect example of such deliberate paraetymological efforts on the part of Tolkien. It is said to be the name of the place "where Giles and Chrysophylax first made [their] acquaintance [and which later] became known throughout the kingdom as Aula Draconaria, or in the vulgar tongue Worminghall" (*FGH* 76-77). The latter is therefore merely an English translation of the earlier, and thus seemingly more authoritative, Latin name which may be rendered as either "the House" (in the meaning of "dynasty"), or "the court" or "royal seat of the Wormings", i.e. the descendants of King Ægidius Draconarius, better known in the vulgar tongue as Old Giles Worming. In reality, of course, there is little truth in the above explanation. Worminghall is in all likelihood a patronymic toponym derived from the name of an otherwise unidentified man called *Wyrma*.[22] Its earliest attested form may be found in the Domesday Book (1086) where it appears as *Wermelle*, the second element being almost certainly *halh* (also spelt *healh*), meaning "nook, secret place".

---

[21] The Ancient Greek word ἐτυμολογία (*etumología*), whence the Modern English word derives, is a compound term which consists of two nouns: ἔτυμον (*étumon*) "true sense" and λογία (*logía*) "study". Hence, it is "the study of the true sense" (of words).

[22] Unfortunately, the name is not attested in any written sources from the period. There is, however, no doubt that it does indeed derive from the Old English noun *wyrm* "serpent, snake, dragon" and is, of course, cognate with the Old Norse name *Ormr*.

Hence, the actual historical name of Worminghall should be translated as "Wyrma's nook".

Needless to say, Tolkien must have been perfectly aware of all this, and so his light-hearted etymological argument is but a clever play on words resting upon the superficial similarity between *halh* and *heall*. In the early twentieth century, when the philological apparatus was not as developed as it is today, such confusions (in this case obviously genuine rather than fabricated) would have been quite common. By bringing up the etymological issue, however, Tolkien does not appear to be so much as criticising any of his fellow scholars, although the ironic reference to the "Four Wise Clerks of Oxenford" (*FGH* 15) might perhaps suggest a more explicit target. Instead, his somewhat implied etymological puns may have been initially motivated by the mysterious "local family game" (*L* 36) he refers to in his letter to C.A. Furth. Although its nature has never been revealed, it is not improbable that in the 1930s, i.e. at the time when *Farmer Giles of Ham* was first conceived as a story, the Tolkiens actually amused themselves by inventing fictional (but not necessarily nonsense) etymologies of the places they visited during their Sunday walks in the Oxfordshire countryside. For professor Tolkien, who is well known to have had a life-long fascination with dragons,[23] the name of Worminghall must have therefore seemed like a potential invitation, a creative spark which would ignite the process of writing of what ultimately became one of his most famous stories outside the Middle-earth canon.

As has been observed, the other of the two place-names whose false etymologies may have been conceived in an analogous way cannot be found in the earliest manuscript version of *Farmer Giles of Ham*. The fact that its origins might not lie in the "local family game" (*L* 36) does not, however, mean that it is not worth looking at. Indeed, the story behind the name of Thame (in reality a troublesome Celtic or even pre-Celtic name of uncertain meaning)[24] is perhaps as amusing as that of Worminghall. Master Ægidius, who in the end

---

[23] In his essay "On Fairy-Stories", Tolkien famously remarks that, as a child, he "desired dragons with a profound desire" (OFS 135).

[24] There are a number of rivers in Britain (Thames, Thame, Tame, Team, Teme etc.) whose root appears to be either Celtic **tam-* "dark" or pre-Celtic **tā-* "melt, flow turbidly" (Mills 454). In reality, the Thame is a north-eastern tributary of the Thames.

becomes the autonomous Lord of Ham (itself an obvious philological pun),[25] is also known in his kingdom under the title of "Dominus de Domito Serpente, which is in the vulgar Lord of the Tame Worm, or shortly of Tame" (*FGH* 74). As the two titles of King Giles get more and more confused, the chief town of the new realm gradually becomes "known by the latter name, which it retains to this day" (*FGH* 76). In this way Ham turns into Thame (pronounced *tame*), a kind of word that must be truly annoying for many a philologist, as it preserves what appears to be an altogether alien graphical element in the form of the letter *h*. Tolkien's "authoritative" explanation, though, soon dispels any conceivable doubts, for otherwise "Thame with an *h* [would obviously be] a folly without warrant" (*FGH* 76). In fact, in this particular word the silent *h* is a folly,[26] a later intrusion from French, which may also be found in, amongst other words, *Thomas*, *Thames* or *thyme*.

Concluding Remarks

There is no denying that the overall character of *Farmer Giles of Ham* was meant to be far less serious than that of his most celebrated works, *The Lord of the Rings*, *The Silmarillion*, or even *The Hobbit*. This is not to say, of course, that it is entirely devoid of any deeper meaning. After all, it subtly touches upon such vital issues as, for instance, the nature of kingship and administration of royal justice (Oziewicz 42-47 and Ferré 71-74). Nonetheless, what most people immediately take notice of is the tale's light-hearted humour, situational as well as verbal. While the former cannot be in any way disregarded, it is naturally the latter that probably constitutes the finest bits of Tolkien's mock-medieval tale, its actual *crème de la crème* and a starting point for many a scholarly analysis.

Due to its succinctness of content, the above examination was not meant to be particularly exhaustive, especially in connection with those of Tolkien's jokes whose nature cannot be described as purely philological. Nonetheless, it is hoped that it does at least succeed in recapitulating some of the most striking aspects

---

25 Cf. Old English *ham* "house, property, enclosure". There are numerous place-names throughout England which incorporate it as a suffix (e.g. Nottingham, Tottenham, Buckingham etc.).

26 Cf. Old French *folie* "madness, insanity". It is a well known fact that Tolkien was not particularly fond of the French language whose "sounds did not please him as much as the sounds of Latin and English" (Carpenter 38).

of onomastic jest to be found in his *Farmer Giles of Ham*, along with their naturally brief and somewhat simplified categorisation. This should perhaps enable its readers to see and, in this way, better appreciate the profound depth of Tolkienian humour which, as has been observed, evinces itself in so many different ways, from the more light-hearted puns on the characters' distinctive personalities and traits, to the more thought-provoking, satirical-like remarks on the nature of kingship and consequences of tyranny. After all, humour is sometimes a serious thing which may stem from an individual's awareness that certain things in life are really important and as such could have far-ranging implications for those who can take the joke.

About the Author

ŁUKASZ NEUBAUER is a senior lecturer in the Department of Humanities at the Koszalin University of Technology, Poland. He specialises in early medieval history and Old Germanic literatures, in particular English poetry and Norse sagas. His publications include academic papers on the metrical structure of Anglo-Saxon verse and animal imagery in Old English battle poems. He is also interested in the Icelandic language and onomastics, and so has written a number of articles on place as well as proper names in Iceland.

Abbreviations

FGH: *Farmer Giles of Ham*, see TOLKIEN 1999

L: *Letters*, see TOLKIEN 2006

OFS: "On Fairy-Stories", see TOLKIEN 1983

Bibliography

BUSSMANN, Hadumod. *Routledge Dictionary of Language and Linguistics*. Abingdon: Routledge, 1998.

CARPENTER, Humphrey. *J.R.R. Tolkien: A Biography*. London: HarperCollins, 2002.

DURIEZ, Colin. *J.R.R. Tolkien: The Making of a Legend*. Oxford: Lion Books, 2012.

FERRÉ, Vincent. "The Rout of the King: Tolkien's Reading on Arthurian Kingship – *Farmer Giles of Ham* and *The Homecoming of Beorhtnoth*." *Tolkien's Shorter*

Works. Essays of the Jena Conference 2007. Ed. Margaret HILEY and Frank WEINREICH. Zurich and Jena: Walking Tree Publishers, 2008. 59-76.

FINNUR Jónsson (ed.). *De Gamle Eddadigte*. København: G.E.C. Gads Forlag, 1932.

GILLIVER, Peter, Jeremy MARSHALL and Edmund WEINER. *The Ring of Words: Tolkien and the Oxford English Dictionary*. Oxford: Oxford University Press, 2006.

HANKS, Patrick, Kate HARDCASTLE and Flavia HODGES. *Oxford Dictionary of First Names*. Oxford: Oxford University Press, 2004.

HOOKER, Mark T. *Tolkien and Welsh/Tolkien a Chymraeg: Essays on J.R.R. Tolkien's Use of Welsh in His Legendarium*. Create Space Independent Publishing Platform, 2012.

MALKIEL, Yakov. *Etymology*. Cambridge: Cambridge University Press, 1993.

MILLS, David (ed.). *A Dictionary of British Place-Names*. Oxford: Oxford University Press, 2011.

OZIEWICZ, Marek. "Setting Things Right in *Farmer Giles of Ham* and *The Lord of the Rings*: Tolkien's Conception of Justice." *Tolkien's Shorter Works. Essays of the Jena Conference 2007*. Ed. Margaret HILEY and Frank WEINREICH. Zurich and Jena: Walking Tree Publishers, 2008. 37-57.

SHAKESPEARE, William. *Macbeth*. Oxford: Oxford University Press, 2008.

SHIPPEY, Tom. *The Road to Middle-earth*. London: HarperCollins, 2005.

TOLKIEN, John Ronal Reuel. *Farmer Giles of Ham*. Ed. Christina SCULL and Wayne G. HAMMOND. Boston and New York: Houghton Mifflin, 1999.

"On Fairy-Stories" in *The Monsters and the Critics and Other Essays*. London: George Allen & Unwin, 1983. 109-61.

The Annotated Hobbit. Edited and annotated by Douglas A. ANDERSON. Boston and New York: Houghton Mifflin, 2002.

The Letters of J.R.R. Tolkien. Ed. Humphrey CARPENTER with the assistance of Christopher TOLKIEN. London: HarperCollins, 2006.

WICHER, Andrzej. *Selected Medieval and Religious Themes in the Works of C.S. Lewis and J.R.R. Tolkien*. Łódź: Łódzkie Towarzystwo Naukowe, 2013.

Anke Eissmann
You cannot pass!

Anke Eissmann
New Hat

Laura Lee Smith

"This of course is the way to talk to dragons": Etiquette-Based Humour in *The Hobbit*[1]

Abstract

The Hobbit frequently calls attention to social conventions within the story, and to the correctness or incorrectness of characters' conduct. The etiquette motif is sufficiently prominent, in fact, that some critics have ventured to discern a strong didactic purpose in it, while others have identified a more parodic intent. This essay considers several etiquette-laced interactions in *The Hobbit*, along with their apparent analogues or precedents in four earlier works of British children's fantasy – *Through the Looking-Glass*, *The Princess and the Goblin*, *The Marvellous Land of Snergs*, and *Winnie-the-Pooh* – and concludes that Tolkien is primarily lampooning ordinary forms of politeness for humorous effect, doubtless to the delight of generations of children who have been pressured to conceal their more selfish tendencies beneath a veneer of courtesy. But is this skewering purely subversive and comical, or is Tolkien perhaps making a deeper point about true politeness and moral courage? Even as they laugh, children are likely to gain a deeper intuitive understanding of the many shades of hypocrisy and sycophancy that so often underlie the outward forms of courtesy. Although true courtesy can be a sign of respect between equals, the powerful have far less need of politeness.

Introduction

For those who may have wondered how to avoid awkward missteps when conversing with dwarves or dragons, Tolkien's narrator provides an invaluable service, as he frequently calls attention to social conventions within the story, and to the propriety of characters' conduct. Particularly in the light-hearted early chapters, the narrator points out Thorin's politeness to the Great Goblin, Gollum's politeness to Bilbo, Gandalf's politeness to the eagles, and the dwarves' efforts to be polite to Beorn. Likewise, the narrator notes that Bilbo is so flustered by

---

[1] The author presented an earlier version of this essay at the Celebrating *The Hobbit* conference at Valparaiso University in March 2013. Liam Daley and Kris Swank kindly commented on the draft when I was readying it for the Valparaiso presentation.

the dwarves' unexpected arrival that he briefly forgets his manners, that Thorin is "rudely interrupted" by Bilbo's inadvertent shriek of distress (*H* 17), and that Beorn is "never very polite" (*H* 112). Yet even as the tale shifts into a more somber register and the narrator's voice recedes, etiquette is not forgotten; Balin notes that the crows are "nasty suspicious-looking creatures at that, and rude as well" (*H* 235), and Dain's people use "polite and rather old-fashioned language" in confronting Bard (*H* 253).

The etiquette motif is sufficiently prominent, in fact, that some critics have ventured to discern a "strong didactic purpose" in it (Stevens and Stevens 59). Specifically, Stevens and Stevens conclude that *The Hobbit* "is a book about good manners for children," which teaches that "everyone should be a good little hobbit, and good little hobbits are polite little hobbits" (65). It is certainly not unreasonable to suppose that Tolkien was interested in good manners and saw value in them. After all, the core principle underlying polite behaviour is the expression of respect and consideration for others (Götz ix), and Tolkien himself suggested that old-fashioned, highly formalized manners actually "made life a lot easier, smoother, and less frictional and dubious; and cloaked or indeed held in check (as table-manners do) the everlasting cat, wolf, and dog that lurk at no great depth under our social skin" (*L* 72).

Nonetheless, it seems clear that *The Hobbit* primarily subverts ordinary forms of politeness for humorous effect. We can get a sense of authorial intent with respect to manners, in the first instance, by looking at the evolution of the characters' interactions in Chapter I and by considering certain aspects of the narrative voice in Chapter II.

The only known surviving portion of Tolkien's original manuscript, which Rateliff has dubbed "The Pryftan Fragment" (3),[2] maps easily to a portion of the opening chapter of *The Hobbit*. It starts in the middle of the unexpected party, just as Bilbo is moved by the dwarves' song, and ends with a suggestion that the company should get an early start on the quest. Many of the ideas and phrasing in *Pryftan* appear essentially unchanged in the final published novel.

---

2 For simplicity, I will cite The Pryftan Fragment as *Pryftan*, and I have amended the quotations to incorporate all changes Rateliff has marked in the text. Certain names in *Pryftan* are disconcertingly different from their final published form; to avoid confusion, I refer to Thorin's antecedent in *Pryftan* as the "chief dwarf" and Gandalf's antecedent as the "wizard".

Bearing in mind that good manners is "the Art of making those People easy with whom we converse" (Swift 34), however, it is striking that the *Pryftan* characters make an effort to conduct themselves with moderation and reasonableness, and a degree of sensitivity toward others. For example, in *Pryftan*, Gloin speaks "in embarrassment" after he learns that Bilbo overheard a dwarf's unflattering remarks about him (*Pryftan* 9). Similarly, when the wizard explains that Bilbo was a fallback choice for the adventure, he hastens to soften the blow with an aside to Bilbo: "I beg your pardon, but I am sure you will understand – dragon slaying is not I believe your specialty" (*Pryftan* 10). Such polite hedges are entirely absent from the opening chapter of *The Hobbit*.

But Tolkien does not merely omit polite hedges in *The Hobbit*; the dwarves and Bilbo now deliberately insult each other, face to face. For example, in both versions, Bilbo is stung when he overhears himself referred to as a "little fellow bobbing [*H*: and puffing] on the mat" who "looks more like a grocer than a burglar" (*Pryftan* 8; *H* 18), and in both versions, he recklessly volunteers for the adventure to salvage his pride. But in *The Hobbit*, Bilbo also takes the opportunity to turn around the statement he has just overheard to insult the dwarves: "As soon as I saw your funny faces on the door-step, I had my doubts" (*H* 19). No such insulting comeback appears in *Pryftan*, even though Bilbo is equally provoked by the insult he has overheard.

Table 1: Bilbo Insults His Guests

Pryftan (8-9)	*The Hobbit* (18-19)
Dwalin to Company (overheard by Bilbo): "if it hadn't been for the secret sign on the door, I should have been sure I had come to the wrong house, *as soon as I clapped eyes on the fat little fellow bobbing on the mat*. He looks more like a grocer than a burglar!"	Gloin to Company (overheard by Bilbo): "if it had not been for the sign on the door, I should have been sure we had come to the wrong house. *As soon as I clapped eyes on the little fellow bobbing and puffing on the mat, I had my doubts*. He looks more like a grocer than a burglar!"
Bilbo to dwarves (in response): "I am sure you have come to the wrong house – but treat it as the right one."	Bilbo to dwarves (in response): "I am quite sure you have come to the wrong house. *As soon as I saw your funny faces on the door-step, I had my doubts*. But treat it as the right one."

In *Pryftan*, as in *The Hobbit*, the dwarves turn to an outsider for suggestions on how to recover their treasure. (Notoriously, the suggestion is to sit on the steps of Erebor until they think of a plan.) In *Pryftan*, this suggestion is elicited, logically enough, from the wizard with a simple and direct question. In *The Hobbit*, however, Thorin directs the question to the least-informed member of the group, framed in a wordier and superficially deferential way: "supposing the burglar-expert gives us some ideas or suggestions" (*H* 21). The narrator describes Thorin's tone as one of "mock-politeness" (*H* 21). Just as politeness involves sensitivity to others and putting other people at their ease, mock-politeness is almost exactly the opposite; it is intended to insult others with *deliberately unconvincing courtesy*. Thorin's mockery has a bitter and cowardly edge to it. Rather than challenging the wizard directly and risking retribution, Thorin indulges a petty and mean-spirited streak by ridiculing powerless Bilbo to demonstrate his dissatisfaction with the wizard's choice.

Table 2: Thorin Ridicules Bilbo

Pryftan (10)	*The Hobbit* (21)
Dwarves to wizard:	Thorin to Bilbo:
"What is your plan" then they all said.	"Very well then," said Thorin, "supposing the burglar-expert gives us some ideas or suggestions." He turned with mock-politeness to Bilbo.

It is also worth noting that the chief dwarf becomes far more self-absorbed, pompous and ineffective in the published work. The alterations make him ruder, and the scene much funnier. Already in *Pryftan*, the chief dwarf is wordy; the narrator remarks that "in the end he would probably have said all he wanted to, and left a little time over for some of the others to have a word" (7). Clearly, the dwarf likes to hear himself talk and takes a while to get to the point; but perhaps no more than some grownups that the average child will meet. But in *The Hobbit*, the chief dwarf is no longer *merely* wordy; he "would probably have gone on like this until he was out of breath" (*H* 17). Thorin, unlike his antecedent, is not about to leave even "a little time" for "others to have a word"; he is entirely self-centered. That is, Thorin lacks the sensitivity and self-control to stop talking of his own accord, as common courtesy requires. Only his own physical limitations – a literal lack of breath – will slow him down.[3]

In sum, the participants in the opening chapter have been exaggerated to the point of caricature in *The Hobbit* – and much of the humour lies in their unmitigated rudeness to each other. As, in its essence, "good breeding consists in concealing how much we think of ourselves and how little we think of the other person" (Twain 345), Tolkien's decision to ratchet up the rudeness to a comical level sets the tone for a discussion of etiquette humour in *The Hobbit*.

---

[3] Consistent with the now comically exaggerated description of the dwarf's long-windedness, this particular speech is about 30 words longer in *The Hobbit*. One small gem is that the introductory phrase "may require explanation" (*Pryftan* 7) becomes "may require *a little brief* explanation" (*H* 17; emphasis added). Of course, Thorin's propensity to speak "until he was out of breath" also helps explain his subsequent delivery of two solid pages of uninterrupted exposition (*H* 22-24), which Tolkien has added to the *Pryftan* story.

With this baseline in mind from the drafting history of Chapter I, let us turn to the narrator's comments on etiquette conventions in the troll scene of Chapter II. The trolls are bigger, stronger, and more ruthless than the Company, and would gladly eat every "burrahobbit" or dwarf they can find. Yet the narrator makes a point of criticizing the trolls' *manners*, of all things, rather than their penchant for killing and eating passing travelers.[4] "Yes, I am afraid trolls do behave like that," the narrator says, when one of the trolls "wiped his lips on his sleeve" (*H* 33). Given the trolls' predilection for dining on sapient bipeds, it is absurd and incongruous to pretend that a mere lapse of etiquette is the greatest imaginable horror to which our heroes are exposed.[5]

The narrator further remarks that trolls do not speak in "drawing-room fashion at all, at all" (*H* 33). Did anyone expect them to? Trolls are known for their coarseness in body, mind and spirit, while drawing-rooms are places for consciously refined and elegant entertaining. But even beyond this essential incongruity, the unnecessary repetition of the words "at all" signals a humorous intent: It is easy to imagine the line delivered in an exaggeratedly fake "upper-class" accent with a pinky extended from an imaginary teacup. The narrator's tut-tutting over the trolls' uncouth speech surely does not in any way encourage children to emulate the refined behaviour appropriate to the formal setting of the drawing-room. Rather, it taps into children's mockery of the perceived stuffiness of "fancy" grown-up manners.

Gail Munde notes that "incongruity is generally recognized as the cornerstone of humor, for without the correct set of expectations the unexpected is not surprising" (220).[6] Likewise, the absurdity and incongruity of references to etiquette in the troll scene suggest that Tolkien's purpose is not primarily

---

[4] Tolkien's narrator in *The Hobbit* is an "intrusive" one, who seems to have greater knowledge and experience than the reader and frequently comments on the story (see generally Thomas 162-65). The narrator's humorously misguided comments in the troll scene, however, suggest early on that readers need not accept the narrator's interpretation and judgments at face value.

[5] There are echoes of *The Marvellous Land of Snergs* in this scene; Tolkien's narrator disapproves of the trolls' failure to use napkins, just as the *Snergs* narrator criticizes an ogre's failure to furnish flatware (Wyke-Smith 78).

[6] "Incongruity" is one of the most widely accepted theoretical bases for humour, along with "superiority" (a sense of superiority over the "butt" of the joke) and "relief" (a sudden release of anxiety or nervous energy) (see generally Carr and Greeves 81-95; Weitz 66-67). Munde also reports, with apparent approval, Michele Landsberg's observation that "children, like all the powerless, find their best release and choicest weapon in humor" (221, 229).

educational; it is only readers' pre-existing understanding and expectations of proper behaviour that allow them to "get" the joke. Sly mockery of the role and importance of manners is doubtless popular with child audiences, since the undeniable "asymmetries of power between grown-up and child" (Briggs and Butts 141) mean that children are inevitably on the receiving end of courtesy lessons from adults. Indeed, Alison Lurie (4) suggests that

> most of the great works of juvenile literature are subversive in one way or another: they express ideas and emotions not generally approved of or even recognized at the time; they make fun of honored figures and piously held beliefs; and they view social pretenses with clear-eyed directness.

Nonetheless, one may well ask whether there is perhaps a deeper purpose to Tolkien's etiquette humour, beyond mere entertainment or parody. After all, his approach to matters of courtesy remains remarkably light and flexible throughout; the narrator explains what is polite among dwarves and eagles, but not what is polite among hobbits or elves, let alone any of their common enemies. And much rudeness, particularly on the part of the dwarves, passes with little or no comment. This essay will consider several etiquette-laced interactions in *The Hobbit*, along with their apparent analogues or precedents in certain earlier works; and look at more "serious" uses of etiquette in *The Hobbit* by way of comparison. In doing so, we will see if we can discern a broader purpose underlying Tolkien's etiquette-based humour.

A Tradition of Etiquette Humour

Naturally, Tolkien's *The Hobbit* did not arise in a vacuum, but amidst the evolving tradition of British children's fantasy literature. Tolkien's etiquette humour can be helpfully compared with that found in four classic tales.

The first two books, Lewis Carroll's *Through the Looking-Glass* and his friend George MacDonald's *The Princess and the Goblin*, were published in the Victorian period, about twenty years before Tolkien's birth. The works have enjoyed an enduring prominence in the history of children's literature (e.g., Lurie 5, 8; Townsend 68-69, 72-73), and it seems likely that they were part of Tolkien's childhood reading.⁷ *Looking-Glass* signals its interest in etiquette early on. Even before the dream-adventure begins, when a kitten tangles up her yarn, Alice criticizes the feline's comportment: "Really, Dinah ought to have taught you better manners! You *ought*, Dinah, you know you ought!" (Carroll 176). Alice makes an effort to speak politely throughout the tale, but the looking-glass creatures lecture her almost incessantly (if nonsensically) on manners. Briggs and Butts note that the Alice books "may be read as a profound scrutiny of systems, including those of social behaviour," and suggest that they reflect "the child's sense of puzzlement at the elaborate codes of the adult world" (141). Much of the humour comes from the looking-glass world characters' over-the-top rudeness to Alice. They indulge in a dizzying variety of interruptions, insults and personal remarks, unreasonable and changeable rules of comportment, refusal to pick up on social cues or give proper answers to straightforward questions, over-literal interpretation of common expressions, and the like.

Politeness is also a recurring theme in *Princess*. The narrator instructs readers that "a real princess is never rude" (MacDonald 21), and both the narrator and the characters comment on instances of courtesy and discourtesy they observe in the story. The etiquette humour in *Princess* is more subtle than in *Looking-Glass*, as it mostly involves a subversion of expectations. For example, it is the social inferior (the nurse) who is far more concerned with observing the formalities of rank than the princess. There is humour, too, in Irene's mistaken effort to be "very polite" to her fairy relative by addressing her as "great-great-great-great-grandmother" (86) – apparently unaware that gratuitous "greats" in this context unflatteringly exaggerate a relative's age, rather than indicating the relative's superlative abilities or eminence.

The second pair, A.A. Milne's *Winnie-the-Pooh* and E.A. Wyke-Smith's *The Marvellous Land of Snergs*, were published about fifty years later, in the 1920s, while Tolkien's sons were young and before his daughter was born.⁸ Although *Snergs* has not achieved the lasting acclaim of the other tales, it must be included, given "Tolkien's own high regard for this now-forgotten story" (Rateliff xxxviii,

---

7 Tolkien referred to both of these works in his correspondence (*L* 460, 481). Although Tolkien appears to have lost his taste for MacDonald later in life, Douglas Anderson identifies *Princess* as a significant source or influence for *The Hobbit* (6).
8 According to Rateliff's analysis, Tolkien began work on *The Hobbit* in 1930 (Rateliff xx), just two years after the publication of *Snergs*, and four years after *Winnie-the-Pooh*.

60), its popularity with the Tolkien boys (Rateliff 47, 59), and its apparent influences on *The Hobbit* (Anderson 6-7) – whether as "an unconscious source-book" for the race of hobbits (*L* 215) or otherwise.⁹ Wyke-Smith's narrator, like MacDonald's, purports to praise good manners and deplore bad manners – but does so in a way that undermines any possible etiquette lesson. We see this, for example, in the narrator's description of Miss Watkyns' attempt to coax "perfect behaviour" from her charges (Wyke-Smith 6). Only two children meet the challenge, and the narrator not only dismisses them as "smug little girls," but also notes that the incentive Miss Watkyns had offered to the children was out of fashion by the time it was awarded (7).

Milne, by contrast with the other authors, does not specifically call attention to his characters' lapses in courtesy in *Winnie-the-Pooh*, but instead plays each episode for gentle humour. As Lurie notes, "the verbal hypocrisies [...] of polite etiquette [are mocked] in Rabbit" (152). Readers may also smile at other etiquette failures among the denizens of the Forest, ranging from Eeyore's pessimistic variations on standard greetings to Kanga's nonsensical responses in any conversation that does not pertain to her own immediate interests. I have not been able to determine whether Tolkien ever read Milne's works,¹⁰ but it makes sense to discuss *Winnie-the-Pooh* and *The Hobbit* together here because the authors depict similar scenes of impolite behaviour, and their works have reached similar prominence in the history of children's literature (Carpenter 211; Townsend 125, 130).

---

9   Hobbits resemble Snergs in their height and love of feasting, but the Snergs live in a land where fairy-tale elements co-exist with humans from multiple time periods. In Wyke-Smith's tale, a much-derided Snerg, Gorbo, befriends two mischievous human children and helps them through a series of scrapes featuring an evil witch, a semi-reformed ogre, and courtly medieval folk.
10 Tolkien was certainly aware of Milne in 1929, at least as the author of a theatrical adaptation that Tolkien disliked (Rateliff 58). And it seems almost certain that Tolkien would have been aware of the Pooh books as "the spectacular British success of the 1920s" (Townsend 125), particularly as he was familiar with other contemporaneous children's literature such as *Snergs* while his children were young. However, despite the boys' predilection for bears (Rateliff 253-54), Jared Lobdell recollects that Christopher Tolkien told him he "had a Pooh-less childhood" (e-mail message to the author, 31 May 2016).

Situational Etiquette in *The Hobbit*

Where etiquette books may promise to guide the reader in how to deal gracefully with common social scenarios, and didactic fiction may depict characters who are rewarded for proper behaviour, Tolkien instead puts his characters into situations where those who attempt to be polite are (at best) not rewarded, may become laughing-stocks, and may even find themselves at a distinct strategic disadvantage.

Close Scrutiny of the Polite Formula

Everyday conversation is laced with "little pleasant phrases," part of a low-level background politeness that signals a generally friendly intent and helps put others at ease (Martin, *Turn-of-the-Millennium* 71; see also Blyth 45). In essence, these stock phrases are not intended to convey any deep meaning beyond a polite acknowledgment of another person's existence. They do not stand up to analysis, and are not intended to; they are, in effect, "ritualistic utterances" which require only the prescribed conventional response (Martin, *Turn-of-the-Millennium* 71). One of the most common, prosaic formulas is the simple "Good morning!" – to which the ideal response is a reciprocal, cheery "Good morning!" Milne and Tolkien both play with this expectation.

In *Winnie-the-Pooh*, Eeyore's response to a polite greeting from Pooh is deeply pessimistic:

> "Good morning, Eeyore," said Pooh.
>
> "Good morning, Pooh Bear," said Eeyore gloomily. "If it *is* a good morning," he said. "Which I doubt" (Milne 72).

The etiquette humour here is subtle, but subversive. If we are not supposed to say how we are really feeling when people ask "How are you?" (Blyth 108; Martin, *Excruciatingly Correct* 206), it is even clearer that we should not question the goodness of the morning when people wish us one. Tolkien improves on Milne's hint in *The Hobbit*, where Gandalf's response to a cheerful "Good Morning!" from Bilbo, who "meant it," is one of dark skepticism (*H* 5). The passing stranger, as yet unidentified to the reader, looks at the hobbit "from under long bushy eyebrows" and demands an explanation:

> "What do you mean?" he said. "Do you wish me a good morning, or mean that it is a good morning whether I want it or not; or that you feel good this morning; or that it is a morning to be good on?" (*H* 5-6).

Bloom points out that Bilbo's greeting is, in fact, "the first thing we hear Bilbo say" in the story, and that Gandalf "is rude enough to overinterpret the remark" (2). As it is also Gandalf's first remark, however, a first-time reader does not necessarily know, quite yet, whether this unusual response springs from a comical misunderstanding or some other source.[11] The reader may balk at this deviation from the polite formula, but Bilbo initially takes it in stride and responds graciously. Or at least he does so until Gandalf discloses that an adventure is in the offing. At that point, Bilbo begins trying to signal to Gandalf (without saying so directly) that the conversation is at an end.

Unfortunately for Bilbo, however, Gandalf is perfectly willing to exploit the gap between the literal meaning of words and their socially coded meaning for his own purposes. Tolkien seems to be taking some hints from Carroll in this regard. For example, when Alice responds to bizarre and unintelligible statements with a polite but puzzled, "I beg your pardon?" the looking-glass creatures take her words literally. Humpty Dumpty, seizing on the word *pardon*, assures her that he is "not offended" (Carroll 267). The White King stops processing the sentence at the verb and informs Alice that "it isn't respectable to beg" (Carroll 280).

Likewise, Gandalf takes Bilbo's "I beg your pardon" literally, and grandly offers to "give you what you asked for. [...] My pardon. I give it you" (*H* 7). Shippey notes that "it is comic to find Gandalf repeatedly ignoring the social code, and acting, as only someone foreign to it would, as if Bilbo meant what he said by phrases like 'I beg your pardon'" (9). It is, of course, implausible that Gandalf wouldn't be familiar with the appropriate polite response. Gandalf is, after

---

11 Miss Manners suggests that those "who insist on taking social idiomatic expressions literally [...] want to strip these remarks of their usefulness and then laugh at their nakedness" (Martin, *Excruciatingly Correct* 206). By contrast, Bloom infers from Gandalf's rudeness that the wizard is "self-important" (2). While an exaggerated sense of self-importance may explain Thorin's initial rudeness to Bilbo, it seems more plausible that Gandalf is acting strategically to obtain Bilbo's assistance. He later uses a different technique, with equal craftiness, to obtain Beorn's assistance.

all, the only member of the Company who knows that the correct reply to the eagles' farewell is the somewhat cryptic wish that "the wind under your wings bear you where the sun sails and the moon walks" (*H* 106).¹²

But Tolkien has taken Carroll's hint in a new direction. The infuriating literalism of Humpty and the White King is simply part of the madness of the looking-glass world, while it is clear that Gandalf is perfectly aware of Bilbo's meaning, and is choosing a response that will throw Bilbo off-balance.

Gandalf also uses another technique, with equal relish, in which he pierces through the polite formula and exposes Bilbo's true intentions. This comes about when Bilbo tries to dismiss Gandalf and end the conversation by saying "Good morning!" and "thank you!" in quick succession (*H* 6). As Shippey notes, this "insincere politeness [...] is socially coded to mean its opposite" (9), but when Gandalf points out what Bilbo is doing, Bilbo denies it. Obviously, it would be impolite for Bilbo to acknowledge in so many words that Gandalf's presence is unwelcome, and as a result he is too embarrassed to admit that Gandalf's interpretation is correct. Thus, Bilbo's own concern for the appearance of proper behaviour traps him into a conversation that he finds more and more alarming, until the only way that he sees to escape is to invite Gandalf to tea. Bilbo then promptly scuttles inside "as quickly as he dared, not to seem rude" (*H* 8). Gandalf's response – "laughing long but quietly" outside Bilbo's door (*H* 8) – suggests that this is precisely the result he had intended. He has, by skillful rudeness, manipulated Bilbo into hosting a tea party.

For this technique to work, Gandalf had to make Bilbo extremely uncomfortable. He undoubtedly counted on Bilbo's intense (and very British) distaste for the impropriety of a *direct* confrontation, as well as Bilbo's fear of offending a wizard.¹³ If Bilbo were more honest, and more courageous, he could easily have avoided this dilemma. Throughout the scene, we see that pre-adventure

---

12 Olsen notes that the "references to 'eyries' and 'wings' show that it is an internal formula – what eagles say to each other upon parting, not what they say to others" (133).
13 The narrator implies that Bilbo's desire "not to seem rude" to Gandalf is at least partly self-protective, since "Wizards after all are wizards" (*H* 8). Five chapters later, when Bilbo fears that he has inadvertently offended the eagles with his babbling, the narrator returns to the theme of self-protective politeness, exhorting readers "not to be rude to an eagle, when you are only the size of a hobbit, and are up in his eyrie at night!" (*H* 102).

Bilbo is overly concerned with the forms of politeness, the appearance of good manners. Knowing this, Gandalf easily keeps Bilbo off-balance and maintains control of the situation.

The Cold Offer, Warmly Received

A very closely related theme is the "cold offer" – one which is extended as a matter of form, but with social cues to make clear that it must be declined. Naturally, there is humour in characters who (like Gandalf) are more than willing to ignore such cues to get their own way.

A classic instance in Milne's novel is Rabbit's comically ineffective attempt to avoid a visit from Pooh. After very elaborate but unsuccessful efforts to convince his friend that he is not at home, Rabbit finally lets Pooh in and very politely invites him to have "a mouthful of something" (Milne 26). This is clearly a mistake, because Pooh silently devotes himself "for a long time" to consuming honey and condensed milk,

> … until at last, humming to himself in a rather sticky voice, he got up, shook Rabbit lovingly by the paw, and said that he must be going on.
>
> "Must you?" said Rabbit politely.
>
> "Well," said Pooh, "I could stay a little longer if it – if you ––" and he tried very hard to look in the direction of the larder.
>
> "As a matter of fact," said Rabbit, "I was going out myself directly."
>
> "Oh, well, then, I'll be going on. Good-bye."
>
> "Well, good-bye, if you're sure you won't have any more."
>
> "*Is* there any more?" asked Pooh quickly. (Milne 26-27)

Rabbit's hypocritical politeness seems to be almost compulsive, offered in spite of repeated evidence that Pooh will blithely ignore every social cue. Pooh, in turn, is a truly terrible guest, one who is fully prepared to lick Rabbit's larder clean, and is able to do so by ignoring Rabbit's unsubtle hints that Pooh's presence is unwelcome and instead seizing on each tepid and meaningless courtesy offered by his reluctant host.

In the opening chapter of *The Hobbit*, Bilbo likewise makes a "cold offer" to the dwarves:

> "I suppose you will all stay to supper?" he said in his politest unpressing tones.
>
> "Of course!" said Thorin. "And after." (*H* 12)

Bilbo's "unpressing tones" make clear that, despite his words, Bilbo would very much prefer that his unexpected guests leave as soon as possible rather than staying for dinner. Where Gandalf actively manipulated Bilbo into doing something he did not want to do, Thorin (like Pooh) accepts an invitation that was insincerely given. Thorin and Pooh disregard social cues and hold an unwilling host to his word; Thorin goes farther than Pooh in inviting himself and thirteen others to partake of hospitality far beyond what is offered.

And what of Bilbo? How does he respond to the liberties Thorin is taking? Here we might turn to Sir Percival in Wyke-Smith's story. Brushing aside the knight's protests, Gorbo places the two children on the horse with Sir Percival, fore and aft, blocking the knight from using his reins or holding his lance. Only after the children are firmly installed does Gorbo consult the knight about the arrangement:

> "I hope this is not incommoding you at all," said Gorbo politely, struck with a sudden idea.
>
> "Oh, no," replied Sir Percival with bitter irony. [...] "Who *would* be incommoded by a little thing like this?" (Wyke-Smith 93-94).

Bilbo is, if possible, even more comically ineffective than the knight in responding to the imposition of one who blithely disregards all social cues. Where Sir Percival finds refuge in bitter irony, Bilbo cannot even reply to Thorin's remarks, but instead starts "almost squeaking with fright" (*H* 13) as the dwarves clear up everything from the tea for the next stage of the adventure.

Proper Deportment for the Prisoner

One situation that is seldom addressed in the etiquette books is the proper conduct of a person who finds himself in the role of captive. Fortunately, MacDonald and Tolkien both help fill this surprising lacuna, by calling attention to the level of courtesy demonstrated by characters who fall into the hands of goblins.

In MacDonald's story, the young miner Curdie is particularly anxious to avoid detection when spying on the goblins. The narrator explains that Curdie does not expect the goblins to "exercise courtesy" toward him, given his well-deserved reputation as their "special rhymester and persecutor" (MacDonald 70). When Curdie literally falls into their midst, however, he addresses the goblin king respectfully as "Your Majesty" in responding (albeit falsely) to questions about his identity and purpose (MacDonald 134). The king's reaction is perhaps surprising; he is "pleased" by this unexpected politeness from a miner, because he "attributed it to the power of his own presence" (MacDonald 134). It apparently feeds his ego to imagine that his presence is so intimidating that Curdie is cowed into submission. But we learn immediately that the king "did not therefore feel friendly" to Curdie (MacDonald 134). The goblin king instead taunts Curdie by ordering him to leave (when he knows Curdie is lost), and then ordering his subjects to seize Curdie when he requests a guide. Under the thinnest veneer of politeness, Curdie and the goblin king do not trust each other; each knows the other is lying and each is awaiting his chance to gain an advantage.

In *The Hobbit*, when the Great Goblin begins interrogating the dwarves about their presence in goblin territory, Thorin responds with "Thorin the dwarf at your service!" – and the narrator quickly reminds us that "it was merely a polite nothing" (*H* 60). Some critics suggest, in analyzing the passage, that Thorin is speaking "from force of habit" (Stevens and Stevens 64). West similarly notes that the words "could be dangerous if taken literally, but it is a formula regularly used [among dwarves] when introducing oneself throughout *The Hobbit*" (6).[14]

---

14 Bilbo uses a different formula, introducing himself to Gollum as "Mr. Bilbo Baggins" (*H* 69). MacIntyre suggests that Bilbo is drawing on "proprieties current in the Shire," which are "as unfamiliar to Gollum as Gollum is to Bilbo" (13). However, Bilbo's formula is equally unfamiliar to Miss Manners, who states emphatically that "one never applies a title of courtesy to oneself," including the title of "Mr." (Martin, *Turn-of-the-Millennium* 51).

But it is misleading to suggest that Thorin's politeness is automatic. After all, Thorin deliberately withheld the greeting when he fell on Bilbo's doorstep and injured his dignity: "Thorin indeed was very haughty, and said nothing about *service*" (*H* 11). Here, by contrast, Thorin's "polite nothing" is surely purposeful. At a minimum, it helps buy him time to think. The goblins are sufficiently wicked and cruel that anyone in their clutches must take care to avoid making them angry. An illuminating contrast can be seen when the dwarves are later captured by the Wood-elves; in that situation, they "did not even pretend to be polite" to the Elvenking (*H* 158). The Wood-elves, though less wise and more dangerous than their kin, are still "Good People" (*H* 154); the dwarves doubtless know that they can get away with rudeness to the elves, as they cannot with the goblins. That is, the Elvenking may (as he does) angrily confine the dwarves, but he will not kill, torture or starve them (*H* 156, 159).[15] The dwarves have no such confidence with respect to the Great Goblin, who (when angered) not only orders his minions to "Slash them! Beat them! Bite them! Gnash them!" but also "rushed at Thorin with his mouth open" (*H* 61).

Both MacDonald and Tolkien are doing something similar here, in calling attention to a prisoner's insincere politeness to his goblin captors; the humour in such exchanges lies in the tension between surface and reality. Good manners in these circumstances are clearly strategic or tactical, rather than sincere. Nor is the prisoner's courtesy rewarded in any conventional sense, as seen in didactic stories. For example, courtesy does not win the goblins' trust or friendship. The tactic seems to be one of stalling for time and avoiding immediate destruction.

Addressing One of Higher Rank

Etiquette requires use of proper titles when addressing an individual of higher rank (see generally Martin, *Excruciatingly Correct* 687-91), and several of our authors play with this concept. When Alice becomes a queen, she scolds herself for being insufficiently dignified – and actually addresses herself as "your Majesty" in doing so (Carroll 317). When the princess of MacDonald's story

---

15 Indeed, the Elvenking's threat to keep the dwarves locked up "until you have learned sense and manners" (*H* 159) is reminiscent of parental punishments such as being sent to one's room.

invites a young miner to call her "Irene," her nurse is indignant and insists that Curdie should address the princess as "Your Royal Highness" (MacDonald 39). But the princess, in turn, is outraged at the suggestion that Curdie should call her by her royal title. Irene's outrage is not due to democratic pretensions, but because she interprets it (literally) as name-calling:

> "My Royal Highness! What's that? No, no, Lootie. I won't be called names. I don't like them. You told me once yourself it's only rude children that call names; and I'm sure Curdie wouldn't be rude. Curdie, my name's Irene" (MacDonald 39).

The joke here, of course, is that the princess has completely misunderstood the convention of addressing royalty by their formal titles and imagines that it is an insult. The low-born Curdie is very well aware of Irene's innocent mistake, as he gives the nurse a glance which shows he enjoys teasing her and tells Irene that "it is very kind of you to let me call you anything" (MacDonald 39).

Polite speech to one of superior rank not only involves use of proper titles, but it often (in books) takes place in an elevated and archaic register, characterized by circumlocutions and use of the vocative *O*, and ornamented with elaborately constructed phrases and compliments. It is easy to skewer this "high" style of speaking through sheer exaggeration or by "misapplying" it to unlikely topics, and Wyke-Smith does exactly that. In *Snergs*, King Merse II's least favorite subject, Gorbo, addresses his monarch respectfully as "O King," and expresses the prescribed wish (i.e., that the king's "shadow be ever a wide one"[16]) – even when the king is heaping insults upon him, such as "O Ornament to the race the other way round" (Wyke-Smith 42). The incongruity and unfairness of this arrangement is rather striking, and is doubtless intended for humorous effect. Wyke-Smith further mocks this convention by mixing formal, archaic speech with modern, colloquial speech. When Merse II asks Joe "what will Miss Watkins (on whom be peace) think of these thy wanderings" (Wyke-Smith 42), he is speaking in the customary formal, archaic register which he uses indiscriminately for purposes high and low. Throughout the scene, a humorous mixture of modern, colloquial

---

16 This is surely echoed, although reimagined, in the Elvenking's farewell wish to Bilbo: "May your shadow never grow less (or stealing would be too easy)!" (*H* 267).

speech with formal, archaic speech is characteristic of both children, as they awkwardly combine the vocative *O* with contemporary slang.[17]

Tolkien similarly draws on a subject/monarch linguistic pattern for Bilbo's conversation with Smaug. As Shippey (38) observes, Bilbo speaks to Smaug "in a much more elevated style than is usual for him" and "Smaug replies more archaically and more heroically than anyone has done in *The Hobbit* so far." Although initially caught off-guard, Bilbo quickly addresses the dragon as "O Smaug the Tremendous" and "O Smaug the Chiefest and Greatest of Calamities" – causing Smaug to remark that Bilbo has "nice manners for a thief and a liar" (*H* 204). Bilbo's use of respectful titles makes sense here, since Bilbo is addressing one who is, as Bard grimly observes to his compatriots, "the only king under the Mountain we have ever known" (*H* 225).

There is much humour in the narrator's comment that riddling talk "of course is the way to talk to dragons," almost as if he were giving etiquette advice to readers anxious to learn the proper forms of discourse for their own future dragon encounters (*H* 205).[18] As hobbit and dragon engage in verbal fencing, each laying traps for the other, they address one another with pretended deference: A single mock-respectful "O Barrel-rider" from Smaug is countered by Bilbo's "O Smaug the Mighty" as well as "O Smaug the unassessably wealthy"[19] (*H* 205-7).

It is even possible to trace tactical changes in their conversation through changes in their forms of address.[20] For Bilbo, the most significant shift occurs when he

---

17 For example: "'I don't know, O King,' replied Joe, hoping he was saying it correctly. 'We just scooted. For fun'" (Wyke-Smith 42-43). Similarly, Sylvia says, "You see – er – O King, Joe and I ran away – for fun – and Gorbo found us," and Joe asserts that "Gorbo's a jolly good sort, O King" (43).
18 Indeed, the narrator, who has previously noted the strategic importance of not antagonizing wizards or enormous eagles through open rudeness, here emphasizes that it is "very wise" not to "infuriate [dragons] by a flat refusal" to reveal one's true name (*H* 205). A flat refusal to respond to a question is, unquestionably, impolite.
19 An apt title, since Smaug's wealth is too vast to assess (measure), and Smaug is also too powerful for anyone to dare attempt to assess (tax) it.
20 Smaug starts with mere name-calling ("thief" and "liar"), rather than titles (*H* 204). As he becomes intrigued with Bilbo's riddling talk, he uses a mock-respectful title and the vocative case ("O Barrel-rider") (*H* 205). As he gains the upper-hand through shrewd guesses and is able to manipulate Bilbo by introducing doubts about his companions, Smaug tones down the titles a notch and abandons the vocative ("Thief Barrel-rider" and "Mr. Lucky Number"). But when he gives himself wholly over to boasting, he enters a more archaic and poetic mode (echoing the Old Testament or a sweeping epic) and refers to Bilbo as "Thief in the Shadows" (*H* 207).

turns to *purposeful* flattery to gain information; at that point, he drops the *O* and refers to the dragon as "Lord Smaug" and "Your Magnificence" (*H* 208). Indeed, Bilbo's use of the honorific "Lord" is surely ironic, because "in speech, 'Lord' or 'Lady' before a given name means that the bearer has *inherited* the title" as the child of a duke, marquess, or earl (Martin, *Excruciatingly Correct* 691; emphasis added). Even if Smaug has appointed himself king under the Mountain, he certainly has not inherited the role, and holds it by might rather than by right.[21]

Smaug primarily speaks with "a kind of elaborate politeness, even circumlocution, of course totally insincere (as is often the case with upper-class English)" (Shippey 37), i.e., a mere "parody [of] polite language" (Kullmann 43). Shippey (38) notes that even as Smaug's tone becomes "familiar, even colloquial," it oozes with contempt and "roundabout mock-courtesy". Yet through all the tonal shifts, Smaug's false politeness suggests that he is not entirely sure who or what he is dealing with, just as Gollum, when he realizes that Bilbo has a sword out of Gondolin, "became quite polite" as he was "anxious to *appear* friendly [...] until he found out more about the sword and the hobbit" (*H* 69; emphasis added).

We see in Chapter XII, from Bilbo's use of flatteringly polite titles, that Bilbo is addressing one who is far mightier than he. But the ring, and perhaps Bilbo's unfamiliar scent, gives Bilbo an edge in dealing with Smaug so that he is not utterly at Smaug's mercy. This elevates Bilbo above the status of mere prisoner (or lunch!) so that he can assume the role of subject addressing a monarch. Smaug's attitude toward Bilbo is reminiscent of Merse II's toward Gorbo, rather than that of a goblin toward a prisoner.

Daring To Be Offended

Etiquette also dictates how one may respond to the impolite behaviour of others, and we again see our authors exploring this concept with humour. In Chapter

---

21 Smaug clearly has not inherited a peerage; and pretending he has earned one would not give him distinction under the British class system. As Miss Manners explains, "the further away the title holder is from earning his distinction, the more distinguished he is considered" and thus, it is ideal to be "the inheritor of a title given to a remote ancestor" (Martin, *Excruciatingly Correct* 690).

4 of MacDonald's novel, the young princess Irene is offended by her nurse's rudeness and informs her, "you are not fit to be spoken to – till you can behave better" (23). However, when the nurse says "I'm sure I beg your pardon" in an offended tone, Irene graciously "let the tone pass, and heeded only the words" (MacDonald 23). Here, the humour lies primarily in MacDonald's inversion of the customary roles, i.e., the child is correcting and disciplining the adult for improper behaviour. Both Irene and her nurse take offense in this scene, but the narrator emphasizes that only Irene is justified in doing so. The nurse certainly has no right to use an "offended tone" when she is requesting Irene's pardon for her own impoliteness. What we may also notice here is that the princess, who has reason to be offended, is quick to forgive, whereas the nurse is quick to take offense.

In Tolkien's tale, it is the dwarves – and especially Thorin – who take offense most readily. As we have seen, when Bilbo opens the door suddenly and Thorin falls on his face with three dwarves on top of him, Thorin "was very haughty" to Bilbo and only after profuse apologies does he finally grunt "pray don't mention it," and stop frowning (*H* 11). Grunting is hardly gracious, but another part of the humour here is also that the characters all erroneously assume that Bilbo was in the wrong for opening the door too abruptly. (The dwarves would not have fallen in, no matter how quickly the door opened, had they stood at a respectful distance after knocking.) Likewise, after Bilbo rescues the dwarves from imprisonment in the Elvenking's realm, Thorin is grumpy, rather than grateful, on being freed from his barrel; the narrator notes that "it was some time before he would be even polite to the hobbit" (*H* 178). Thorin is particularly quick to stand on his dignity and to unleash his displeasure on the hobbit by withholding common courtesies.

By contrast, the dwarves show great restraint in the presence of Beorn. They scrupulously heed Gandalf's warning that "you must all be very polite when I introduce you" to Beorn (*H* 108). But when they offer Beorn their service, his response is rather rude. Beorn immediately sees through the form of politeness and (like Gandalf with Bilbo in the opening chapter) points out the truth of the situation, noting correctly that he does not need the dwarves' service, "but I expect you need mine" (*H* 112). Beorn's brusqueness only escalates as the dwarves continue to arrive and offer him their service. Olsen (134) notes, correctly, that "Beorn's rudeness to Thorin and Company shows, in part, that he does not fear them." But an important converse is true as well. When Beorn reaches the point of simply laughing at the dwarves and ordering them to "sit down and stop wagging," the dwarves promptly obey, "not daring to be offended" (*H* 114-15).[22]

In everyday life, quickness to take offense, and to express that offense through sullenness or grumpiness, is a sign of immaturity and is (naturally enough) seen most often in children. MacDonald inverts the expectation in the relationship between the young princess and her nurse; and Tolkien again expands on MacDonald's hint. His dwarves, though fully grown, respond like children when they do not get their own way[23] – except when their self-interest counsels otherwise. Thus, they feel free to sulk and scowl at harmless Bilbo, but not at dangerous Beorn.

Counterpoint: Rudeness as Benchmark

While Bilbo (unlike the dwarves) generally makes efforts to be reasonably polite, it is notable that skillful use of rudeness marks two significant points in Bilbo's development.

Indeed, rudeness is Bilbo's primary weapon in Chapter VIII, his first real "heroic" endeavor, when he saves his companions from the spiders of Mirkwood. He wields Sting and throws stones, but ultimately prevails "by taunts and trickery, not by combat" (MacIntyre 15). Bilbo's strategy consists of inventing insulting songs "on the spur of a very awkward moment" (*H* 147) to taunt the spiders into blind rage and draw them off. Bilbo's taunting poetry for the spiders somewhat echoes Curdie's taunting poetry in *Princess*. In MacDonald's world, rhyming verse is the miners' main weapon against the goblins. While Curdie's songs are, in Irene's estimation, "rather rude" (MacDonald 41), their

---

[22] Indeed, through Beorn's eyes, readers may see the dwarves' overscrupulous politeness as ridiculous (*H* 114; Olsen 133). Critically, Beorn helps the Company only because he becomes interested in Gandalf's story. Although his interest is heightened by the interruptions (*H* 116), his reaction to the dwarves' obsequious bowing and offers of service is merely that of annoyance and amusement; thus, he orders the dwarves to stop, once he is through laughing at them.

[23] [The "immature" sulking could also be linked to pre-modern behaviour, as found in numerous protagonists in the Icelandic sagas. It is, however, more likely that Tolkien, in the context of *The Hobbit*, had primarily the behaviour of children in mind. – Eds.]

effectiveness appears to lie in the rhymes themselves. That is, it appears that the goblins are extremely discomfited by poetry because they "have no more voice than a crow" (MacDonald 36) and "could not make any" verses of their own (MacDonald 49). The rudeness appears to be almost incidental, a byproduct of Curdie's genuine contempt for them.[24] As Curdie explains, "if you're not afraid of them, they're afraid of you" (MacDonald 36). Tolkien has reinvented rhyming verses as weapons for Bilbo, whose deliberate use of rude names such as "Attercop" and "Tomnoddy" makes the spiders "frightfully angry" (*H* 147); it is now the rhymes that appear to be merely incidental. Although the notion of using rudeness as a weapon is somewhat absurd, it is a benchmark of Bilbo's growing heroism.

A second significant turning point, reflecting Bilbo's increasing self-confidence, occurs just four chapters later. Just as Gandalf rudely punctures Bilbo's polite nothings in Chapter I by calling attention to Bilbo's true intentions, Bilbo does much the same to Thorin in Chapter XII, and it signals an important shift in their relationship. Thorin has begun a grand speech on the theme of "Now is the time for our esteemed Mr. Baggins [...] to earn his Reward" (*H* 195). The narrator quickly deflates Thorin's "magniloquent speech" for the reader, and then Bilbo further mocks Thorin's polite hypocrisy (Shippey 42-43). As Tolkien writes:

> It certainly was an important occasion, but Bilbo felt impatient. By now he was quite familiar with Thorin too, and he knew what he was driving at.
>
> "If you mean you think it is my job to go into the secret passage first, O Thorin Thrain's son Oakenshield, may your beard grow ever longer," he said crossly, "say so at once and have done!" (*H* 195)

Bilbo now sees through Thorin's grand words, and publicly reveals their emptiness while parodying a courtier's flattering speech; and yet he also now has the courage to volunteer for the task with eyes wide-open.[25]

---

24 Curdie does "not value the enmity of the goblins in the least" (MacDonald 46), and unwisely dismisses them from his calculations.

25 This is not the last time that Bilbo pierces through Thorin's polite nothings; in the descendant-of-rats scene, Bilbo challenges Thorin about the "service" he had promised to Bilbo (*H* 251-52). Shippey (44) notes that Bilbo thereby "punctures dwarvish greeting formulas in much the same way that Gandalf punctured his own at the beginning."

Conclusion

The "good" characters presented in *The Hobbit* are, as Shippey (49) notes, "far removed from standard presentations of virtue as thought suitable for child readers – no doubt one reason why the book has remained so popular." Precisely the same can be said of Tolkien's presentations of etiquette in *The Hobbit*; these are not simple, one-size-fits-all applications of rules of custom and courtesy, but instead, comically and subversively, they show that manners can and do change to fit different circumstances and different purposes. Superficially polite words may be used to insult, to deceive, to satisfy tradition, or to show genuine respect;[26] others' polite words and actions (whether or not sincerely meant) may be reciprocated, pierced, or ridiculed; and the forms of politeness may be withheld, or even entirely abandoned in favor of undisguised taunts and insults.

We have seen that what constitutes polite behaviour among the denizens of Tolkien's world is somewhat arbitrary, a matter of convention removed from its literal meaning. Moreover, a person who is overly concerned with polite behaviour, like Bilbo at the beginning of *The Hobbit*, can be manipulated into situations he would prefer to avoid. Not only do we see that politeness can be hypocritical; we also see Bilbo suffering the consequences of his own insincere politeness when the Company takes him at his word. It is the impolite characters, Gandalf and Thorin, who prevail in the initial tussles with Bilbo; and much of their success in bullying him into an adventure is owed to their ruthless disregard of courteous behaviour. Bilbo himself soon learns to deploy rudeness strategically against the spiders of Mirkwood.

Nor is adherence to polite formulas rewarded elsewhere in *The Hobbit*. Thorin's politeness to the Great Goblin, the dwarves' politeness to Beorn, and Bilbo's politeness to Smaug – none of these efforts "pay off" in any tangible way. They fool no one, and win no friends, through their efforts to be polite.

---

26 For example, when Balin learns that Bilbo has managed to slip by him undetected, he takes off his hood to Bilbo and reintroduces himself with the words "Balin at your service" (*H* 87). The implication is that the ordinarily empty polite formula now has meaning, because Bilbo has managed to earn Balin's respect with his stealth. In a similar vein, the use of the vocative *O* and elaborate titles is merely false and flattering in Bilbo's encounter with Smaug, but becomes serious and formal in the halls of the Elvenking, as the king has gained a genuine affection and respect for the unlikely burglar (*H* 267).

In fact, where Tolkien breaks away most completely from his predecessors is in this additional layer of Realpolitik: politeness is most consistently displayed from the less powerful to the more powerful. This mirrors the traditional experience of children who have rules of politeness imposed on them regardless of whether the adults follow such rules consistently or not. Like children, the dwarves are peevish and sulky, and even downright rude to Bilbo and the Elvenking because they can get away with it; but they are scrupulously polite to Beorn and the goblins, as their self-interest dictates. Over the course of the tale, we can even see levels of politeness change as the power balance changes in different relationships. Gollum and Smaug put on a show of politeness as they take Bilbo's measure; and a defining moment in Bilbo's relationship with Thorin occurs late in the story when Bilbo pierces Thorin's courteous words, much as Gandalf did to Bilbo and Beorn did to the dwarves. Simply put, in Tolkien's world, as in our own, the powerful have far less need for politeness.

About the Author

LAURA LEE SMITH received her J.D. magna cum laude from Boston University School of Law. She lives and works in New York City, and is also enrolled part-time at Signum University/Mythgard Institute, an online center for graduate-level scholarship in speculative fiction. She has published book reviews in *Mythlore* and *Mythprint*, and has presented Inklings-related papers at several conferences. Her essay "Who Deserves the Truth? A Look at Veracity and Mendacity in Harry Potter" appears in *Harry Potter for Nerds II*, edited by Kathryn McDaniel and Travis Prinzi (Unlocking Press 2015).

Bibliography

ANDERSON, Douglas A. *The Annotated Hobbit.* Revised and expanded edition. Boston and New York: Houghton Mifflin Company, 2002.

BLOOM, Harold. "Introduction." *Bloom's Modern Critical Views: J.R.R. Tolkien*, New Edition. Ed. Harold BLOOM. New York: Bloom's Literary Criticism/ Infobase Publishing, 2008. 1-2.

BRIGGS, Julia and Dennis BUTTS. "The Emergence of Form (1850-1890)." *Children's Literature: An Illustrated History.* Ed. Peter HUNT. Oxford and New York: Oxford University Press, 1995. 130-166.

BLYTH, Catherine. *The Art of Conversation: A Guided Tour of a Neglected Pleasure.* New York: Gotham Books, 2009.

CARPENTER, Humphrey. *Secret Gardens: A Study of the Golden Age of Children's Literature.* Boston: Houghton Mifflin, 1985.

CARR, Jimmy and Lucy GREEVES. *Only Joking: What's So Funny about Making People Laugh?* New York: Gotham Books, 2006.

CARROLL, Lewis [Charles DODGSON]. *Through the Looking-Glass, and What Alice Found There.* 1871. Ed. Martin GARDNER. *The Annotated Alice.* New York: Bramhall House, 1960. 167-345.

GÖTZ, Ignacio L. *Manners and Violence.* Westport, CT and London: Praeger, 2000.

KULLMANN, Thomas. "Intertextual Patterns in J.R.R. Tolkien's *The Hobbit* and *The Lord of the Rings.*" *Nordic Journal of English Studies* 8.2 (2009): 37-56. Open Journal Systems. 9 Nov. 2013 <http://ojs.ub.gu.se/ojs/index.php/njes/article/view/338/335>.

LURIE, Alison. *Don't Tell the Grown-ups: Subversive Children's Literature.* Boston, Toronto & London: Little, Brown and Company, 1990.

MACDONALD, George. *The Princess and the Goblin.* 1872. London: Puffin Books, 2010.

MACINTYRE, Jean. "'Time shall run back': Tolkien's *The Hobbit.*" *Children's Literature Association Quarterly* 13.1 (Spring 1988): 12-17.

MARTIN, Judith. *Miss Manners' Guide for the Turn-of-the-Millennium.* New York, London, Toronto & Sydney: Simon & Schuster, 1990.

Miss Manners' Guide to Excruciatingly Correct Behaviour, Freshly Updated. New York and London: W. W. Norton, 2005.

MILNE, A.A. *Winnie-the-Pooh.* 1926. London: Puffin Books, 2005.

MUNDE, Gail. "What Are You Laughing At? Differences in Children's and Adults' Humorous Book Selections for Children." *Children's Literature in Education* 28.4 (1997): 219-233.

OLSEN, Corey. *Exploring J.R.R. Tolkien's The Hobbit*. Boston and New York: Houghton Mifflin Harcourt, 2012.

RATELIFF, John. *The History of the Hobbit*. Boston and New York: Houghton Mifflin, 2007.

SHIPPEY, Tom A. *J.R.R. Tolkien: Author of the Century*. Boston and New York: Houghton Mifflin, 2000.

STEVENS, David, and Carol D. STEVENS. *J.R.R. Tolkien: The Art of the Myth-Maker*. San Bernardino, CA: The Borgo Press, 1993.

SWIFT, Jonathan. "On Good-Manners and Good-Breeding." Vol. IX of *Works*. Dublin: George Faulkner, 1758. 34-44.

THOMAS, Paul Edmund. "Some of Tolkien's Narrators." *Tolkien's Legendarium: Essays on the History of Middle-earth*. Ed. Verlyn FLIEGER and Carl F. HOSTETTER. Westport, CT: Greenwood Press, 2000. 161-81.

TOLKIEN, J.R.R. *The Hobbit*. 3rd ed. 1966. Boston and New York: Houghton Mifflin, 2007.

The Letters of J.R.R. Tolkien. Ed. Humphrey CARPENTER, with the assistance of Christopher TOLKIEN. Boston and New York: Houghton Mifflin, 2000.

"The Pryftan Fragment." *The History of the Hobbit*. Ed. John D. RATELIFF. Boston and New York: Houghton Mifflin Company, 2007. 7-11.

TOWNSEND, John Rowe. *Written for Children: An outline of English-language children's literature*. 6th American edition. Lanham, MD & London: Scarecrow Press, 1996.

TWAIN, Mark [Samuel CLEMENS]. *Mark Twain's Notebook*. 1896. Vol. 22 of *The Complete Works of Mark Twain*. New York: Harper & Brothers, 1935. Internet Archive. 27 Nov. 2013 <https://archive.org>.

WEITZ, Eric. *The Cambridge Introduction to Comedy*. Cambridge: Cambridge University Press, 2009.

WEST, Richard C. "'And She Named Her Own Name': Being True To One's Word in Tolkien's Middle-earth." *Tolkien Studies* 2 (2005): 1-10.

WYKE-SMITH, Edward Augustine. *The Marvellous Land of Snergs*. 1928. Mineola, NY: Dover Publications, 2006.

Gandalf looked closer are the smaller writing and read...
"Forgotten your password? Press staff here to reset".

Graeme Skinner
The Doors of Durin

Graeme Skinner
The Force

Evelyn Koch

Parodies of the Works of J.R.R. Tolkien

Abstract

With J.R.R. Tolkien's works being among the most read texts of the twentieth and twenty-first centuries, and the film adaptations of *The Lord of the Rings* and *The Hobbit* by Peter Jackson being incredibly successful as well, there is naturally an abundance of parodies. This paper does not attempt to list them all but to look at how parody works, and what strategies are involved to create a parody of Tolkien's works. Thus, I have categorised some of the parodies according to their underlying strategy: as textual or social parody, and whether they involve strategies of exaggeration/understatement, whether they substitute heroes and villains with non-heroes or non-villains, whether they make the quest ridiculous or trivial, make fun of place names and proper names, or add vulgarity or obscenity to the original text.

Introduction

The fifth season of *Epic Rap Battles of History* (2016) by Nice Peter & EpicLLOYD features an episode with J.R.R. Tolkien and George R.R. Martin duelling each other with words. The latter accuses Tolkien that "all your bad guys die, and your good guys survive! We can tell what's gonna happen by page and age five! Tell your all-seeing eye to find some sex in your movies (Yeah). Ditch the Goonie, and cast a couple boobies! There's edgier plots in that David the Gnome. [...] You went too deep, Professor Tweed Pants. We don't need the back story on every fucking tree branch." Tolkien's literary works are parodied here in a nutshell; and it is one of the latest additions to the ever growing universe of parodies of Tolkien's works or Tolkien himself. One of the first published parodies was Henry N. Beard and Douglas C. Kenney's *Bored of the Rings* (1969). Ever since then, Tolkien's solemn literary style has spawned a plethora of parodies in various forms and guises,[1] be it books, comic strips, videos, or radio series like *Hordes of the Things* (1980) by Andrew Marshall and John Lloyd. The release of Peter Jackson's film adaptation of *The Lord of the Rings* (2001-2003) created a further surge of spoofs, parodies, and satires. Since there appear to be gazillions of Tolkien parodies by now, especially on the internet, only some of them can be considered here, otherwise this paper would just turn into a very long, and indeed, boring list.[2]

Defining Parody

Before turning to the actual parodies in more detail, we should briefly take a look at what actually constitutes a parody. *The Oxford Dictionary of Literary Terms* defines parody as "a mocking imitation of the style of a literary work or works, ridiculing the stylistic habits of an author or school by exaggerated mimicry" (s.v. "Parody"). Yet this definition is rather vague. Martha Bayless defines parody more precisely

> as an intentionally humorous literary (written) text that achieves its effect by (1) imitating and distorting the distinguishing characteristics of literary genres, styles, authors, or specific texts (*textual parody*); or (2) imitating, with or without distortion, literary genres, styles, authors, or texts while in addition satirizing or focusing on nonliterary customs, events, or persons (*social parody*). (3)

So whereas textual parody is more concerned with an actual parody of the text, social parody makes fun of the impact a certain text (or film) has on society and culture. *The Soddit* (2003) by Adam Roberts[3], for example, is for most of its parts a straight textual parody. The opening sentences of the book stay very close to the beginning of *The Hobbit*:

> In a hole, in a highly desirable and sought-after portion of the ground (the hole two doors along went for three hundred thou last month, near enough, although admittedly it was double-fronted and had a newly turfed roof) lived a soddit, the hero of our story. His name was Bingo 'Sac' Grabbings. Not a name he chose for himself, of course, but one decided on by his mother. Easy

---

1 This paper is based on a presentation Markus Raddatz and I gave in Thomas Honegger's seminar "Representing Middle-earth" at the Friedrich-Schiller-University Jena in January 2016. I would like to thank Markus Raddatz for researching many of the parodies that are examined here.
2 For more parodies, see Sherrylyn Branchaw's paper about *The Stupid Ring Parody* in this volume, and also Bratman (2007).
3 Roberts chooses, of course, A.R.R.R. Roberts as a synonym.

for her to say, of course; she didn't have to live with it all through school and adult life. Parents, eh? (Roberts 3).

The parody is achieved here by using a rather chatty tone and by frequent digressions to trivial and unimportant information. But *The Soddit* also contains elements of social parody. One of the many subheadings of the book title is "Let's Cash In Again", referring to the fact that nowadays everything remotely connected with Tolkien can be turned into money, especially when it comes to film adaptations. It has to be kept in mind that parody imitates and transforms an original work at the same time (Dentith 3), as can be seen in the aforementioned example from *The Soddit*. It repeats another work with a critical distance and is "characterized by ironic inversion" (Hutcheon 6). Yet this does not tell us anything about the quality, i.e. the desired comic effect of the parody. There are various strategies to create a parody, often with varying success.

We should also mention that the understanding of a parody requires specific knowledge on the part of the audience. They have to be acquainted with the various conventions, the style, and themes of a certain genre or author in order to be able to fully appreciate the parody (Hutcheon 94). What is more, the original text has to have recognisable traits in order to be parodied. Mediocrity is hard to parody. In a way, parody condenses the most outstanding characteristics of a text, and confirms the status of the original. So, parody is not only about downgrading or making fun of the original, but it is entirely possible to conceive a parody as homage to the original. How important it is to be acquainted with the original text in order to understand that we are dealing with a parody becomes clear in the following case. One of the already older parodies on the internet is *A Brief Synopsis of The Lord of the Rings* which has the appearance of being one of the countless websites like sparknotes.com or shmoop.com that offer synopses and interpretations of literary works for students who cannot be bothered with reading a whole book. So *A Brief Synopsis of The Lord of the Rings* is much more a parody of these websites than of the actual Tolkien novels. In the synopsis, the reader is led completely astray. Much of the information offered seems very similar to the original text, but there is ever so much nonsense added, like for example: "Frodo discovers that the witches have destroyed the village of Bree, and the Witch-king uses a magic spell to burn down the home of their old friend Tom Bombadil" or "next they are driven into the dark forest of Lothlorien, where they are imprisoned by the beautiful but evil Queen Berúthiel. They make their escape when Berúthiel's good sister, Galadriel, frees them from their prison-cell and floats them down the river in barrels" (Flying Moose of Nargothrond n.p.). A reader has to be aware of the fact that Queen Berúthiel is mentioned only once in passing by Aragorn in the chapter "A Journey in the Dark". He says that Gandalf "is surer of finding the way home in a blind night than the cats of Queen Berúthiel" (*LotR* 311). Thus Berúthiel is mentioned but she is not a protagonist in *The Lord of the Rings*, and the escape in barrels is from *The Hobbit*. What happens if the reader is not aware, becomes clear in an article by Ian Markham-Smith about Cate Blanchett's role as Galadriel, published in the London *Sunday Times* on 26 July 2000. The journalist writes about Blanchett's character: "for the uninitiated, Galadriel is the good sister of the evil but beautiful Queen Beruthiel, who imprisons the Fellowship of the Ring in the forest of Lothlorien. In the book, Galadriel frees them from her sister's clutches" (Markham-Smith n.p.). Probably, the journalist wanted to save time, and just googled the relevant information, found this synopsis, and simply copied out the information. Without the knowledge of the original text he was apparently completely taken in. Thus, parodies can also appeal to and test our knowledge. Particularly in the realm of the Tolkien fandom, understanding a parody with very specific allusions to Tolkien's works might be more appealing to some fans than a parody that just re-stages scenes from Jackson's adaptations and adds a few fart jokes.

When sifting through the various parodies, it becomes quickly apparent that most of them are parodies of *The Lord of the Rings* and *The Hobbit*, because many more people have read those books than, say, *The Silmarillion*. And of those works the majority are rather parodies of the film than of the books. Again, many people may have seen the films, or are at least familiar with the idea of them, so they are instantly more recognisable. For instance, there are two books called *The Wobbit*, one by Paul A. Erickson (2011), and one by the makers of *The Harvard Lampoon* (2013). Whereas Erickson's work is a straight textual parody of the book, *The Wobbit* from 2013 was conveniently published at a time when Peter Jackson's film adaptation of *The Hobbit* played in the cinemas. It is no coincidence then that the first chapter of the book is named "An Unexpected Trilogy" (1). Of course, there are other textual parodies in book form such as the already mentioned *The Soddit* (2003) and *The Sellamillion* (2004) by the same author, the latter one being one of the lesser frequent parodies of *The Silmarillion*.

Strategies of Parody

Strategies of Textual Parody

When it comes to applying specific strategies to achieve a parody, exaggeration of an original work by overdoing its recognisable features immediately springs to mind (Dentith 32). For example, in a sketch from the BBC comedy programme *Dead Ringers* (2002-2007), the returned Gandalf the White confronts Saruman who then tries to eliminate him immediately, only for Gandalf to come back as "Gandalf the Tartan" presenting Saruman with a whole colour chart in which he may return if Saruman tries to kill him again. Yet the same can be achieved by understatement, as well. In the BBC Radio 4 comedy *Elvenquest* (2009-2013) the villain Lord Darkness, unmistakably reminiscent of the Dark Lord, is played with remarkable understatement by Alistair McGowan. His Lord Darkness never goes into the typical villain mode, i.e. speaking gruffly with a deep voice whilst being imposing and also a little bit mysterious, but he is very sober, often even bored, and speaks with a nasal voice that would be more fitting for a middle-aged civil servant who cannot be bothered.

More specific strategies for parodying the content of a text involve substituting the hero, or indeed, villain of the original text with a non-heroic person or anti-hero (or "anti-villain") who performs non-heroic (or non-villainous) deeds (Tigges 133). For instance, the German comedy show *Die Wochenshow* (1996-2002) re-dubbed sequences from Peter Jackson's *The Lord of the Rings* in Swabian dialect. Frodo is renamed "Otto" here, and his greatest dream is phrased as: "oinmol in seinem Läbe will der Otto uff en großes Rockfeschtival."[4] Consequently, he has to get permission from his father to go there. So here Frodo is turned into an everyday, rather provincial guy who strives for his father's approval to go to a local rock festival rather than the one who will save

---

4 "Only once in his life Otto wants to attend a big rock festival." *[my translation]*

the world from evil. By setting the parody in a very mundane, even provincial setting, the non-heroic qualities of the main characters are especially emphasised. The use of local dialects with strong connotations of provincialism only adds to this setting.⁵ There are parodies not only in Swabian, but there is also the Swiss film *The Ring Thing* (2004) directed by Mark Schippert, which plays out entirely in Swiss German. Another *Lord of the Rings* parody by the comedy duo Elsterglanz, "Auf Achse" (Track 8) from the album *Der Scharlachrote Buchstabensuppe* (2005), uses the dialect from the area of Mansfelder Land in Saxony-Anhalt.⁶ The comedy created by the use of these dialects exploits the clash between two opposing concepts. On the one hand, we perceive the setting and traits of high fantasy as created by Tolkien; on the other, we hear the characters talk to each other in an everyday way, as if we were, for example, meeting a neighbour in a supermarket. The use of such dialects immediately takes away a lot of the enchantment connected with the genre of fantasy; and it effectively undermines the solemnity of Tolkien's work. The strategy of replacing the hero with a non-hero is used in the *Sesame Street's Lord of the Crumbs* (2013), too, which features Cookie Monster, a non-heroic person *par excellence*, on his quest to remember a cookie recipe and trying to prevent himself from gobbling up all the ingredients beforehand.

When it comes to making the villains look less evil, we already mentioned the character Lord Darkness from *Elvenquest*. Lord Darkness loses a lot of his supposed menace because we witness him frequently doing everyday things like writing his shopping list, or facing mundane problems such as losing his keys or going on a diet. This makes him appear much more human and less terrifying. Another good example as a case in point is Jamie Thomson's *Dark Lord* series for which, up to now, three volumes have been published, *Dark Lord: The Teenage Years* (2011), *Dark Lord: A Fiend in Need* (2012), and *Dark Lord: Eternal Detention* (2014). What creates the parody here is the non-villainous appearance of the Dark Lord. He is cast out from his own world into our contemporary world, and finds himself trapped inside the body of

---

5 Here, I mainly refer to parodies in various German dialects, since being a native speaker of German, I am acquainted with more examples from this field than in other languages.
6 This dialect is often mistaken as Saxon dialect. On YouTube there are various uploads of this parody with the tagline "Herr der Ringe auf Sächsisch". Even worse, many people in Germany may perceive this as standard "East German" dialect.

a schoolboy. Therefore, no one takes him seriously anymore; and people misinterpret his name as Dirk Lloyd. He also lacks the usual gimmicks, and indeed the infrastructure of a villain striving for world domination, i.e. evil minions to carry out his plans – be it rampaging Orc hordes or enslaved Nazgûl – or a dark fortress, which is anything but homely looking, ideally surrounded by desolated wasteland. Thomson's Dirk Lloyd still has the character of an arch-villain, yet his appearance and the unfamiliar context he has been put into make him non-threatening, and also a little ridiculous.[7] Although Thomson takes a big parodic swipe at villains in fantasy literature in general, Tolkien's Sauron still is the blueprint for all of them. Another ridiculous villain can be encountered in a parody of Peter Jackson's *Lord of the Rings* films by British comedy duo French and Saunders from 2002. There, a Ringwraith rides on a really tiny pony which instantly makes him appear funny, rather than threatening.

Furthermore, the aim or reward of the quest, or indeed stages of the adventure itself, can be rendered mundane, ridiculous, "trivial, pointless or absurd" (Tigges 133). This is, for example, the case in the aforementioned *Lord of the Crumbs* episode from *Sesame Street* in which Cookie Monster has to bake some cookies with the help of Gandalf and Galadriel without eating all the ingredients before the dough is finished. Likewise, in the Swabian parody of *The Lord of the Rings* films the re-named Otto alias Frodo wants to attend a local rock festival; and the biggest obstacle on his way is his obstinate father. In a parody called *Gandalf: You Shall Not Pass* (2013), by the Polish YouTuber Sylwester Wardęga, who trades under the pseudonym SA Wardega, Gandalf's fight with the Balrog from Peter Jackson's *The Fellowship of the Ring* is re-staged in the primary world. We see somebody vaguely dressed as Gandalf who walks onto some rails only to stop a train with his staff whilst declaiming "You shall not pass!" and "Go back to the shadows!" He then summons the rest of the Fellowship from the bushes to guide them safely across the railtracks. The conductor of the train is clearly not amused and threatens to call the police. The comedy of this parody lies in

---

7 "The man who had spoken leaned closer, looking him over. (Stupid human. Didn't the fool realise who he was dealing with?) Immediately, he tried ripping the man's throat out with his iron-taloned Gauntlets of Ineluctable Destruction, but it was no good, he just didn't have the strength. Then he noticed he wasn't wearing any gauntlets, or even gloves. His hands were pink, pallid and pudgy, with neat little white nails, like those of a wretched little human boy! You couldn't even rip out the throat of a rat with those hands, let alone a fully grown human warrior. He groaned in despair." (Thomson 16)

its everyday context. We see the Fellowship not on the Bridge of Khazad-dûm, but on some rails in what is probably the Polish countryside. Gandalf does not face a Balrog like in the film, who is aflame and cracks his whip, but an ordinary train conducted by an understandably disgruntled train driver. The absurdness of this "adventure" is emphasised by the seriousness of the actors who still perform like they were in a high fantasy adventure. In episode 15 from season 18 of *The Simpsons*, "Rome-old and Juli-eh" (2007), Bart and Lisa erect a castle made out of cardboard boxes which they had scrounged from used UPS boxes. An enraged UPS driver reprimands them for the unlawful use of the boxes, and threatens retaliation if they do not return them. Of course, Bart and Lisa want to keep their cardboard castle and are prepared to defend it. Later, an army of UPS drivers arrives and starts an attack on the castle. The whole battle is clearly reminiscent of the Battle of Helm's Deep from Peter Jackson's *The Two Towers*. The parody of this piece is achieved by using the strategy of making the whole adventure rather mundane and trivial, i.e. UPS drivers attempting to retrieve their cardboard boxes. At the same time, the tone of the parodied film in question is kept. We hear elevated operatic music in the background, and one of the UPS employees even rides on a dragon.[8]

In this context, a very specific strategy to parody Tolkien's works is to make fun of the many place and proper names which are featured in Tolkien's texts. The remarkably high density of place names and proper names makes an excellent target for parody. Almost every parody in book form includes a map at the beginning on which all the place names of Middle-earth are mocked. In *The Soddit*, a mountain range is called "Upsn Downs"; there is "The Snug of Smug", "The Gulf of Gulp"; for George Eliot fans there is a place called "The Mill" next to a river called "The Floss"; 1990s Brit-Pop fans might spot a place called "Oasis" next to one named "Blur", and so on (Roberts 1). In French and Saunders' parody of Peter Jackson's *The Fellowship of the Ring*, there is a map right at the beginning featuring place names like "Murky Brown Pläce", "Forest Gump" and "Victoria Wood". In *Elvenquest*, the Questers come upon

---

8 Of course, there were no dragons at the Battle of Helm's Deep. The dragon here is probably reminiscent of the fell beasts on which the Nazgûl ride. Yet since these beasts look a little dragon-like in Peter Jackson's films, and because the depiction of a fell beast would require more intimate knowledge with Tolkien's universe, the makers of *The Simpsons* presumably opted for a more recognisable dragon in this case as a sign for the audience that we are dealing with the genre of fantasy.

places like "Grazak-Dun" or the "kingdom of Premenstrua" in a world that is called "Lower Earth". For *Hordes of the Things*, Andrew Marshall and John Lloyd devised their own coherent naming system in that they name their characters after bath or pharmaceutical products, so we have "Radox the Green", "Badedas the Blue", "Matey the White", or "Crown Prince Veganin". We find a similar approach in Henry N. Beard and Douglas C. Kenney's *Bored of the Rings*. There, characters are named after soft drinks ("Moxie Dingleberry" and "Pepsi Dingleberry"), corn chips ("Frito Bugger"), pharmaceutical products ("Bromosel" and "Serutan"), or other things we might encounter in a supermarket or at a chemist's.

Another frequently applied strategy is to render the original text obscene or vulgar. This is indeed one of the most frequently applied strategies, at least when it comes to parodies on the internet, although it is not always one of the most successful ones, i.e. if success is measured by how funny a parody actually is. One of the most popular German fandubs, i.e. a version of a film re-dubbed by amateurs, is *Lord of the Weed – Sinnlos in Mittelerde* (2003-2005). Here, long sequences of Peter Jackson's *Lord of the Rings* films are re-dubbed in various parts so that the film gains a whole different meaning. As can be expected from the title, all peoples in Middle-earth are preoccupied with smoking weed, and that is not Shire weed, but marijuana most of the time. Bilbo Baggins aka Don Bilbo is a proficient dealer who likes to impart his knowledge only too gladly to the younger Hobbits. Gandalf is stoned all the time and likes to blast techno music from his horse cart when he rides through the Shire. Sauron is the worst of them all with respect to marijuana consumption. He rolls himself the biggest joint of them all. Further, we learn that the one ring is only sought after so intensely in Middle-earth because it possesses the miraculous property to inject THC directly into the bloodstream of the person who wears it. Among all the various fandubs, *Lord of the Weed* is one of the better examples, because it has a coherent story line, and the connection to smoking weed is not a million miles away from Shire weed-smoking Hobbits, although, as with so many of these internet videos, the longer it runs, the more tiring it gets. Watching Gandalf & Co. using youth slang and foul language, smoking weed, and doing silly things might be amusing at first, but the humour quickly wears off.

Since sex is a topic that is broadly omitted in Tolkien's work, it is not surprising that many parodies make use of it. In *Lord of the Piercing* (2002), a sketch first premiered at the MTV Movie Awards, Jack Black and Sarah Michelle Gellar play Elves who are intercut into the scene from the Council of Elrond in Peter Jackson's *The Fellowship of the Ring*. Jack Black's character confesses to having used the one ring to get himself a genital piercing, but the ring can, of course, only be destroyed in the fires of Mount Doom if it is not attached to Jack Black's private parts anymore. In the end, Sarah Michelle Gellar's character solves the problem by ripping the ring off from where it does not belong. This setting provides ample opportunities for sexual innuendo and bawdy humour. This sketch is characteristic for using just the strategy of making a text obscene or bawdy. Neither the content nor the style of the original text itself is parodied, but sexual innuendo or vulgar language is added to the text to render it different and ridiculous. Of course, this strategy only works if the original text is not already drenched in obscenities itself. Another parody using this strategy is the Swiss film *The Ring Thing* (2004) directed by Mark Schippert. This feature-length parody of *The Lord of the Rings* films shows binge-eating, weed-smoking, or nymphomaniac Elves, and revels, amongst other things, in belches, the excretion of various bodily fluids, and naked bottoms. Needless to say, it gets a little tiring after a while, and the bawdy humour appears to be an end in itself rather than contributing to a spot-on parody. A much better working example using this strategy is Cassandra Claire's *Very Secret Diaries*[9], another parody of *The Lord of the Rings* films. Claire re-writes the stories of the various characters from *The Lord of the Rings* as slash[10] fan fiction, i.e. she invents romantic, or most of the time not-actually-so-romantic, attachments between the mostly male characters. Her conceit of the whole Fellowship already being or turning gay and trying to get off with each other is based on very good observations of the characters as depicted in the films. She exaggerates their mannerisms[11] and adds sexual or romantic desires between the characters, an exaggeration which spoofs the traditional notion of heroic bonds of honour

---

9   For a more detailed analysis of *The Very Secret Diaries* see Kroner (2010) and Branchaw in this volume.
10 For the origin and definition of the term see Kroner 109-111.
11 To give an example from Aragorn's diary: "Day One: Ringwraiths killed: 4. V. good. Met up with Hobbits. Walked forty miles. Skinned a squirrel and ate it. Still not King." (Claire n.p.)

between men in high fantasy.¹² But still, the original traits and behaviour of the characters are recognisable (Kroner 113). Claire's parody works on several levels. On the one hand, it serves an audience acquainted with Peter Jackson's adaptations of *The Lord of the Rings*; "on the other hand it is also a parody of fan fiction, especially of slash fiction" (Kroner 113). So, fans of slash fiction might read the parody on a different level and spot various allusions to this genre, e.g. "the tendency of the fan fiction community to turn everything into slash no matter how unlikely the pairing" (Kroner 114). Thus, people with a prior knowledge of *The Lord of the Rings* films and slash fiction might get the most out of this parody. Not always does it have to be vulgar or obscene; sometimes it suffices to be just plain silly in order to create a parody. One of the most clicked[13] parodies of Jackson's *The Lord of the Rings* on YouTube is the video *They're Taking the Hobbits to Isengard* (2005) by Erwin Beekveld. With techno music playing in the background, Legolas' line "they're taking the Hobbits to Isengard" from Jackson's *The Two Towers* is looped *ad nauseam*. This is indeed an example how to distort an original work effectively. The video has elicited an abundance of videos responding to it, among them a ten hour version of the video and an actual response by Orlando Bloom which lifted the clip to another metafictional level.

Strategies of Social Parody

So far, we have looked at strategies that create a textual parody, but the conventions of a genre and the literary style of a text can be stressed in a parody, too, by ridiculing them, or by deliberately deviating from genre conventions. This aims at creating a social parody. An excellent example for social parody is a sketch by Dawn French and Jennifer Saunders from an Easter special of their programme *French and Saunders* in 2002. Again, instead of directly spoofing Tolkien's *The Fellowship of the Ring* novel, they opted for the adaptation by Peter Jackson, since it had only been playing in cinemas during the previous months. French and Saunders' parody focuses on the metalevel, on the mechanics of how a film works, and what stakes are involved in the production surrounding

---

12 For instance, from Aragorn's diary: "Day 28: Beginning to find Frodo disturbingly attractive. Have a feeling if I make a move, Sam would kill me. Also, hairy feet kind of a turn-off." (Claire n.p.)
13 By June 2016 the clip had had 21,448,931 hits.

it, rather than on the plot or content. For instance, we see Frodo (played by Dawn French) wearing enormous plush foot prostheses so (s)he may pass as a Hobbit. French and Saunders especially like to make fun of the difference in size between the Hobbits and Gandalf. Apart from Frodo, all the Hobbits are played by children. In the scenes between Frodo and Gandalf, Frodo is replaced with a small puppet in some shots. In another scene, Gandalf is placed in the foreground to appear taller, and Frodo in the background to appear smaller. All this is indeed very well observed, since Peter Jackson also relied on these tricks to make the Hobbits appear smaller than the other characters. In the parody by French and Saunders this illusion is frequently and deliberately broken; for example when Frodo just stands up, walks up to Gandalf, and thus allows us to see that he is actually the same size. Another shot shows how the Hobbits hide behind a tree stump so the Ringwraith may not spot them. Only here, it is a very poor stump to hide behind. Later, the Hobbits even hide beneath a single branch. Frequently during the sketch, the fourth wall is broken, and the audience realises how much we actually suspend our disbelief in the original. When Gandalf delivers to Saruman a lengthy monologue involving a plethora of apparently unintelligible names and places, for example, he also says the aside: "Try to stay with me, darling. Could you just try!" So in this case, the actors are actually communicating in a self-reflexive manner about the roles they are playing, and how to properly perform them. For instance, one of them recommends: "Less panto! Less panto!" In the scene of the Council of Elrond the roles of the actors are even more highlighted. The Elrond in this sketch declaims his entire life story in an exaggerated thespian manner which provokes two participants of the council to fall out of character and just talk together as fellow actors rather than characters in a Tolkien adaptation:

- What's he [the actor of Elrond] done before?
- Nothing much. I think he might have done it on the radio.
- [...] Very actory.

Another comment later is: "I think it's very Harry Potter what he's doing." When Gandalf is hanging on the edge of the Bridge of Khazad-Dûm, he also mutters to the production team: "Take the stepladder away, darling." Ultimately, we are constantly put on a meta-level above the mere content of the adaptation of *The Fellowship of the Ring*, and thus, the French and Saunders parody is an excellent example of self-reflexive social parody.

Another good example of social parody is the Facebook and Twitter page *Orcs of New York* by Harry Aspinwall. He uses Tolkien's Orcs to parody the blog and Facebook page *Humans of New York* in which ordinary people and their often inspiring life stories are portrayed, and which gained huge popularity through social media. Aspinwall describes his parody as "[g]iving a face to the Mordor diaspora in New York, one orc at a time" (n.p.). Orcs are photoshopped into pictures of actual places in New York; and the Orcs are also often dressed in human clothes. These pictures are accompanied by captions such as

> - I can't watch Game of Thrones at home. My grandfather keeps coming in and being like 'That's not how you really stab a manfilth with a sword.'
>
> - My daughter comes home from college and she's all 'Dad, I'm a vegan.' Great, now she won't eat my famous manflesh stew. I'm kidding, I'm kidding. I know you guys love those kind of jokes.
>
> - I saw a *Lord of the Rings* parody play called 'Fly, You Fools' on Friday night. I'm always a little skeptical of *Lord of the Rings* and fictional portrayals of Orcish people by humans, but these guys did an excellent job. And one of the actors was actually Orcish, so I have to give them props for that.
>
> - We've come over for our son's graduation. We're from a suburb of Osgiliath. This is our first time in New York! (Aspinhill n.p.)

The Orcs here are humanised and non-villainous, but they still do not fit into the environment of a modern metropolis like New York, and this is what creates the comedy in the end. References to "manflesh stew" and "how you really stab a manfilth with a sword" also betray that the Orcs are not completely tamed.

With a book title like *Fifty Shades of Grey* it was, of course, only a matter of time until parodies involving Gandalf the Grey would spring up. One fan video on YouTube called *50 Shades of Gandalf the Grey*, for instance, edits scenes featuring Gandalf in Jackson's *The Lord of Rings* into the trailer for the film adaptation of *Fifty Shades of Grey*, thus creating the impression Gandalf was the said Mr Grey from the title. Again, one of Tolkien's characters is used here to parody a completely different work.

Social parody also involves parodies of the author himself, and here the fictitious rap battle between George R.R. Martin and J.R.R. Tolkien mentioned at the beginning of this paper is a good example of this kind of social parody. The comedy created here stems from the fact that two authors are engaging in a rap battle and that they are dissing each other's work in a way only rappers with a certain street credibility would do. We would not expect this from a distinguished Oxford professor like J.R.R. Tolkien. However, when we keep in mind that we are dealing with two authors who write fantasy literature inspired by the Middle Ages, such dissing would not actually be totally out of character, because what we term a *rap battle* today would have been called a flyting duel in the Middle Ages and earlier ages. "To put it simply, flyting occurs when two or more people are contesting each other by the means of creative insults, the more inventive, the better; and it further follows a kind of ritual structure" (Koch 2). Flyting can be found in Ancient Greek epics such as *The Iliad*; it is used in medieval Germanic literature like *Beowulf* and Old Norse poetry and sagas; it reached its artistic zenith in the verbal duels of Scottish poets such as "The Flyting of Dunbar and Kennedy" (c. 1500) during the sixteenth century before it fell out of fashion because of its extremely rude language. If we compare the structure of a flyting poem like "The Flyting of Dunbar and Kennedy" to the flyting of Martin and Tolkien, we actually find striking similarities. In "The Flyting of Dunbar and Kennedy" the Scottish poets William Dunbar and Walter Kennedy want to establish who is the better poet by means of a flyting duel. They have to come up with the most creative rhymes, make up new words, invent highly creative insults, and thus prove they have a better way with words than the other. Sounds familiar? This is exactly what the rap battle between Martin and Tolkien is doing. Here, the creativity is measured in a way by the most inventive allusions to each other's works. For instance, Tolkien comes up with the line "C. S. Lewis and I were just discussing how you and Jon Snow... both know nothing!", thus referencing Martin's work and at the same time establishing his academic superiority. The fictitious rap battle between Martin and Tolkien is another case of highly self-reflexive social parody that is concerned with the impact which Tolkien's (and Martin's) works still have on our culture; and in the end, Tolkien puts Martin in his place again. So even in this kind of parody, the makers admit and confirm Tolkien's dominant literary position in this specific field of our culture.

In this paper I have shown that there is a vast abundance of parodies of Tolkien's works with most of them focussing on Peter Jackson's film adaptations, because even more people are acquainted with the films than with the books. I have also shown that there are notably different approaches to create a parody, and have categorised some of the parodies presented here according to the strategies used. The enormous number of parodies of Tolkien's works confirms his status as one of the most important and well-known authors.

About the Author

EVELYN KOCH holds an M.A. in English and American Studies from the University of Jena, Germany. She is a PhD candidate in English Literature at the University of Bayreuth, Germany, and is working on how astronomy and cosmology are represented in Early Modern English literature. Her further research interests include medieval and Early Modern literature in general, landscape in literature, and the works of J.R.R. Tolkien and George R.R. Martin.

Bibliography

Primary Sources

50 SHADES OF GANDALF THE GREY. 24 Feb. 2015. 14 June 2016.
>https://www.youtube.com/watch?v=uqTFGUn4U8c<.

ASPINWALL, Harry. "Orcs of New York." 2015-2016. 14 June 2016.
>https://www.facebook.com/orcsofnewyork/<.

BEARD, Henry N. and Douglas C. Kenney. *Bored of the Rings.* First published 1969. New York et al.: Touchstone, 2012.

BEEKVELD, Eric. "They're Taking the Hobbits to Isengard." 2005. 15 June 2016.
>https://www.youtube.com/watch?v=uE-1RPDqJAY<.

CLAIRE, Cassandra. "The Very Secret Diaries." 2001-2003. 10 June 2016.
>http://cassieclaire.livejournal.com/<.

DEAD RINGERS. 2002-2007. "Crimewatch on Lord of the Rings." 20. Dec. 2008. 31 May 2016.
>https://www.youtube.com/watch?v=_4-4fyGQ2JM<.

DIE WOCHENSHOW. 1996-2002. "Herr der Ringe Trailer - Headbanger Festival (Schwäbisch)." 06. Nov. 2011. 31 May 2016.
>https://www.youtube.com/watch?v=1S9A-65aAhU<.

ELSTERGLANZ. "Auf Achse." *Der Scharlachrote Buchstabensuppe*. 2005. 05. Feb. 2011. 01 June 2016.
>https://www.youtube.com/watch?v=ITYpOSw9sJw<.

ELVENQUEST. Writs. Anil Gupta and Richard Pinto. BBC Radio 4. 2009-2013.
>http://www.bbc.co.uk/programmes/b00w7kgn<.

FLYING MOOSE OF NARGOTHROND. "A Brief Synopsis of The Lord of the Rings." *The Tolkien SarcasmPage*. 1996-2008. 30 May 2016.
>http://flyingmoose.org/tolksarc/homework.htm<.

FRENCH AND SAUNDERS. "The Egg." Dir. Ed Bye. Writs. Dawn French and Jennifer Saunders. 29. Mar. 2002. 8 May 2016.
>http://www.dailymotion.com/video/xcwty_lord-of-the-ring-partie-1_fun<,
>http://www.dailymotion.com/video/xczln_lord-of-the-ring-partie-2_fun<,
>http://www.dailymotion.com/video/xczly_lord-of-the-ring-partie-3_fun<.

HORDES OF THE THINGS. Writs. Andrew Marshall and John Lloyd. BBC Radio 4. 1980.
>http://www.bbc.co.uk/programmes/b00cnjz5<.

LORD OF THE PIERCING. 2002. 9 June 2016.
>https://www.youtube.com/watch?v=8Uztj3vp-RI<.

LORD OF THE WEED: SINNLOS IN MITTELERDE. 2003-2005. 09 June 2016.
>https://www.youtube.com/watch?v=0JHw01WUFQo<.

MARKHAM-SMITH, Ian. "Tolkien about me, my elf and I – and Middle Earth." *The Tolkien SarcasmPage*. 26 July 2000. 30 May 2016.
>http://flyingmoose.org/tolksarc/blanchett.htm<.

NICE PETER & EPICLLOYD. "J. R. R. Tolkien vs George R. R. Martin." *Epic Rap Battles of History*. Season 5. 02 May 2016. 8 June 2016.
>https://www.youtube.com/watch?v=XAAp_luluo0<.

ROBERTS, Adam. *The Soddit*. London: Gollancz, 2003.

SA WARDEGA. "Gandalf: You Shall Not Pass." 15. Dec. 2013. 2 June 2016.
>https://www.youtube.com/watch?v=cVy7YeeqGZQ<.

SESAME STREET. "Lord of the Crumbs." 09. Dec. 2013. 2 June 2016.
>https://www.youtube.com/watch?v=8nN9lNJuqG4<.

THE HARVARD LAMPOON. *The Wobbit*. New York et al.: Touchstone, 2013.

THE RING THING. Dir. Mark Schippert.Writs. André Küttel, Christoph Silber, Dominik Kaiser and Thorsten Wettcke. 2004. 14 June 2016.
>https://www.youtube.com/watch?v=MdDPHays2Qg<.

THE SIMPSONS. "Rome-old and Juli-eh". Dir. Nancy Kruse. Writ. Daniel Chun. 2007. 8 June 2016.
>https://www.youtube.com/watch?v=h5yjhF0Bjbo<.

THOMSON, Jamie. *Dark Lord: The Teenage Years*. London et al.: Orchard, 2011.

Secondary Sources

BAYLESS, Martha. *Parody in the Middle Ages: The Latin Tradition*. Ann Arbor: University of Michigan Press, 1996.

BRATMAN, David. s.v. "Parodies." *J.R.R. Tolkien Encyclopedia: Scholarship and Critical Assessment*. Ed. Michael D.C. DROUT. New York et al.: Routledge, 2007. 503f.

DENTITH, Simon. *Parody*. London and New York: Routledge, 2002.

HUTCHEON, Linda. *A Theory of Parody: The Teachings of Twentieth-Century Art Forms*. First published 1985. Urbana and Chicago: University of Illinois Press, 2000.

KOCH, Evelyn. "Flyting in Shakespeare's Plays." *academia.edu*, term paper, 2015. 16 June 2016.
>https://www.academia.edu/24403196/Flyting_in_Shakespeares_Plays<.

KRONER, Susanne. "'Still Not King' – The Very Secret Diaries: Tolkien Fan Fiction Between Book-verse and Movie-verse." *Inklings: Jahrbuch für Literatur und Ästhetik* 28 (2010): 107-117.

THE OXFORD DICTIONARY OF LITERARY TERMS. Ed. Chris BALDICK. s.v. "Parody." Oxford Reference, 2008. 30 May 2016.
>http://www.oxfordreference.com/view/10.1093/acref/9780199208272.001.0001/acref9780199208272-e-843<.

TIGGES, Wim. "Romance and Parody." *Companion to Middle English Romance*. Eds. Henk AERTSEN and Alasdair A. MACDONALD. Amsterdam: VU UP, 1993. 129-152.

Kay Woollard
Party Piece

Sherrylyn Branchaw

Strategies of Humour in *The Stupid Ring Parody*

Abstract

Begun in 2002 in response to the release of the first New Line Cinema film in December 2001, *The Stupid Ring Parody* bills itself as the "Earth's largest Tolkien parody." At over 300,000 words, its claim is likely to be correct. *Stupid Ring* is written in the form of a screenplay, and it follows *The Lord of the Rings* closely, parodying virtually every episode. Given the length and depth of the parody, and the obvious appreciation of and close attention to Tolkien's works with which it was written, *Stupid Ring* provides a fertile ground for examination of the many and varied strategies of humour employed by its creators. Drawing as it does on material from the film, from the greater body of Tolkien's legendarium beyond *The Lord of the Rings*, from the fandom culture that developed around the films, from other *The Lord of the Rings* parodies, and from other works of humour from popular culture, *Stupid Ring* is broad enough in scope to be the subject of several papers. In this paper, I study the construction of the parody as a text, by exploring the following strategies of humour: breaking the fourth wall; metatheatrical commentary by the characters/actors; engagement with the fan culture of which the parody is a part, and use of source materials.

Introduction

The Stupid Ring Parody is an online parody of *The Lord of the Rings*. Inspired by New Line Cinema's *The Fellowship of the Ring* (December 2001), the parody was begun in 2002 by a group of fans on a Netscape message board. Some 70-odd names are credited as co-authors of the parody. *The Stupid Ring* is over 300,000 words long, and exhaustive in parodying virtually every episode to be found in the books. It bills itself as "The Earth's Largest Tolkien Parody", and I, at least, have found no parody to challenge this claim.

The stupidring.com domain lapsed some time between July and October 2012. As a result, *Stupid Ring* is now only available in a cached format on the Internet Archive at http://web.archive.org/web/*/http://stupidring.com. The

Internet Archive is a service that crawls the web and periodically takes snapshots of sites for just this purpose: so that Tolkien scholars can write papers about parodies hosted on sites that are no longer available. Any date after July 30, 2012 yields only a cache of a broken page for http://stupidring.com, but snapshots from prior dates preserve the parody in its original glory. *Stupid Ring* is thus now the digital age's equivalent of a lost manuscript, in its way similar to Tolkien's fictional *Red Book of Westmarch*.

The strategies of humour employed by *Stupid Ring* are numerous, ranging from low humour about bodily functions to self-referential metafiction. When setting out to write this paper, I was faced with an abundance of options for potential topics. For instance, I could have chosen to write about the translation of the culture of recent decades to Middle-earth: the use of technology such as video tapes to replay flashbacks at the Council of Elrond; the framing of Sauron and Saruman in corporate language, such as Saruman appropriating Gandalf's key-card; and above all the self-awareness of the characters that they are not supposed to have this technology, living as they do in a pre-industrial society.

Another paper could have been written on the use of stylistics, including the juxtaposition of high tone with low content – "In the Elvish tongue they are called books." This juxtaposition is used in connection with the device, standard in parodies, of making the wise characters from the books appear foolish and incompetent. A study of stylistics could also have explored the use of diction to cast various characters into stereotypical groups familiar to the reader. The Rohirrim, for instance, speak in a parody of cowboy dialect ("But if'n you get kilt, don't bother."), and the Ents like hippies[1] ("Hey that's cool, man. I can dig it."). Tolkien used the same device, in a more restrained manner, of distinguishing the hobbits' speech, Gollum's speech, and the Orcs' speech from the more formal diction of the traditionally epic heroes for humorous effect.

---

1 While in *praeteritio* mode, I cannot resist drawing attention to the psychedelic effects of Entdraught; the protest slogans of the Ents: "Down with Saruman", "Give Trees a Chance", "No Orcs are Good Orcs", "Make Loam, Not War", "Ban the Eye", "Go with the Flow (of the Isen)", "Hell No, We Won't Plow!", "Trees have got to be FREE!!", "Feelin' Grovey", "Just Dig It, Don't Dig it UP!"; and the allusion to Woodstock in "this one entmoot back in '69. Oh man that was like so far out!…It was pretty short though, only lasted like three days man…Back then it was about peace and love man, not like nowadays."

Another device used by Tolkien that was translated into parody is music. Just as Tolkien's characters express themselves in song, so do the characters of *Stupid Ring* – only they are reworking popular music. For instance, when Legolas sings of his longing for the Sea, he does so by parodying a Beach Boys song. Fruitful comparisons could be made to Tolkien's own use of songs, particularly those sung by the hobbits, for humorous effect, especially "The Man in the Moon", which is based on a nursery rhyme from the real world.

Since it should be clear by now that it would be impossible to do justice to all the strategies of humour employed by *Stupid Ring* in a single essay, I have elected from this embarrassment of riches to focus on the parody as a text by examining its structure; its relationship to its sources, including Tolkien's writings, the New Line Cinema films, *Lord of the Rings* fan culture, and the parody itself; and the metafictional devices of humour employed in the parody.

1. Structure of the Parody

Stupid Ring is constructed in the form of a screenplay. This decision is owed in part to the film that inspired it. At the same time, the parody's structure follows the book, because it is broken down into the same six books with the same chapters. The header of each chapter gives a roman numeral indicating the book, and an arabic numeral indicating the chapter, so in this paper I use (SR II.5) to indicate the fifth chapter of the second book in *Stupid Ring*.

In its plot, the parody follows the book rather than the film: e.g. Bombadil is present, Faramir never tries to take the Ring, and Aragorn never falls off a cliff nor does he meet Arwen in a dream. The dialogue, however, is inspired as much by the film as the book, to the point where the reader can't tell whether this is a parody of a film or of a book.

The schizophrenic indecision of *Stupid Ring* between film and book extends to the characters as well. To take Frodo and Sam as representative characters, they are sometimes presented as real hobbits named Frodo and Sam, in the manner that Tolkien's characters perceive themselves; sometimes as actors Elijah Wood and Sean Astin, playing fictional characters in a film based on a fictional book written by J.R.R. Tolkien; and sometimes as fully fictional characters in a web parody based on a fictional book written by Tolkien. For this reason, there are complex interactions between the several major metafictional categories of speakers in *Stupid Ring*:

- the characters of *The Lord of the Rings*
- the film actors
- the film crew
- fictional narrators
- the authors of the web parody
- ad hoc characters

One category in this list of textual levels is missing: J.R.R. Tolkien himself. His name is invoked only a handful of times by speakers, always with respect, and he is never given a speaking part. The reason is obvious: the authors of the parody clearly have no desire to make him a figure of fun, and reverence is simply not as funny as irreverence. Therefore, references to Tolkien are kept both few and inoffensive.

Interactions take place between any and all categories except between actors and characters: Elijah Wood never talks to Frodo Baggins, though he sometimes talks *about* him. Instead, the dialogue, which is consistently presented in the screenplay in this manner,

Frodo: [dialogue]

is sometimes delivered from the point of view of Frodo the hobbit and sometimes from Elijah the human actor. There are no cases of

Elijah: [dialogue]

in the screenplay. In most cases, either it is possible to tell from context whether "Frodo" is speaking as a hobbit or as an actor playing a hobbit, or it doesn't matter, because the dialogue would suit equally well a character speaking from the heart or an actor delivering a line. But there are a few striking cases in which the same piece of dialogue makes sense only if both contexts are taken into account simultaneously.

For instance, at the Council of Elrond, Bilbo observes that "apparently we're skipping over my story, which, I may add, is the only one so far that's been a best-seller" (*SR* II.5). In this line, Bilbo is speaking not only as someone who has lived the events of *The Hobbit* and written them, as in Tolkien's canon, but as someone who has enjoyed the material successes of the published volume that Tolkien enjoyed in the real world. Since Tolkien makes Bilbo one of the characters responsible for metafictional commentary, he is an appropriate choice for crossing the genre boundaries in *Stupid Ring*.

Faramir is given an even more mind-bending line that breaks the wall between film and book. When Frodo assures him that Boromir's scene in Moria was popular with the fans and enjoyed a moving soundtrack, Faramir observes that the silver lining of his brother's death is that he can make a killing selling Boromir's merchandise on eBay. In this case, the speaker labeled "Faramir" speaks both as someone who has lost his brother to the events of the plot – which does not apply to the actor David Wenham – and as someone with merchandise and access to eBay, which could not possibly apply to Faramir. It is a sort of category mistake that produces a humorous effect because it is so blatantly illogical.

Because of the frequent switches between Frodo as actor and Frodo as character, and the occasional blending of characters and actors as in Faramir's speech, I will use the umbrella term of *speakers* in the essay when it is unimportant, or impossible, to distinguish between actor and character in the parody.

2. Source Material

The sources of *Stupid Ring* that pertain to Middle-earth are four: the books by Tolkien, the films by New Line Cinema, the fictional works by Tolkien fans to be found on the internet, and the parody itself, insofar as later elements of the parody build on earlier elements that are original to the parody. There are numerous other sources that are drawn on for humorous effect, particularly movies and popular music, like Monty Python and the Beach Boys, but since they are not directly related to *The Lord of the Rings*, they fall outside the scope of this essay. Given this abundance of material, the *Stupid Ring* authors had a wealth of options when it came to selecting elements from the source material for the best humorous effect. The following sections explore some of the choices the authors made that resulted in a parody of such richness and, insofar as a subjective matter like humour can be judged, hilarity.

2.1 The Books as Source

In its use of source material, the *Stupid Ring* parody is in a much more fortunate position than the film. The parody has the collected works of Tolkien, the film itself, and the works of fandom to draw on. The film does not have any rights to use material from *The Silmarillion* or *The History of Middle-earth*, only *The Lord of the Rings* and *The Hobbit*. Much use was made of the appendices to *The Lord of the Rings* in the films, but, for instance, the Valar could not be named. The parody suffers no such constraints, and the characters freely make phone calls to Mandos and receive fan letters from Manwë.

Where Tolkien scatters references to his mythology to create a sense of depth in his world, *Stupid Ring* has the director give characters extra reading to do as background for the film, and Pippin – perhaps to be understood in his Billy Boyd persona – perpetually needs references explained to him, as he has not done his homework. Sometimes his companions taunt him by refusing to explain references like the cats of Beruthiel to him. Then, in the end, he shocks everyone by catching up.

As did the makers of the films, the makers of *Stupid Ring* took advantage of the material in the appendices. One notable metafictional use of the source material occurs when Legolas insists on being called by his "true, untranslated name," rather than "Greenleaf Greenleaf" or "Leggy". He means "Legolas", the name by which he is known in the book and film, but the hobbits deliberately misunderstand him and jump on the bandwagon of untranslated names.

> Merry: Right! In that case you can call me Kalimac Brandagamba.
> Sam: And I think I'd prefer to be called Banazir Galbasi.
> Frodo: And you can call me Froda.

By doing this, the characters are drawing attention to the many layers of fictionality: they are in a parody of a film of a book that purports to be based on a manuscript of lost history written by real people named Froda and Bilba.[2] Later on, there is a delightful – to the scholarly fan – moment of pedantry in

---

[2] Interestingly, an onomastic joke is made in the film as well by creative use of the source material. In the beginning of the *Fellowship* film, Bilbo scoffs that Frodo is "a Baggins, not some block-headed Bracegirdle from Hardbottle." In the final chapter of the books, "The Grey Havens", we learn that the much-loathed Lobelia Sackville-Baggins' own people are the Bracegirdles of Hardbottle.

which Legolas addresses the question of whether he is in fact the same Legolas as the one who appears in the history of Gondolin, and he observes that the identification was made by Tolkien only in a single draft (*SR* II.5). This is, of course, the kind of reference that the film-makers do not have the rights to make even should they want to.

2.2 The Films as Source

The differing source material of the book and film gives the parody yet another opportunity for humour: competition between the two. Since the film sometimes gives lines spoken by one character in the book to a different character, this leaves the speakers in *Stupid Ring* fighting over who gets to deliver a line. Sometimes they are forced to go the way of the movie, and they grumble. Frodo solves the riddle of the doors of Moria by asking Legolas the word for *friend* in Elvish, to which Gandalf retorts, "which I've known the whole time, and if anyone bothers to read the book, they'll see *I* in fact was the one to figure it out" (*SR* II.4). Sometimes entire scenes are fought over, as when Glorfindel, from the book, and Arwen, from the movie, both show up to rescue Frodo from the Black Riders, and they have an argument over who is best qualified to do so. The argument, naturally, culminates in silliness and lack of dignity. Arwen spooks Glorfindel with "Oh no! A Balrog!", making him squeak and jump. As with Legolas, the potential identification of Glorfindel with an elf of the First Age is closed to the film-makers. This scene is later invoked as an explanation of a plot point: why Glorfindel is not chosen as one of the Nine Walkers. In Tolkien's work, Glorfindel's absence is because force of arms and skill are to play a lesser role than the loyalty of friends. In *Stupid Ring*, the justification given is that if Glorfindel goes, then Arwen will insist on coming, and there is a unanimous agreement among the members of the Fellowship that no one wants to put up with her being lovey-dovey with Aragorn, while at the same time she and Glorfindel engage in constant one-upmanship. For a parody that repeatedly harps on its lack of continuity – even to having a character known as Continuity Girl show up periodically to lament its lack – it does show some moments of creative continuity that are in neither film nor book.

In addition to having characters fight over lines, the parody finds many creative ways of working lines in indirectly. Aragorn goes all the way around the Midgewater Marshes while making the hobbits go through, and explains on the other side that he is allergic to midge bites, but there would be a riot from the audience if Sam's line "What do these things eat when they can't get hobbit!" weren't included (*SR* I.11). Sam indirectly works one of his lines in when, having noticed that the parody is diverging from the book, he wonders: "So how are we going to work in that really cool line about how Winter is nearly gone and time flows on to a spring of little hope?" to which Frodo smiles and replies, "I think you just did, Sam" (*SR* II.9).

In keeping with the running theme of making the wise appear incompetent, Gandalf forgets a snappy comeback that he would have liked to have delivered to Denethor. Then, too late, he remembers. He delivers his speech about being a steward of all living things in Middle-earth… to Pippin, alone in their room (*SR* V.1). Without doubt, there is not a reader who has not had this experience and cannot empathize with Gandalf, or empathize with his explanation that there's something about Denethor's eyes that is intimidating. He is right, of course, but Tolkien's Gandalf is immune to it.

When Wormtongue makes his first appearance, his lines have to be shoehorned in, because his actor is a big fan of Ian McKellen, quotes lines from movies McKellen was in twenty years before, and breaks character to ask if he can get his autograph. Gandalf (recall that all lines are attributed to speakers by the names of Tolkien's characters, even when they are speaking from the persona of an actor) has to nudge him to deliver his lines (*SR* III.6).

2.3 Fandom as Source

Both generic features of fandom and specific works of fandom serve as source material for *Stupid Ring*. Generically, the idea that some of the characters are sexually attracted to or even in sexual relationships with other characters is a popular one in fandom, and it opens an obvious door to humour: sexual innuendo. The intense male bond between Frodo and Sam has inspired not only a multitude of fanwork linking them in a romantic fashion, but even scholarly works that provide a queer reading of *The Lord of the Rings*, or study the fanworks produced by queer readings. See for instance Smol (2004) and Abrahamson (2013).

Innuendo hinting at same-sex relationships among the members of the Fellowship is unrelenting throughout *Stupid Ring*, but for the most part it is leveled at the characters by the narrators of the parody, and the characters are put in the position of defending themselves against these allegations. In keeping with the general practice of the parody that the dialogue is radically different from the book or even the film, but the action is much the same, Sam still marries Rosie, Sam's friendship with Frodo remains platonic, and Legolas and Gimli are left entirely ambiguous. One humorous strategy I admit falling for five times in a row consists of a sequence of dialogue between Frodo and Sam that, out of context, sounds like it could only be about sex. Then the moment of revelation comes, and the reader learns that the characters were ordering a drink called "Sex on the Beach", or some such other innocent activity. The reader is thus prompted to take responsibility for reading too much into the dialogue, while the characters' behaviour remained entirely above board.

This disparity between dialogue and plot means the parody is open to a purist interpretation as well as a queer-friendly interpretation. The characters can be read as fighting back against the dirty minds of the readers – as when Sam protests that *he is* the one who gets married and has thirteen kids (*SR* I.10) – in keeping with the interpretation that practically everyone agrees Tolkien had in mind when writing. Alternatively, the parody can be read as delighting in pointing out every place where the homosocial culture with its intense male friendships, which was familiar to Tolkien in the early twentieth century, lends itself more readily to a homosexual interpretation to a modern audience. On the one hand, the intended audience of this parody includes readers of fanworks wherein the sexuality is explicit, and the innuendo is aimed at their entertainment. On the other hand, the deep respect shown by the authors for Tolkien himself and their desire to honour his work manifests in giving him a voice, as it were, to argue his position, and letting him win in the end. The only occasion on which a sexual encounter takes place in *Stupid Ring* that is not based on anything in Tolkien's work is heterosexual and is handled with a gravity and maturity that contrasts with the humour that is lavished on every other reference to sex in the parody. It is unfortunately beyond the scope of a paper on strategies of humour to treat this passage in detail, but the "Many Partings" chapter of *Stupid Ring* is worth reading for this episode.

Moving from generalities to specific fan works, one piece that was a major influence on *Stupid Ring* is "The Very Secret Diaries". It is a short piece of fandom humour by Cassandra Claire that purports to be the collected diaries of the Fellowship members. "The Very Secret Diaries" became extremely popular in *The Lord of the Rings* fandom, and famous lines from it are often quoted on the internet without reference, the reader being expected to be familiar with the source. The phrase "Stupid Ring" occurs frequently in Boromir's diary, along with "Stupid Orcs," and "Stupid Aragorn," when he is grumbling about things that don't go his way. Thus, even the very title of *Stupid Ring* is indebted to "The Very Secret Diaries".

The major strategy of humour in these diaries is innuendo, implying or outright asserting the existence of sexual relationships between anyone and everyone in Middle-earth. From "The Very Secret Diaries" comes the notion that Aragorn is a "pervy hobbit-fancier" who has an unreciprocated interest in Frodo, that Sam "will kill him if he tries anything," and especially the frequent references to strawberry-scented bath soap and/or bubble bath, used in "The Very Secret Diaries" by Sam in his romantic interludes with Frodo. These allusions, along with references to Gandalf's "pointy hat", are most frequent in the first volume of *Stupid Ring*, after which the parody finds its own voice. Table 1 contains counts of each "Very Secret Diaries" reference per *Stupid Ring* book, showing a clear decline in frequency as the parody progresses.

Table 1
"The Very Secret Diaries" References by Book

	Book 1	Book 2	Book 3	Book 4	Book 5	Book 6
strawberry bath	11	16 (Fully 11 of which are from a rendition of "Strawberry Baths Forever" to the tune of the Beatles' "Strawberry Fields Forever.")	4	6	1	3
Sam will kill him if he tries anything	2	0	1	0	0	0
pervy hobbit-fancier (with occasional variations on "hobbit", such as "pervy elf-fancier.")	4	2	1	1	1	2
pointy hat	4	4	0	0	2	2

Though "The Very Secret Diaries" is a marvellous and deservedly famous piece of humour, *Stupid Ring* benefits when it gains confidence in its own power to entertain and ceases to lean so heavily on its crutch. When I recommend *Stupid Ring* to people, I advise them that it starts slow but picks up around the "Strider" chapter. The humour after that point becomes more independent – which is not to say without frequent allusions to popular culture – and complex. Running gags begin to build on themselves, giving the parody the option of either letting the reader finish the sentence, or building up expectations only to subvert them. The parody, in other words, begins to use itself as a source.

2.4 The Parody as Source

One device used by the authors of *Stupid Ring*, the makers of the New Line films, and by Tolkien himself in editing his own texts, is taking something that makes an appearance only once in the source and scattering references to it throughout. In Tolkien's case, once he decided on Arwen as Aragorn's betrothed at the end, he had to scatter references and allusions to her in the text he had already written, so that it would not be completely unforeshadowed. The film took material from their story in Appendix A and incorporated it into the main storyline, as well as expanding on Arwen's role by giving her more frequent appearances, far beyond anything in the books. The later *Hobbit* films from New Line Cinema, released well after the writing of this *The Lord of the Rings* parody, used this technique to even greater effect: emphasizing the importance of the Arkenstone from the beginning, and showing prejudice against elves as one of Thorin's notable character traits throughout the story. *Stupid Ring* takes this technique and goes wild with it. Isolated incidents that made sense in their context are extracted from that context and repeated in the most absurd ways. For instance, after the narrow escape from the Barrow-Wight, the hobbits are described by Tolkien as running naked and free over the grass. In *Stupid Ring*, "naked time" becomes a very important pastime that the hobbits, especially Pippin, need regular doses of. *Parth Galen* is etymologized by an indulgent narrator as "'Parth' means 'place of the little people' and Galen means 'running naked'," to which information the hobbits respond with joy and proceed to do just that (*SR* II.10).

But the best use of this device is Merry as real estate developer. In Tolkien's work, Merry helps Frodo buy a house at Crickhollow, as a cover for his leaving Bag End. This is an isolated incident that makes sense in context. In keeping with their strategy of expanding such incidents into important character traits, the *Stupid Ring* authors give Merry the profession of real estate developer. He goes on his journey through Middle-earth with an eye for how this or that piece of land could be developed into a strip mall or a water park. At first, this seems to be simply a running gag, like Pippin's naked time. Over the course of the parody, however, it grows into much more.

In the first place, Tolkien's landscapes often *do* present a threat to the travellers, and Merry's frequent speculations about the potential of various undeveloped landscapes provides a consistent motivation. In the books, the trees of the Old Forest feel more threatening after Frodo sings a song about woods failing. Caradhras strikes at the Fellowship either because of Sauron's desire for the Ring that Frodo carries, or because the mountain itself has always been known as malevolent. In the film, the snowstorm is caused by Saruman, who desires to force the Company to take the Gap of Rohan and bring the Ring within his reach. In *Stupid Ring*, all these events are inspired by Merry's comments about developing the unspoiled landscape to make a profit, and the others learn to start shushing him before he can get started. Sometimes his proclivities are even brought up when he is not around, as when Frodo, admiring the moon over the Forbidden Pool, mulls, "I bet Merry would have a few things to say about this place" (*SR* IV.6).

Moreover, the repetition of Merry's obsession increasingly falls into line with Tolkien's themes. Tolkien is known for his love of undeveloped or lightly developed nature and for his hatred of the industrialism that Saruman represents. New Zealand was selected as a site for filming in part because it offered a variety of landscapes that were well suited to a depiction of the largely uninhabited realms of Middle-earth. When Merry wants to replace these landscapes with commercialized developments as places for making money, we are meant to find it humorously incongruous that one of the heroes is proposing such a thing. Yet in its way, it is consistent with Merry's description of the ongoing battle between the Old Forest and the Brandybucks, who earned the trees' hatred by burning them and driving them back from tilled land. Flieger, in writing about this episode, points out the ways in which we are led to see the Old Forest as the enemy because we identify with the hobbits, but to see Saruman as the enemy because we are led to identify with the Ents. Tolkien's presentation of the issues of man versus nature is not simple. Thus Merry is a good spokesman for the side of development in the parody.

Matters come to a head in "The Scouring of the Shire", where Merry's oft-envisioned but still unrealized desires for development come up against the reality of what Saruman has done to the Shire.

> Merry: Come on guys! I only wanted to build a couple of strip malls ... not like this ... Okay, I see the light! Strip malls are VERY BAD THINGS. (*SR* VI.8)

Because Merry *is* a hero, though, his trajectory is given a satisfactory resolution. In the final chapter, when Sam is leading the rebuilding of the Shire, Merry's development skills are put to good use. First he tries building fitness centers, but hobbits being hobbits, no one ever finds time to attend. Then he replaces them with restaurants, and he is said to make a killing.

Merry's trajectory has now gone beyond mere parodying of the source and into creative generation of new subplots. Perhaps most impressive is how closely it follows the original by changing only the dialogue and leaving the action mostly alone. The same landscapes are still threatening in the same way; they remain untouched by Merry's wishful thinking; the Shire is devastated by Saruman with no help from Merry (as he protests); and the hobbits, led by Sam, rebuild the Shire after driving out the ruffians. Other than the detail of Merry's restaurants, the externalities of Tolkien's world remain largely the same, yet the parody has managed to contribute to the characterization, plot, and theme, all in the pursuit of humour.

3. Metafiction

Much of the use of source material for humour in the previous section involved various metafictional and metatextual devices: for example, the desire of various parties to work their lines into the parody, and the ongoing tension between the presentation of the parody as a book, a film, or a web parody. Metafiction is a major font of humour in *Stupid Ring* that yields a diverse range of humorous strategies, including commentary on strategies of humour and on the relative effectiveness of those strategies.

The Lord of the Rings itself makes use of a metafictional strategy by means of the conceit that the events described therein really happened and were written down by Bilbo, Frodo, and Sam in a story. A manuscript recording this story was later found and translated into English by J.R.R. Tolkien. Several times in the story, the characters refer to the fact that they are having adventures which are being written down by Bilbo, that these adventures will be the subject of songs – if anyone survives to sing the songs or hear them – and that their adventures are a continuation of other adventures they themselves have heard or read about in stories. Frodo and Sam even have a famous discussion culminating in Sam asking Gollum whether he would prefer to be the hero or the villain of the story. However, while these conversations draw the reader's attention to the fact that these are fictional characters, the characters do not see themselves as fictional. They are presented as real people whose real stories – albeit possibly greatly distorted by some tellers – happen to be told by others after the fact. This perception of themselves is consistent with Tolkien's conceit that this is not a work of fiction but a piece of lost history.

During the journey to and from Mordor, Sam observes more than once that he and Frodo are continuing the story of Beren, Eärendil, and others, and that such stories don't always turn out pleasantly for the people living in them. This passage is parodied to full effect, of course, and one of the strategies employed is having Frodo and Sam reference stories and genres that would be familiar to the reader, not to Frodo and Sam. These include fairy tales such as the gingerbread man who is eaten by a fox, self-help books such as the imaginary *Gollum's Guide to Skin Care and Grooming*, and films such as *Frodo and Sam's Excellent Adventure*. While we expect Middle-earth to have folklore, and perhaps stories of similar plots, we don't expect the details to be the same. Tolkien invokes epics of his own making to increase the reader's sense of the importance of Frodo and Sam's quest; the parody uses less prestigious genres to mock it.

In a final meta-meta-meta stroke, the characters make us question which events "really" took place. Near the end, in a discussion of Bilbo's book that is based on a similar discussion in canon, when speculating about what forms the stories will take in the hands of later storytellers, Frodo predicts: "You know storytellers, they'll probably find a few more wild things to polish the story…maybe talking trees, and wild men who know algebra[3]…" Until now, the reader has been

---

3 G-b-G: "Wildman wild, not stupid. I am great headman Ghan-buri-Ghan. Count many things. Know set theory, differential calculus and Drakes Equation. Count stars in sky and measure doppler shift" (*SR* V.5). Cf. Tolkien's "Wild Men are wild, free, but not children…I am great headman. Ghân-buri-Ghân. I count many things: stars in sky, leaves on trees, men in the dark" (*RK* 104).

accepting that the encounters with talking trees and wild men are events that "really" took place on some level in the parody, just as the events of *The Lord of the Rings* "really" took place in the books. Only now is the reader given reason to question whether the narration might be unreliable. The Ents are part of Tolkien's canon, so if the encounter with Merry and Pippin is not meant to be understood as something that "really" happened to Merry and Pippin, it must have been a later introduction into the textual history some time during the 4,000 years between the *Red Book* and *The Lord of the Rings*. But when Frodo and Sam question the wild men knowing algebra whom Merry has already encountered, it leaves the reader wondering what is being questioned. Merry's veracity? Frodo and Sam are still in Mordor and haven't even heard Merry's story. One possible reading is that the characters are again mocking the silliness of the web parody authors, but that explanation doesn't account for the talking trees. Whose credibility is being undermined is a meaningless question to ask, of course: these parody characters are well aware of their own fictional status, in a way that Tolkien's Frodo and Sam are not. Like the Wenham-Faramir merger described earlier, the humour is all the funnier for its logical impossibility.

3.1 Strategies

The characters themselves comment on the strategies of humour used in the parody. At one point, a "Dick Clark narrator" shows up to ask the characters to rate the songs that the parody authors wrote, and Legolas gives one of the authors, Russ, a 4 (*SR* III.6). Sam questions whether the "yokels with a keyboard" might neglect to bring Gollum back, because it's a parody, and Frodo predicts that Gollum will be back, because "the possibilities for silliness with Gollum's character are endless" (*SR* IV.2). A narrator wonders aloud whether a gag is still running, complaining that it's hard to keep track (*SR* II.3). When the parody reaches the point where Tolkien's Sam describes Gollum on the river Anduin as a log with eyes, the Sam of the parody provides a helpful visual:

$$[[[[[]]\ )\text{-}8$$

When Frodo asks Sam how he did that, Sam answers, "It's a web-based parody, Mr. Frodo. We can do all sorts of things" (*SR* II.9).

The speakers, thanks to their self-awareness of the various fictional media – book, film, and parody – are also able to comment on the plausibility of, and reasons behind, various plot devices devised either by Tolkien or by the creators of the movie. For instance, Elrond insists that choosing the members of the Fellowship is an important task that will require time, and the decisions cannot be made spontaneously at the Council just so the audience can have a feel-good moment.

> Elrond: Do you think I'm going to say something all dramatic just to give you all a warm fuzzy? Just imagine, a randomly selected bunch stands here together like they're getting a portrait made, I look all proud and say: "They will be the Fellowship of the Ring!" [snort] (*SR* II.2)

Obviously, *Stupid Ring* is offering commentary on the reasons behind the deviation of the movie from the book. But the Elrond of the parody has to give in to pressure, and he sighs: "This is going to be a long epic" (*SR* II.2). Compare Sam's "It's been a long trip" later in the parody, when he laments that he is running out of gafferisms (*SR* IV.7). In this case, Sam is commenting on a use of humour employed by Tolkien in the book, and while doing so he is speaking from the perspective of a real person who has gone on foot from the Shire to Mordor. His use of "trip" stands in contrast to the use of "epic" by Elrond. Unlike Sam, Elrond is speaking from the perspective of either a character or an actor who sees himself primarily as a character or actor within a story. The parody thus is able to comment on strategies of humour from a variety of perspectives.

3.2 Competition

Unlike Tolkien's restrained metafictional allusions to the fact that the characters are in a book, *Stupid Ring* pulls out all the stops when it comes to metafictional techniques. As hinted at in section 1, the speakers in *Stupid Ring* cannot decide whether they are actors playing hobbits, real hobbits, or fictional characters in a web parody. In the first two cases, they see themselves as real people, just as you or I do, whether they be real people in Middle-earth about whom fictionalized accounts of their adventures will be told, or real people in Hollywood playing fictional characters written by one J.R.R. Tolkien. In the third case, however, they show explicit awareness that they are at the mercy of the parody authors, and that these authors can make them do things. Nevertheless, the line is blurred by such utterances as "You're no more fictional than they [the authors] are!" (*SR* I.8). The line of free will is blurred still further by the similarities between the parody characters, who have to do what the authors write them doing, and the actors, who have to follow a script. At times, even the characters in Middle-earth show rare fictional self-awareness by commenting on how their free will is restricted by Tolkien's authorial decisions – though it can be hard to tell whether this should be interpreted as the character himself aware of his own fictional status, versus an actor wondering how much freedom he has in representing his character.

This metafictional chaos is itself employed strategically for humorous effect. Each of the sets of speakers listed in section 1 has its own motivations, and humour often arises from conflicts among their interests and attempts to maintain or upset the balance of power. The parody authors want as much silliness as possible. The film crew wants the actors to deliver their lines. The actors want good working conditions. The characters want to complete their quests with as little hardship and as much praise as possible. The ad hoc characters are generally there to serve a single purpose: e.g. the attorneys' purpose is to represent their clients. The narrators are a mixed bunch (for example, the beaver narrator wants to gnaw wood), but mostly they are marked by a desire for the actors to cooperate, deliver their lines, and stop arguing.

Though the actors never speak *to* their characters, all other categories of speakers mix it up more or less freely, with few constraints. The actors go on strike and negotiate with the film crew for better working conditions. The actors/characters threaten to shoot the narrators if they don't comply with their wishes, and at least one narrator does actually find himself in danger from stray missiles on a battlefield. One ad hoc attorney, making a nuisance of himself by attempting to defend Gollum on the charge of entering the Forbidden Pool, is promptly defenestrated at Faramir's command (*SR* IV.6). Manwë later comments in a letter that, though he is otherwise a big fan of the Faramir chapters, this was not a nice move on Faramir's part (*SR* IV.6). Yet another attorney accuses a narrator of plagiarizing a passage directly from Tolkien and forces the narrator to rephrase (*SR* III.6).

As noted, the characters interact with the parody authors by insulting them (*SR* I.8). They do so as a way of fighting back against treatment that they don't like, in refutation of the observation that they are all at the mercy of the people at the Netscape board. In fact, the autonomy of the characters is a matter of some debate, as evidenced by the following exchange among Frodo, Sam, and the parody author Idril.

> Sam: She does have a point.
> Frodo: Is she making you say that?
> Sam: No, really.
> Idril: Thanks Sam, really!
> Sam: Look, a large bag of M&Ms! Cool! (*SR* IV.2)

Idril's ability to manifest at will Sam's wish of a large bag of M&Ms leaves in some doubt how much autonomy Sam had to refuse her. On one level, obviously Frodo is able to argue with her. On another level, the reader is well aware that she is the one making Frodo argue with her. Juxtaposing these two levels of reading the text – the one in which we readers suspend disbelief and pretend the story is real, with the one in which we rationally know the author controls everything – is a frequent device for achieving humour in this parody.

The main advantage of the frequent switching of contexts in *Stupid Ring* is the flexibility it affords. The speakers can comment on any aspect of the embedded story that they wish: from the creation of Bilbo to the creation of Tolkien, from the creation of New Line Cinema to the creations of internet fans. Yet another advantage, though, is the fact that the switching itself affords opportunities for humour. With their typical disregard for continuity – a fact that is not only commented on but lamented by the ad hoc Continuity Girl – the characters overtly contradict every expectation they have led the audience to have about this parody. They derive humour from the very fact that they can't decide what context they are in or how they should behave. For instance, after five books of constant interference from the characters/actors, a frustrated narrator exclaims in book six, "Alright! I'm sorry! I was trying to get your plight across to the audience. I think in NORMAL movies the characters don't listen to the narrator anyway" (*SR* VI.3). After this, when everyone is becoming genre-savvy in the many genres, Sam comments that the screenwriters have imposed a moratorium on self-insertion and therefore cannot be called on directly (*SR* IV.7). After uncountable references throughout the parody to sets, props, makeup crews, trailers, scripts, and Peter Jackson, Éowyn says flirtatiously to Aragorn, "Darn. I wish we were in the movie… I could show you the moves I've learned… and maybe you could show me some new ones" (*SR* V.2).

3.3 Suspension of Disbelief

One of the disadvantages of context switching is that it has the potential for reducing reader engagement. One doesn't have to believe a story is real in order to enjoy it, but if one dwells on the fact that the story is fictional, that none of the perils are a real threat, and that the characters have no free will because they are utterly at the mercy of the author, it becomes difficult to sustain interest. Tolkien differentiated between "primary belief", a belief about the real, external world, and "secondary belief", a belief in a constructed world. In his essay "On Fairy-Stories", he emphasizes the importance of not breaking secondary belief. In a fairy story, he argues, breaking the reader's belief in the magic of Faerie breaks the story. For this reason, he believed that stage drama was poorly suited to most depictions of fantasy, because the audience would be too aware of the primary world and the devices used to achieve the effects. Tolkien, in his own work, keeps us believing in the realness and vitality of his characters. Even when Frodo and Sam are aware that their adventures are part of a story, it is only in the sense that, say, Julius Caesar might have been aware that stories would be told about his deeds.

Stupid Ring, in contrast, makes the conscious choice to break secondary belief frequently for humorous ends. Tension builds in the plot, and then *Stupid Ring* reminds us that none of this is real. One genre-savvy character will reassure another character that he is too important to the plot to die, or at least that he is sure to last until an epic climax and get a dramatic scene worthy of his death. Reasoning such as "you went for the cutest one, who obviously isn't meant to die in this scene" (*SR* II.4) is used to break suspense. Other times, the characters speak from the perspective of the actors, who are not going to die even if they portray the death of their character. The technique works, though it violates Tolkien's precepts, precisely because the genre is humour. Humour operates by presenting us with the unexpected. Our experience reading literature teaches us to expect that the author wants us to take the plight of the characters seriously, and the reader who refuses to play along and insists that none of this is real is being cheated of the literary experience. Therefore, *Stupid Ring* challenges these expectations by leading us down the accustomed path of being invested in the perils of the characters, then yanking the rug from under us by making us laugh at the absurdity of our own investment. Moreover, the way it reminds us that there is little danger to certain characters in certain scenes is by invoking the very expectations we have formed over years of experience with stories.

Having defused tension in this manner, *Stupid Ring* uses two techniques to restore it. One is that genuine, non-parody stories also violate expectations by killing off characters for a tearjerker effect, for shock value, for plot necessity, or for any number of reasons. Screenwriters also often choose to make their films diverge from the books on which they are based. Accordingly, *Stupid Ring* frequently reminds us that even if the actors know what happened in Tolkien's book, they do not necessarily know what will happen in the film, for they haven't been given the script for later scenes. Similarly, we the parody readers, even if we have read the book and seen the New Line films, do not know what liberties the parody will take. It is, in fact, a remarkably faithful parody. The dialogue is radically different, but the actions remain virtually unchanged. Nevertheless, the first time reader of *Stupid Ring* does not know this, and even for the repeat reader, it is a good reminder that the parody authors had the freedom to change anything they pleased.

The second means used by *Stupid Ring* for offsetting the effects of reminding readers that nothing is real is to choose specific occasions on which to honour Tolkien's great moments of moving emotion. For instance, the Rohirrim go on strike because their losses in battle have been treated with too much callousness by the film-makers/parody writers, and they have to be enticed back with promises of better treatment (*SR* III.8). As Frodo and Sam journey through Mordor, a narrator protests, in response to complaints that he is being too negative, that he is trying to get their plight across to the audience. He asks if they would prefer he make light of their situation (*SR* VI.3). Making light of situations is exactly what the parody is all about, but that very fact makes it all the more effective when on one occasion they violate expectations and choose to pay homage to the magnitude of Frodo's accomplishment in traversing the Black Land. Similarly, when the Ring is destroyed and all the world celebrates, or when he departs from the Grey Havens in a scene of sorrow mingled with hope, one character will express concern that the narrators or parody authors will make fun of them, but will be reassured that even the authors are too overcome with emotion to ruin the moment. In these cases, the humour comes at the expense of the parody authors themselves, while leaving the mood generated by Tolkien intact. And of course, these fans would not have written a parody of such length and depth had they not been deeply in love with Tolkien's work, which their tears highlight. Moreover, the very contrast of their handling of these scenes with their flippancy in other scenes lends greater weight to the moments where they abstain. These are the authors who turned Boromir's death into an "I am your father" revelation from Aragorn[4] (*SR* II.10). If even these authors, *Stupid Ring* seems to say, tear up at the final parting of Frodo from his friends on the shores of Middle-earth, then the power of the Grey Havens scene is real.

I hope to have shown with this and other examples that *The Stupid Ring Parody* employs a number of sophisticated strategies for humour, including the absence of humour to intensify rare moments of emotional depth. It rewards not only reading but close reading and analysis, and it stands as a great tribute to the works of J.R.R. Tolkien and New Line Cinema, as well as a monument to the creativity and devotion of Tolkien's fans. I hope finally to have inspired some readers of this paper to check out the parody and enjoy a good laugh.

About the Author

Sherrylyn Branchaw holds a PhD in Indo-European Studies from UCLA. She worked as a lecturer in the Classics department at UCLA before leaving academia to become a database administrator at a tech company. She continues researching and publishing as an independent scholar.

---

4 Aragorn later turns out, in Arwen's words to him, to be someone who will benefit from the streak of celibacy she imposes on him as a married man: "judging by the number of young men who look exactly like you." In support of her observation, Beregond has been introduced by this point in the narrative as "Beregond, son of Arag- I mean, Baranor."

Bibliography

ABRAHAMSON, Megan B. "J.R.R. Tolkien, Fanfiction, and 'The Freedom of the Reader'." *Mythlore* 32.1 (2013): 55-74.

CLAIRE, Cassandra. "The Very Secret Diaries." 2001-2003. <http://cassieclaire.livejournal.com>.

FLIEGER, Verlyn. "Taking the Part of Trees: Eco-conflict in Middle-earth." In *J.R.R. Tolkien and His Literary Resonances*. Eds. George CLARK and Daniel TIMMONS. London: Greenwood Press, 2000. 147-158.

SMOL, Anna. "'Oh... oh... Frodo!': Readings of Male Intimacy in *The Lord of the Rings*." *Modern Fiction Studies* 50.4 (2004): 949-979.

The Stupid Ring Parody. 2002. Originally at <http://stupidring.com>. Archived at <http://web.archive.org/web/20120209025111/http://www.stupidring.com/parody/index.html>.

TOLKIEN, J.R.R. "On Fairy-Stories." In *Tree and Leaf*. London: Unwin Hyman, 1988. 9-73. (The original essay was first delivered as a lecture in 1939, and first published, somewhat enlarged, in 1947.)

The Return of the King. Originally published 1955. New York: Ballantine Books, 2012.

Davide Martini

Humour in Art Depicting Middle-earth

Abstract

Tolkien's humour is predominantly verbal, yet we can also find humour in the illustrations to and paintings inspired by his work. This essay provides a brief over-view of the development of illustrations of Tolkien's texts in general and then focusses on the figure of Gollum in particular. In Gollum's case, the publication history gave rise to an often humorous tradition of illustrations that attained independence of the later text-based descriptions found in *The Lord of the Rings* and the later editions of *The Hobbit*.

Did I put humour into my Tolkien pictures? Not more than Tolkien put into his text, I suppose. People may find that many of my characters look rather funny, but they are not intended to be funny. It is rather that my style of drawing is 'lighthearted', so to speak: it avoids overdoses of seriousness where the subject – Tolkien's story – is already serious enough. My style walks on tiptoes where others prefer to march in on sturdy boots.
(Email from Cor Blok to the author on 9/7/2015.)

Cor Blok, *The Cow Jumped over the Moon* (1960)

In 1961, after seeing five examples of Blok's work, Tolkien commented to Rayner Unwin:

> I thought them most attractive [...] I should very much like to see some more, in the hope that some more will be as good as The Battle of the Hornburg. The other four I thought were attractive as pictures, but bad as illustrations. But I suppose it is impossible to hope, nowadays, that one might come across an artist of talent who would, or would even try to depict the noble and the heroic. (Scull & Hammond, *Reader's Guide 422*)

About *The Lord of the Rings*

Before speaking about humour in illustrations inspired by Tolkien's subcreation, a distinction between the two novels that open the gates to Middle-earth, *The Hobbit* and *The Lord of the Rings*, has to be made. Let us put, from the very beginning, the posthumous *The Silmarillion* aside, since the pictures in the only illustrated version of the book, the one by the Canadian Ted Nasmith in 1998, can be described as many things but certainly not 'funny'.

Ted Nasmith, *The Hill of the Slain* (1998)

Science fiction and fantasy artists face a daunting task: to depict the unknown, the unreal, and the impossible, and make it believable, compelling, and beautiful. They are asked to envision imaginary places, populating them with strange, wonderful beings, and they must do it all on a deadline. That's a tough job. (Haber 8)

Illustrations inspired by *The Lord of the Rings* appear systematically in the United States since the 1975 *Tolkien Calendar*, illustrated by Tim Kirk. In the following we will take into consideration at first only those published pictures inspired by Tolkien's masterpiece. Kirk was followed by the artists Frank Frazetta, Stephen Hickman and, most notably, the Brothers Hildebrandt. They all produced a continuous output of Tolkien-related artwork, yet without creating any 'amusing' pictures.

The American pictorial art of the 70s illustrating Tolkien's works is the product of fifty years of experiments in SF-Fantasy illustrations, most prominently found on the covers of pulp magazines and also, later, on those of the paperbacks.

Cover-art by Frank Frazetta for the ACE edition of *The Buccaneer*

SF-Fantasy artists like Allen St. John, Frank R. Paul, Virgil Finlay, and Richard Powers aimed at making their creations 'realistic' and believable, a purpose which proved inimical to comical elements.

In 1962, the stunning artwork of Frank Frazetta makes its appearance on the covers of books by ACE publishers. Frazetta endeavours to incorporate

Frank Frazetta, *The Witch King and Éowyn* (1975)

in his pictures aspects of the noble and the heroic, which, at first sight, seems to correspond to what Tolkien has been looking for (cf. his comment on Cor Blok's pictures quoted on page 180). In his pictures, Frazetta successfully captured the imaginary worlds and thus functioned as a point of departure for those who became interested in Fantasy illustrations in the US. His illustrations of *The Lord of the Rings* (1975), comprising a portfolio of seven pictures, combine his penchant for muscular heroes and scantily clad women with whimsical hobbits.

Michael William Kaluta, in his biographical essay on Frazetta, writes the following about the public's reaction to the artwork:

> When short-lived Denver, Colorado publisher Middle Earth commissioned Frazetta to create an art portfolio inspired by J.R.R. Tolkien's classic trilogy they inadvertently ignited a firestorm of criticism from the legion of *Rings* fans who took issue with Frank's liberal interpretation of the story. Accustomed to his versions of fantasy characters becoming definitive, he was somewhat mystified by the controversy surrounding the folio. 'Wow, I thought the Burroughs fans were particular,' Frazetta muses [sic], 'but the Tolkien fans were *really* picky.' (Kaluta 58)

Frazetta's 'photographic idealism', which was highly successful for the muscular pulp-fiction heroism (and aesthetics) of Conan & Co., was, as the reaction of both dedicated fans and possibly general readers shows, obviously felt to be less suitable for presenting the understated Aragorn or Boromir and to run counter to Tolkien's (and many of his readers') more Pre-Raphaelite attitude towards the depiction of women.

More discreetly, and with roots in the Art Nouveau (think Aubrey Beardsley, Arthur Rackam, John Bauer, and Kay Nielsen), we find on the other side of the Atlantic James Cauty drawing his famous *The Lord of the Rings* poster. Commissioned by Athena International in 1976, it depicts Middle-earth in a realistic and convincing way – as will do other artists later on for David Day's *Tolkien Bestiary* (1979).

Illustration for David Day's *Tolkien Bestiary* by Ian Miller (1979)

The intention of the English artists, although choosing different solutions from the American tradition, remained the same: giving Middle-earth a realistic feel and look, this time by adding dramatic elements drawn in Indian ink. This aspect is clearly visible in Ian Miller's artwork.

Compared to the images found in the earlier *The Lord of the Rings* illustrations, neither the images from the 80s such as those from Roger Garland, Chris Achilleos, Angus McBride, nor those from the 90s such as illustrations by Alan Lee, Ted Nasmith, John Howe or Donato Giancola show an increase of the fun-factor. The only improvement to be found in the more recent artwork is a shift towards a more concrete and vivid dramatization of the scenes depicted – which will later inspire Peter Jackson's screen adaptations.

Roger Garland, *Lord of the Nazgûl* (1983)

Moreover, it must be noted that the artists' and art directors' favourite scenes are not dealing with situations that lend themselves easily to a humorous treatment: they prefer the emotionally moving parts of the novel. A good case in point is the journey through the Mines of Moria. Most artists focus on the orcs, the cave-troll and the balrog.

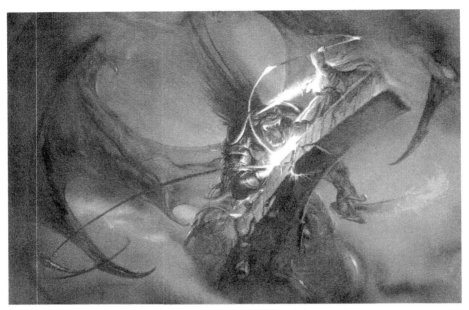

John Howe, *The Bridge of Khazad-dum* (1995)

Rarely will the viewers be able to see scenes meant by the artist to put a smile on their faces. Thus, the picture "Tom Bombadil" by the brothers Greg and Tim Hildebrandt for the third *Tolkien Calendar* (February 1976) is the only 'funny' piece among the forty-two illustrations found in the three *Tolkien Calendars*. This may be no coincidence since Tom Bombadil is also in the works of other artists often depicted in a light-hearted, humorous way.

We find quite a few humorous examples, by the Brothers Hildebrandt and other artists, among the illustrations for the first nine chapters of *The Lord of the Rings*, i.e. until Frodo meets Strider in the Prancing Pony and suffers the mishap with the Ring. Strider's "Why did you do that? Worse than anything your friends could have said! You have put your foot in it! Or should I say your finger?" (*LotR* 157) marks a turning point in the mood of the narrative. After that, and similar to the character of Frodo, the illustrations too will become sombre and are utterly devoid of any fun until the end of the novel.

Greg and Tim Hildebrandt, *Tom Bombadil* (1976)

The Hobbit

J.R.R. Tolkien, the first Illustrator of *The Hobbit*

While those artists who began to illustrate *The Lord of the Rings* drew on fantasy art and the works of the original *fin de siècle* in order to give Middle-earth consistency and substance by means of their artwork, the matter is different with *The Hobbit*. This difference is mainly due to the fact that *The Hobbit* is first and foremost a children's book, as Rayner Unwin famously stated in his 1936 report written for his father, Sir Stanley Unwin:

> Bilbo Baggins was a Hobbit who lived in his Hobbit hole and never went for adventures, at last Gandalf the wizard and his Dwarves persuaded him to go. He had a very exiting (sic) time fighting goblins and wargs. At last they get to the lonely mountain; Smaug, the dragon who guards it is killed and after a terrific battle with the goblins he returned home—rich! This book, with the help of maps, does not need any illustrations it is good and should appeal to all children between the ages of 5 and 9. (Unwin 74)

In spite of young Rayner's opinion that the story needed no illustrations, *The Hobbit* arrived in bookstores on 21 September 1937 with ten black and white illustrations by Tolkien himself. The artwork's humour is debatable. This may be mainly due to Tolkien's focus on the landscapes Bilbo crosses during his adventures rather than on character-illustrations as such. Although painted landscapes are known to evoke various kinds of emotions, humour isn't one of them, mainly because humour is linked to the human condition, and it is very hard to make the viewer smile at a landscape painting.

J.R.R. Tolkien: detail from *The Hall at Bag End*

Between the publication of Allen & Unwin's second impression and the first American edition of *The Hobbit*, Tolkien produced five watercolours, which had been requested by the American publisher, Houghton Mifflin. Tolkien depicts Bilbo in three out of the five colour illustrations. However, he does not add any elements that would have served to help towards a better characterisation of his protagonist.

Tolkien's intention to keep the 'burglar' of his story out of the limelight in his pictures becomes clear in the way he presents him. Thus, in *Conversation with Smaug*, Tolkien shows only Bilbo's silhouette, shrouded in a cloud (symbolising his ring-induced invisibility) and "fat in the wrong places" (*L* 35). He shows him 'zombified' next to the Lord of Eagles in *Bilbo woke up with the early sun in his eyes*; and only gives us a view of Bilbo's back riding a barrel in *Bilbo comes to the huts of the Raftelves*. One explanation for this could be that Tolkien, whilst fully able 'to draw' his main characters with words, lacked the technical skills required to draw hobbits and men well enough so that the drawings would meet his own standards.

In March 1938, when the American publisher asked Tolkien to provide some drawings portraying hobbits in order to promote the novel, "he replied saying that he was not competent enough to do so, and to prove it (to himself) he drew on the telegram a very inadequate pencil sketch of a hobbit [...] with the face left blank and with ears rather more than 'slightly' pointed" (Hammond and Scull 99). Tolkien's artwork lacks humour, even now that the illustrations show a greater presence of the figure of the Hobbit. In a letter to Susan Dagnall at Allen & Unwin in 1937, he wrote the following:

> I have redrawn (as far as I am capable) one or two of the amateur illustrations of the 'home manuscript', conceiving that they might serve as endpapers, frontispiece or what not. I think on the whole such things, if they were better, might be an improvement. But it may be impossible at this stage, and in any case they are not very good and may be technically unsuitable. It would be kind if you would return the rejected. (*L* 14)

The letter to Allen & Unwin Publishers is dated to the 4th January 1937 and helps us to better understand Tolkien's attitude towards illustrations in and for *The Hobbit*. The letter suggests that Tolkien worries about pictures and images that could compromise his subcreation. Such illustrations, as Tolkien fears, harbour the risk of involuntarily rendering the protagonists ridiculous in the eyes of the reader. To quote Tolkien, "illustrations do little good to fairy-stories" (OFS 70). What is at stake is the enchantment of Middle-earth. Humour, or rather ridicule, can undermine its credibility and threaten its very existence.

Illustrations and drawings Tolkien made for *The Father Christmas Letters* and *Mr. Bliss* prove that he was very well capable of producing humorous illustrations.

J.R.R. Tolkien, illustration to the Father Christmas Letter for 1928

This corroborates the thesis that the decision to omit all humour from the illustrations to *The Hobbit* was a conscious one, as can be seen by Tolkien's comment on Virgil Finlay's illustration *Rescue by the Eagles*:

Virgil Finlay, *Rescue by the Eagles* (1964)

> Though it gives prospects of a general treatment rather heavier and more violent and airless than I should like, I thought it was good, and actually I thought Bilbo's rather rotund and babyish (but anxious) face was in keeping with his character up to that point. After the horrors of the "illustrations" to the translations [of *The Hobbit*] Mr. Finlay is a welcome relief. As long (as seems likely) he will leave humour to the text and pay reasonable attention to what the text says, I expect I shall be quite happy.
> (Tolkien to his British publisher 11 October 1963, quoted in Anderson 154)

It comes therefore as no surprise that the humorous tone of several illustrations of translations of *The Hobbit* irritated Tolkien and he refers to them as "horrors".

After Tolkien: The first Illustrators of *The Hobbit*

Those who illustrated *The Hobbit* after 1937 seem primarily interested in capturing the reader's attention. This shifts the focus away from the text to the graphic representation of the characters and settings.

The first time Bilbo makes an appearance in an illustration is on the dust jacket of Foyles Children's Book Club edition of *The Hobbit* (1942).

Dust jacket of Foyles Children's Book Club edition of *The Hobbit* (1942)

The unknown artist presents Bilbo in profile and shows him with a Tin Tin style quiff, dressed as a horseman as if he just came back from horse riding around the Shire. Tolkien is said to have remarked, "Surely the paper wasted on that hideous dust-cover could have been better used."[1] The first full-scale illustrations of *The Hobbit* come five years after this tentative beginning in the very first translation of the book (into Swedish) which appeared in 1947.[2]

> I suppose hobbits need some description nowadays, since they have become rare and shy of the Big People, as they call us. They are (or were) a little people, about half our height, and smaller than the bearded dwarves. Hobbits have no beards. [...] They are inclined to be fat in the stomach; they dress in bright colours (chiefly green and yellow); wear no shoes, because their feet grow natural leathery soles and thick warm brown hair like the stuff on their heads (which is curly); have long clever brown fingers, good-natured faces, and laugh deep fruity laughs [...]. (*H* 4)

---

1 http://www.latimes.com/books/jacketcopy/la-jc-75-years-of-the-hobbit-photos-20120920-004-photo.html, which credit The Tolkien Library for the quote from Tolkien.
2 It also represents the very first translation of any of Tolkien's books.

A colour picture of Bilbo appears on the cover of *Hompen*, the Swedish translation of *The Hobbit*, and the illustrator Charles Sjöblom adorned Bilbo's left ear with a pirate's earring.

Charles Sjöblom, cover illustration for *Hompen*,
the Swedish translation of *The Hobbit*, featuring Bilbo (1947)

Inside, we have black and white illustrations by Torbjörn Zetterholm which show Gandalf, Bilbo (now without earring), some of the dwarves of the Company and a group of orcs that resemble savage aboriginals.

Torbjörn Zetterholm, Gandalf and Bilbo (1947)

All these pictures are well drawn and often characterized by a light touch of humour. One illustration is of special interest for the development of the depiction of Gollum. The drawing shows Bilbo's first encounter with the slimy creature in the depths of the Misty Mountains.

Torbjörn Zetterholm, Bilbo and Gollum (1947)

Zetterholm, a landscape painter, architect and illustrator who illustrated, among others, a selection of Hans Christian Andersen's tales, is the first artist to portray Gollum. In Zetterholm's picture, Gollum's height is exaggerated to approximately 6 metres, therefore rendering Bilbo's sting practically useless. In a letter to Rosemary, a young fan in 1948, Tolkien commented on how "huge" (Scull and Hammond, *Chronology* 328) this Gollum was, dwarfing Bilbo. This is mainly due to the fact that the first edition of *The Hobbit* (1937) lacks a precise description of Gollum and it is thanks to the omission of detailed information on this creature that we can enjoy today some of the funniest sequences in the history of illustrations inspired by Tolkien's novel. Before embarking on an extensive discussion of the history of 'Gollum illustrated' we have to re-read what Tolkien wrote in 1937:

> Deep down here by the dark water lived old Gollum. I don't know where he came from, nor who or what he was. He was Gollum—as dark as darkness, except for two big round pale eyes. He had a boat, and he rowed about quite quietly on the lake; […]. He paddled it with large feet dangling over the side, but never a ripple did he make. (Anderson 118)³

This at least partially explains why Zetterholm felt free to create one of the artistically most original depictions of this character. He thus, together with Horus Engels, stands at the head of a tradition that takes great liberties with the text when it comes to portraying Gollum. Thus in 1946 Horus Engels wrote to Tolkien about a German translation of *The Hobbit* and illustrated his letters with drawings of his own, one of them showing Bilbo confronting an (again) oversized Gollum.⁴

Letter with illustrations showing Gandalf, the Three Trolls, and Bilbo and Gollum, from the German artist Richard Horus Engels (1946)

---

3 For a comparison of the original 1937 text and the later adapted description of Gollum, see Douglas Anderson's *The Annotated Hobbit*, pages 118-19.
4 Tolkien, in a letter to Sir Stanley Unwin (7 December 1946), remarks: "I continue to receive letters from poor Horus Engels about a German translation. He does not seem necessarily to propose himself as a translator. He has sent me some illustrations (of the Trolls and Gollum) which despite certain merits, such as one would expect of a German, are I fear too 'Disnified' for my taste: Bilbo with a dribbling nose, and Gandalf as a figure of vulgar fun rather than the Odinic wanderer that I think of …" (*L* 119).

Eleven years after Tolkien's rejection of his first artistic project, Horus Engels makes a comeback in 1957 with his 24 illustrations for the first German translation of *The Hobbit*. Engels' illustrations include additional characters to the ones encountered in the Swedish translation. However, he keeps the giant Gollum, who is so fat that he seems stuck in his little boat and looks comical rather than frightening.

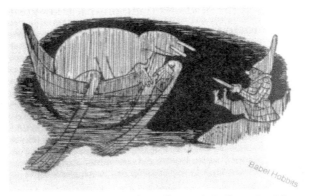

Richard Horus Engels, Bilbo and Gollum (1954)

In 1960, Jan Młodożeniec's attractive pictures are published in the first Polish translation: in the top left-hand section of page 92 Gollum's huge head appears,

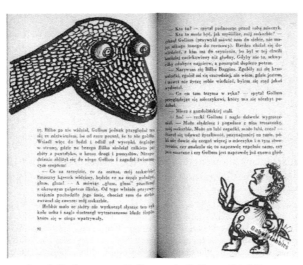

Jan Młodożeniec, Bilbo and Gollum (1960)

resembling that of a dinosaur or a lizard – it is so big that in order to show the entire creature at least two pages would be required. Bilbo, at the right-hand bottom of page 93, looks definitively unpleasantly surprised and gives the impression that he suffers from a stiff neck.

Let us now look at some of the marvellous illustrations of the second Swedish edition of *The Hobbit*, published in 1962. These illustrations were drawn by the well-known Finnish illustrator Tove Jansson, who is best known as the creator of the Moomins, a family of white, roundish fairy-tale characters that resemble hippopotami. Her interpretation of Gollum shows a creature that looks a bit like a dazed, huge Barbapapa, comparable in size to the Gollum in the first Swedish translation.

Tove Jansson, Bilbo and Gollum (1962)

In the same year the Portuguese translation with the title *O Gnomo* was published. António Quadros populates Middle-earth with his big-nosed creatures and gives us a slightly reduced Gollum who is now merely twice the size of Bilbo. To make up for this 'loss', Quadros has his Gollum grow a thick black beard and three teeth so big and set wide apart that Bilbo's sword Sting could easily serve as a toothpick.

António Quadros, Bilbo and Gollum (1962)

António Quadros' "horrible" pictures (Tolkien's very own expression, as reported by Clyde Kilby in *Tolkien and the Silmarillion* 23) constitute, in my mind, some of the funniest interpretations of Tolkien's text so far.

The 1964 adaptation of *The Hobbit* contains Ferguson Dewar's attractive pictures from *The New Princess and Girl* magazine. He provides a portrait of Gollum which is so far the most 'correct', even though Gollum sports a Pinocchio-style nose and wears a mime suit, which makes him look rather like a burglar-spy from the 1960s James-Bond movies.

Ferguson Dewar, Bilbo and Gollum (1964)

The British illustrator Dewar is also the first who gives Gollum the right size, which is likely due to his familiarity with Gollum as he is presented in *The Fellowship of the Ring*, which had been published in Britain in 1954. Tolkien gives the following description, which complements and clarifies the text of the 1937 *The Hobbit*.

> Trying to find his way out, Bilbo went on down to the roots of the mountains, until he could go no further. At the bottom of the tunnel lay a cold lake far from the light, and on an island of rock in the water lived Gollum. He was a loathsome little creature: he paddled a small boat with his large flat feet, peering with pale luminous eyes and catching blind fish with his long fingers, and eating them raw. (*LotR*, Prologue 11)

Illustrations in Japan are, even ten years after the publication of *The Lord of the Rings*, still a far cry away from depicting Gollum as imagined by Tolkien and owe more to the monsters in contemporary movies than to the descriptions in the primary texts.

In 1965, Ryuichi Terashima's Indian ink drawings show again an oversized Gollum that seems to have wandered off from Jack Arnold's set of *The Creature from the Black Lagoon*. The Japanese artist is also the first one who reduces the level of caricature, preferring more realistic pictures. This results in an attitude that is at odds with those illustrators who, so far, were amused by as well as amusing in their depiction of Gollum.

Ryuichi Terashima, Bilbo and Gollum (1965)

Tolkien approved of the choice, as Clyde S. Kilby notes in his *Tolkien and the Silmarillion* (23), observing how Tolkien "was pleased with the Japanese translation of *The Hobbit* and showed me with particular satisfaction the frontispiece which portrayed Smaug falling convulsively over Dale."

Also in 1965, in the midst of the so called 'War over Middle-earth' which was started by ACE Books' unauthorised publication of Tolkien's epic in a cheap paperback edition in America, Tolkien had to revise the text in order to be able to register his copyright of a new edition. In the course of the revision process he elaborates the description of Gollum, who now becomes a small slimy creature.

However, most illustrators did not pay any attention to Tolkien's new additional pieces of information and instead of a reduction of Gollum to his correct size we notice a progressive deformation not only of Gollum but also of other characters.

To digress briefly, let us take a brief look at some other (often involuntarily) humorous examples of illustrations of the other protagonists in *The Hobbit*. Exceptional in their light-hearted expression of *joie-de-vivre* are the 'nudist dwarves' in the first Czech edition of 1979. Jiri Salamoun, the illustrator, depicts Thorin & Co. obviously enjoying the opportunity to take a bath and foreshadows Peter Jackson's problem of how to depict dwarvish underwear.

Jiri Salamoun, Dwarves taking a bath (1979)

Shifting our focus back to the main protagonist of *The Hobbit*, we find Bilbo's hairy legs from Belomlinskij's illustration for the 1976 Russian translation making a comeback in M. Czernyszew Indian ink illustrations drawn for the first Soviet Learners-of-English-edition in 1982. Bilbo not only sports furry legs but also wears an "I love Bilbo" T-shirt and a pair of shorts.

M. Czernyszew, Bilbo (1982)

In the first Moldavian edition from 1987, Igor Hmelnickij decides, in true Doctor-Moreau-fashion, to complete Bilbo's transformation by providing him with a face that is half-lion and half-monkey.

Igor Hmelnickij, Bilbo (1987)

Bilbo is shaved again in the 1990 Russian edition, but the book-illustrations retain his hairy legs.

A. Markewica, Bilbo (1990)

Ferguson Dewar had anticipated this new trend in his illustrations for the *New Princess Magazine* of 1964, where Bilbo sports a "Jackson Five" afrostyle hairdo.

For the second German edition in 1971, Klaus Ensikat keeps the long sideburns but he does away with Bilbo's curls of the English version. Instead he gives him a top hat and dresses him in elegant clothes for the meeting with Gollum. The latter now has now been turned into a gigantic toad, whose size is second only to Młodożeniec's 'dinosaur' from the 1960 Polish translation.

Klaus Ensikat, Bilbo and Gollum (1971)

After this time, the great majority of *The Hobbit* illustrations come from the territory of the former USSR. The reason for this can be found in the existence of several *samizdat* versions, i.e. unauthorised translations and bootlegged copies of the novel.

The first illustration of Gollum from 1976 by Mikhail Belomlinskij is hardly recognisable.

Mikhail Belomlinskij, Gollum (1976)

Furthermore, he creates a cheerful-looking Bilbo in black and white with hairy legs like a chimpanzee.

Mikhail Belomlinskij, Bilbo (1976)

Markewica's illustrations are drawn in a humorous vein. This becomes clear already from the cover that features a dragon carrying a teapot and a bunch of flowers – reminiscent of Grahame's Reluctant Dragon rather than Smaug.

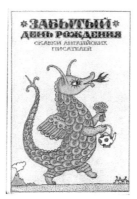

A. Markewica, cover for *The Hobbit* (1990)

The volume features also a fairy (maybe in anticipation of Peter Jackson's Tauriel?)

A. Markewica, An Elf? (1990)

and a hardly recognisable Gollum who looks like a gherkin on legs.

A. Markewica, Gollum (1990)

In 1991, the year that marked the end of the USSR, N. Fadeieva published an extremely funny series of pictures presenting a Bilbo that wanders wide-eyed (maybe reflecting the feeling of 'flabbergastedness' that many readers must have felt in these times of change). Moreover, Gollum is oversized once again and seems to belong to a species not clearly identifiable (but certainly not related to hobbits).

N. Fadeieva, Bilbo and Gollum (1991)

After the upheavals of the early 90s had diminished and the newly founded Russian Federation inherited most of the territory of the defunct USSR, we have the publication of an edition illustrated by Dar'ya Yudina.

Dar'ya Yudina, Gollum (1994)

In this 'beast fable' version, Bilbo gets rid of his bristly hairs – a prickly characteristic during the Iron Curtain-years – in order to turn into a figure that has more in common with a hamster than a hobbit. Of special interest is the illustration that portrays Bilbo like a hamster armed with a dress sword standing opposite Gollum who here resembles a ferret turned ferryman Charon.

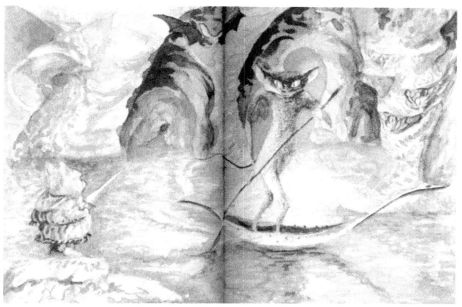

Dar'ya Yudina, Bilbo meets Gollum (1994)

Last but not least, A.W. Smirnowa's whimsical illustrations in the 2006 edition present Bilbo with a rather pronounced set of ears that make him look like a mouse, and Gollum who not only seems to be suffering from nummular dermatitis or a similar eczema, but who sports a carrot-like nose.

A.W. Smirnowa, Bilbo and Gollum (2006)

And we can be sure that the 'story goes on'. Much of the humour inherent in the illustrations of Tolkien's work is accidental and has its origin in the early ignorance about Gollum's actual appearance. Yet neither the availability of fuller descriptions of the protagonists' appearance nor the influence of Peter Jackson's movies has been able to uproot the persistent strain of humorous and often quite idiosyncratic pictures – and we can look forward to enjoy the appearance of further leaves on that tree.

About the author

DAVIDE MARTINI is an expert in Tolkien-related art and curator of numerous fantasy art exhibitions. Between 2002 and 2005 he was the brains behind and curator of the itinerant exhibition 'Images from the Middle Earth', the world's first collection uniting works illustrating Middle-earth by international artists. Since 2006 he has been the art director of the Greisinger Museum in Switzerland. He has selected and built the art collection, managing the disposition and its presentation inside the museum. In 2012 he wrote the first essay presenting the history of illustrations of Middle-earth for the conference-exhibition *Lucca Comics & Games* art catalogue and has, since 2013, explored aspects of Tolkienian art in his radio show *Art History of Middle-earth* and is directing conferences on the history of this fascinating art genre. He is furthermore owner of the Dama Collection, the second largest collection containing artworks inspired by Tolkien's Middle-earth, which has been shown in prestigious locations.

Bibliography

Anderson, Douglas (ed.). *The Annotated Hobbit*. Revised edition. Boston and New York: Houghton Mifflin, 2002.

Haber, Karen. "Introduction." In *Masters of Science Fiction and Fantasy Art*. Edited by Karen Haber. Beverly, MA: Rockport Publishers, 2011. 8-9.

Hammond, Wayne G. and Christina Scull. *J.R.R. Tolkien: Artist and Illustrator*. London: HarperCollins, 1995.

Kaluta, Michael William. "Frazetta." In *Testament. The Life and Art of Frank Frazetta*. Edited by Arnie Fenner and Cathy Fenner. Grass Valles, CA: Underwood Books, 2001. 38-65.

Kilby, Clyde S. *Tolkien and the Silmarillion*. Wheaton, Illinois: Harold Shaw Publishers, 1976.

Scull, Christina and Wayne G. Hammond. *The J.R.R. Tolkien Companion and Guide: Reader's Guide*. Boston and New York: Houghton Mifflin, 2006.

The J.R.R. Tolkien Companion and Guide: Chronology. Boston and New York: Houghton Mifflin, 2006.

Tolkien, John Ronald Reuel. "On Fairy-Stories." In *Tree and Leaf*. London: Unwin Hyman, 1988. 9-73. (The original essay was first delivered as a lecture in 1939, and first published, somewhat enlarged, in 1947.)

The Hobbit. London: HarperCollins, 1995.

The Letters of J.R.R. Tolkien. Ed. Humphrey Carpenter, with the assistance of Christopher Tolkien. Boston and New York: Houghton Mifflin, 2000.

Unwin, Rayner. *George Allen & Unwin. A Remembrancer*. Ludlow: Merlin Unwin Books, 1999.

Patrick Wynne
Mordor Lemonade

Patrick Wynne
Grendel's Mom

Jared Lobdell

Humour, Comedy, the Comic, Comicality, Puns, Wordplay, 'Fantastication', and 'English Humour' in and around Tolkien and His Work, and among the Inklings

> **A Recollection on humour in Tolkien's coterie.**
>
> "Humour in and around Tolkien's Work" – that is a very broad topic indeed, though the humour itself may not always be broad – and frequently is not. Let us separate our task here into two halves (or perhaps not-halves), the typology and definition of "humour" and the definition and exploration of "in and around Tolkien's Work," and look at what we mean by these "halves or halve-nots." After that we can go on to our discussions – and, doubtless, qualifications.

Humour, Comedy, etc.

First, the definitions of humour in this paper are built in part on material covered in Chapter Five of my *Rise of Tolkienian Fantasy* (2005), "Blackstick, Prigio, and 'It': Comic and Fantastic," given originally as a paper at the 1987 Conference on the 50th Anniversary of *The Hobbit*. It is built in part on subsequent work on what I have called the Tolkienian pun, as well as on some further study of punning among the Inklings – particularly Lewis, Dyson, Coghill, and, of course, Tolkien. And it is built on a construct of English humour based on Stephen Potter (*Sense of Humour*) and Nikolaus Pevsner (*The Englishness of English Art*). Note that this last particularly includes Lord David Cecil, among the Inklings.

Though Potter is more closely C. S. Lewis's contemporary than Tolkien's, his work – and Pevsner's – gives a valuable point from which to view the humour of observation which is part of Tolkien's strength, notably with the Hobbits. That this is extended through what may be considered *buffo* interludes in the *serio* narrative (revealing the aspects of carnival in the whole creation) is to be expected in light of the origins of some parts of Tolkienian fantasy in Victorian (Christmas) children's books. This also explains the route to the comic through "comicality" – an impulse actually quite different from the English humour of observation. Finally, the *eucatastrophe* can occur as well (using Frye's *mythoi*) in Comedy as in Romance – to one of which genres *The Hobbit* and *The Lord of the Rings* unquestionably belong.

We should begin by defining our terms. By *Comedy* we mean essentially Northrop Frye's *Comedy* – that is, the *mythos* (story-pattern) allied with the spring, ideally with the country-side or country-village, ending usually in a sorting-out or *penseroso* mode. It has affinities with Romance, the mythos of the summer and the country-town, which also frequently ends with a sorting-out or in a *penseroso* mode. (Of the contrapuntal *mythoi* of the fall and winter, Tragedy and Satire, we will consider only Satire, and that only as an adjunct to considering satire in its lower-case sense, for there is a strong element of satire, of course, in Lewis's work, some in Tolkien's, and at least a breath in Coghill and Dyson.)

By the comic, we mean not a reference to comedy *per se* and certainly not to comedy in Northrop Frye's sense, but to the risible, to things that we laugh at or (if no more) smile broadly at. The comic thus includes jokes, slapstick, shaggy dog stories, wordplay (so that puns are a subcategory), Groucho Marx's eyebrows and leer, Vaudeville – and it also includes, or at least borders on (marches with) certain forms of humour, and particularly the humour of exaggeration, in "tall stories" and "yarns" of the Davy Crockett type. This "comic" may even include a kind of "inspired silliness" though it is more likely in film and on stage than in writing – some critics have suggested that we can include here the chase sequences in Buster Keaton's *The General* and some passages in *Charley's Aunt* or the Pink Panther films or Flanders and Swann, who, in their song "Design for Living", ask: "Well, why not … collect those little metal bottle-tops, and nail them upside down to the floor? This will give the sensation … of walking … on little metal bottle-tops turned upside-down." And yes, this is the same Swann who did *The Road Goes Ever On* and the opera from *Perelandra*.

By "comicality" we mean something like the attitude which sees the "comic" lurking everywhere – or almost everywhere, an attitude of mind one might say. Sometimes it may be forced, and certainly an unwearying comicality may be as difficult to take as Chesterton's *unwearying* paradox and unwearying "fantasticality" (see my *Rise of Tolkienian Fantasy* 83). The Clown's face may be only painted into a smile – and even if not painted, the laugh-lines may harden and the attitude become a fixed shell. What was once inspired silliness may become ponderous silliness. His Excellency, Gilbert's Played-Out Humourist, is a tragic (as well as a hopeless and quixotic) figure.[1]

The word "pun" we should not need to define. The *Tolkienian* pun is the use of a word so exactly as to produce a kind of cognitive dissonance (if perceived) that illuminates meaning – as in "the tale of years" where "tale" has the double meaning of "tale" and (an original meaning) "tally" – the kind of playing with words one would expect of an historical philologist. (Another example occurs in the punning last line about "Great Charles's Wain" in his comic – or at least humourous – poem on Charles Williams – see below.) We will look at how this wordplay fits in with Tolkien's comicality, with his "carnival" (which is not particularly English – may even be Kentuckian), with the "comic" in his works, with the *mythoi* of Comedy (*The Hobbit*?) and Romance (*LotR*), and with English humour.

All of this brings us to the matter of *English* humour, as defined by Potter, with some assistance from Sir Nikolaus Pevsner. Here we should pause to look at Potter's suggestions on the birth of English humour: here he is in a lyrical passage (Potter 12-15):

> [One of the rewards of the academic student of English literature] is the appreciation of first bursts, and there was never such a first burst as happened to the English in the fourteenth century. Humour came suddenly to our literature without warning […] No Eng. Lit disciple will ever believe there is a greater innovator in any art than Chaucer in his. There is the language he chose, the dialect of that language […] the making rhythm out of that language, the attitude to his writing […] the eye turned intently to the contemporary reality of life […] the recognition of the sacred importance of detail, the recognition that character is […] a fusion into small unpredictable traits […] no need to add humour to these attributes which together make Humour itself.

By humour, then, we mean essentially what Potter has meant, which is quite closely related to what the art-historian Sir Nikolaus Pevsner has meant by "the Englishness of English Art" (Pevsner 24 and *passim*). For Pevsner, Englishness in the arts is defined (1) by the belief that the intention of art is to teach and (2) by the belief that the most effective teaching is done through

---

1 Cf. *Quixotic is his enterprise and hopeless his adventure is / Who looks for jocularities that haven't yet been said: / The world has joked incessantly for over fifty centuries: / And every joke that's possible has long ago been made.*

the detailed observation of daily life. This is clearly allied to what Potter has called the humour of observation, whose chief exemplar he finds in Boswell's *Life of Johnson*.

Humour – and most especially "English humour" – is thus, in this sense, a creature of both realism (for the observation) and immediacy. Of course, it shades off into the comic, as we will see – and can be shaded off into the satirical. But it is important to remember that this humour may be funny (as in the patter songs in Gilbert and Sullivan), yet it is usually far removed from anything like comic slapstick which, on my side of the Atlantic, at least, is better called "slapstick comedy".

In and around Tolkien's Works: Inklings Humour

It is time now we start on the second part of the title – "in and around Tolkien's Work." Though it can and doubtless will be otherwise interpreted (as, for example, meaning "humourous" comments or even whole creations directed at *The Lord of the Rings* – as with the *Harvard Lampoon* parody years ago), we will be looking here at those who worked and wrote around Tolkien, as well as at his own works, at least from *Roverandom* (1925-1927) on. That is, we are looking at our subject not only in connection with Tolkien's *Werke*, but with his working, one might say among those he worked with or who worked with or around him. Those who worked with and around him include, of course, C.S. Lewis, Nevill Coghill, Hugo Dyson, and possibly others of the Inklings. These three, at least, loved puns as much as Tolkien did, though doubtless their puns were less "Tolkienian" (and antiquarian) than his. The Chaucerian Coghill and the comedian (or comic) Dyson were somewhat different of course, but Tolkien (gently) and Lewis (not nearly so gently) were satirists. In fact, if we were to take Lewis's humour as representative of "humour in and around Tolkien's work," we would be finding far too savage and almost Swiftian satire as our exemplar.

Lewis, of course (in the XIth of the *Screwtape Letters*) discussed the various sources of human laughter – but he discussed them with Screwtape's voice, and one of his points is that humour and laughter do not have a necessary relation in either direction. In fact, the whole definition is infernal, and thus for our purposes misleading – and it is discussing laughter and the question of sexual concerns and incongruity: but because it is someone at least "around Tolkien" and the discussion uses the word "humour," we had best look at it, if only to dispose of it. Here's a summary of the passage. The "causes of human laughter" are divided into Joy, Fun, the Joke Proper, and Flippancy. Joy is found "among friends and lovers reunited on the eve of a holiday;" Fun "is a sort of emotional froth arising from the play instinct." The Joke Proper, which "turns on the sudden perception of incongruity," is more promising for Hell. Hell uses jokes or humour "as a means of destroying shame." Flippancy (from Hell's point of view) is best of all because among flippant people, the joke is always assumed to have been made: "they talk as if virtue were funny." There is of course one great problem with all this.

It is from the voice of Screwtape in the *Screwtape Letters*, a book written to mock the Devil ("the Devil, the Proud Spirit, cannot endure to be mocked"). The book is itself a humourous satire based on the premise that the Bureaucracy (Lowerarchy) of Hell has no Sense of Humour, by an Anglican Irishman whose favourite humourist was the Anglican Irish satirist, Dean Swift. That is, humour is holy, the comic even is holy, and all Comedy tends toward the Divine. Lewis was, of course, preeminently a satirist, as we have noted. He was also a word-player, a punster (though that word has been degraded, I think). We will come to that shortly, along with other Inklings word-players (punsters?), but for the moment let us look at Lewis and Tolkien as satirists, remembering that we have reversed our entire frame of reference and that we are speaking of the holy, not the hellish, view of humour.

Lewis's unfinished Ulster novel is satirical; *The Pilgrim's Regress* is satirical (even in title) if not a satire: as Lewis's disciple James Blish has taught us, out of Northrop Frye's four mythoi, science-fiction is the satirical (and obviously much of *Out of the Silent Planet* is broadly satirical); *Screwtape* and *The Great Divorce* fit well into the satirical category; the time-travel fragment Walter Hooper called *The Dark Tower* is a satire in which Faerie takes on the attributes of the Nazi state; *Perelandra* almost triumphs over Lewis's strong satirical impulse, but it returns revived in *That Hideous Strength*, parts of which are almost Swiftian (as are parts of "The Dark Tower"). Even in Narnia there is quite enough satire for my taste, at least, though not perhaps so evident. But what of Tolkien: the two, after all, are not twins.

A Brief Look at Tolkien

Let us look briefly at *Farmer Giles of Ham*. True, it is possible to mistake merely Oxonian humour for satire, because the tone appears satirical. To take an example rising four centuries old, when Bishop Corbet, laying hands on a bald man's head, asked his chaplain Lushington for resin (used on bowling balls), we can see satire lurking, as we can with Tolkien's account (in *The Hobbit*) of Bandobras Took's striking off the Goblin chieftain Golfimbul's head at the Battle of Greenfields (S.R. 2747) and the head went down a rabbit-hole and the game of golf was invented. The Lushington story satirizes Corbet's worldliness (or at least presents it satirically); the Golfimbul story satirizes traditional accounts of game inventions or other historical developments with only traditional – and no real historical – bases. Tolkien thought better of it a quarter-century later, but he never got around to making a final change. His most Oxonian joke, I should say, is in *Farmer Giles*, about the definition of blunderbuss by the four wise Clerks of Oxenforde (the editors of the *Oxford English Dictionary*, now so-called). Here we should probably look at two of the other essays in this book (my thanks to the authors for making them available to me before publication).

Particularly, I want to suggest that what Łukasz Neubauer calls "pseudo-classical reframing" in his discussion of Tolkien's onomastic humour in *Farmer Giles* is similar to what I noted above as satirizing tradition when there is no true historical basis for it – only with the Latinizing of Famer Giles of Ham into Aegidius Agricola de Hammo (and the other Latinizations, including Dominus de Domito Serpente) the objects of the satire are the monkish chroniclers who did the Latinizing in our real world (if that is what it is). I am aware that Professor Neubauer (93) thinks Tolkien not much of a satirist, but I beg to differ. Consider how Aegidius (Giles), who, as Neubauer (94) points out,

> becomes the autonomous Lord of Ham (itself an obvious philological pun), is also known in his kingdom under the title of 'Dominus de Domito Serpente, which is in the vulgar Lord of the Tame Worm, or shortly of Tame' [*Farmer Giles*, p. 74]. As the two titles of King Giles get more and more confused, the chief town of the new realm gradually becomes 'known by the latter name, which it retains to this day' [*Farmer Giles*, p. 76].

The other essay I have in hand is Laura Lee Smith's "'This is, of course, the Way to Talk to Dragons': Etiquette-Based Humour in *The Hobbit*" (also in this volume). Once again, I am calling the author's findings into my own service, with thanks. The author calls this "lampooning ordinary forms of politeness for humorous effect" – and while "lampooning" may be *le mot juste* here, I think I might rather say "satirizing" because the impulse and effect seems to me very similar to that of "Aegidius Agricola de Hammo, Dominus de Domito Serprente" (or "Lobelia Sackville-Baggins" or – but this is from our real world – "Archibald Willingham de Graffenreid Clarendon Butt," Teddy Roosevelt's aide who went down on the *Titanic*).

The 'Tolkienian' Pun

Not all of this, of course, deals directly with humour, even Tolkienian humour – but the humour of what I have called the Tolkienian pun, the exact application of an original exact meaning of a word now often otherwise used, is inherent in the literal interpretation of words of politeness now often (nay, nearly always) otherwise (conventionally) used. Besides the use of the "tale of years" with reference to "tally," and the whole complex of word-plays in his punning reference to "Great Charles's Wain" in his verses on Charles Williams, there are other cases in point we may come to in good time. But in the mean time (Tolkienian pun?), we will look at another form of wordplay, rhymed (often epigrammatic – very often "light") verse, including Tolkien's limericks and his verses on Williams, Lewis's great Nonsense patter-poem, Coghill's light – and epigrammatic – verses going all the way back to his notes for Gordon's classes and up to his Masque (we might even make some reference to his Chaucerian "translations"), Williams in his epigrammatic modes in poetry (and – leading back into prose humour – in his reviews and columns, though Williams is no Strix). Thereafter we will return to the puns, and here we come back to Dyson, which will lead us back to Nonsense, remembering that roaring cataract thereof for which "Hugo" was famous.

One of my favourite examples (unforced in context but needing considerable introduction) occurs in Tolkien's O'Donnell Lecture, "English and Welsh"

(1955): Tolkien is referring to himself as an amateur in Welsh (Tolkien, *The Monsters and the Critics* 167):

> I speak only as an amateur and address the *Saxon* not the *Cymry*; my view is that of a *Sayce* and not a *Waugh*. I use these surnames – both well known (the first especially in the annals of philology), since *Sayce* is probably a name of Welsh origin (*Sais*) but means an Englishman, while *Waugh* is certainly of English origin (*Walh*) but means a Welshman: it is in fact the singular of *Wales*.

The "Sayce" reference is presumably to Archibald Henry Sayce (1845-1933), Deputy Professor of Comparative Philology at Oxford, but in 1955 it might also be to Olive Lenore Sayce of Somerville, who edited the Second (1954) Edition of Joe Wright's *Grammar*. And for Waugh, in Tolkien's world, we need only look to Evelyn, who found a very different kind of sustenance in the Roman Catholic Church, and his son Auberon, one of the more antagonistic reviewers of *The Lord of the Rings*. No wonder Tolkien would rather speak as (or be) a Sayce than a Waugh. (See the article on "The Welsh Language" in the *J.R.R. Tolkien Encyclopedia*.)

'Inklings' Puns and Wordplay and 'Inklings' Wit in General

Only one Barfieldian line comes to my mind in this context ("ontology recapitulates philology")[2] and not much from Lord David, so for our purposes discussing humour in and around Tolkien and his work, the in-and-around Inklings are Tolkien himself (of course), Lewis, Coghill, and Dyson. To represent Lewis's *extempore* wordplay we have his response to the Portuguese guest at High Table venturing to eat haggis, who compared himself to a "gastronomic Columbus" – "the comparison is wayward in your case – why not a Vascular Da Gama?" To represent Dyson, when partridge was served at High Table in place of the announced duck – "Ah, *le mallarde imaginaire!*" And for Coghill, the description of Tolkien's great work as "hobbit-forming." But these were not solo examples. Let us note here the scene in *That Hideous Strength* when there comes to St. Anne's, "the lord of Meaning himself, the herald, the messenger,

---

2 This was a comment in conversation with me: I do not recall having seen it in print, though it may have been printed: on this I bow to those more expert than I.

the slayer of Argus [...] the angel that spins nearest the sun. Viritrilbia, whom men call Mercury and Thoth" (Lewis, *Hideous Strength* 322).

Here is what happens in the kitchen at St. Anne's:

> Now of a sudden they all began talking loudly at once, each, not contentiously but delightedly, interrupting the others. A stranger, coming into the kitchen, would have thought they were drunk, not soddenly but gaily drunk: would have seen heads bent close together, eyes dancing, an excited wealth of gesture. What they said, none of the party could ever afterwards remember. Dimble maintained that they had been chiefly engaged in making puns. MacPhee denied that he had ever, even that night, made a pun, but all agreed that they had been extraordinarily witty. If not plays upon words, yet certainly plays upon thoughts, paradoxes, fancies, anecdotes, theories laughingly advanced yet (on consideration) well worth taking seriously [...] Mother Dimble always remembered Denniston and her husband as they had stood, one on each side of the fireplace, in a gay intellectual duel, each capping the other, each rising above the other [...] never in her life had she heard such talk – such eloquence, such melody [...] such toppling structures of double meaning, such skyrockets of metaphor and allusion. (Lewis, *Hideous Strength* 321)

Recalling that when the lord of Meaning comes upon Ransom and Merlin upstairs (Lewis, *Hideous Strength* 321), it is "a rod of coloured light, whose colour no man can name or picture" that darted between them – it is my belief that the colour was that of the flames at Pentecost (which also had a skyrocket quality). Tolkien, Lewis, Coghill, even Dyson (by contagion perhaps), and I daresay others of the Inklings, knew the Word-play that is Holy Wit. (What Word? John 1: Ἐν αρχη ην ὁ λόγος καὶ ὁ λόγος μρος τόν θεόν καὶ ὁ λόγος ὁ θεός. Or, in English: In the beginning was the Word, and the Word was with God, and the Word was God.) But let us briefly look at the Inkling whose death (in Major Lewis's opinion) effectively ended the Inklings. Let us look at Charles Williams, and then come back, *via* our Carolinian detour, to Tolkien's humour.

It was from Williams even that I learned something of the British view of and friendship for (as well as opposition to) Islam – as much as from his coeval Aircraftman Shaw or from the Henty books of my youth – and perhaps for that reason particularly remember Palomides. Williams, in *Taliessin through Logres*, begins "The Coming of Palomides" as follows:

> Talaat ibn Kula of Ispahan
> taught me the measurement of man
> that Euclid and Archimedes showed,
> ere I took the Western road
> across the strait of the Spanish seas.
> Through the green-pennon-skirted Pyrenees,
> from the sharp curved line of the Prophet's blade
> that cuts the Obedience from the Obeyed,
> I came to the cross-littered land of Gaul.
> Gospels trigonometrical
> measured the height of God-in-man
> by the swinging hazels of Lateran
> [...]
> (Williams, *Arthurian Poems* 33)

That is what I think of, initially, when I think of Charles Williams as poet (and someday I'll figure out who Talaat ibn Kula was, though he may also be a Williams-ish joke) – and of course the rhymed tetrameters imply (and provide) a kind of wit (Kindwit?). Of Williams as theologian (also witty), I think of "Hell is inexact" and "This also is Thou" and "Neither is this Thou" – and I remember that it was Williams who tried to interest Lewis in Kierkegaard – but curiously, Lewis would rather read Sartre (in French, as it happens). I recall the passage in *The Descent of the Dove* (201-2), speaking of the Church and Voltaire (I hear echoes of Chesterton):

> For thirteen hundred years she had not been in a position to be attacked from outside; there had, in fact, been no outside. She had been denounced only by her members, even if they were heretical members, except where the alien cymbals of Islam had challenged her. But the clash of these new cymbals refused membership – in favor of a God not so unlike the God of Islam. Intellectually the cymbals were a little brassy. Voltaire seems actually to have thought on a low level; he did suppose that the fact that there were a thousand reputed Saviors of the world proved that there was no Savior of the world, and that the different circumstances and natures of many mothers of many gods disproved the Virginity of the Mother of God. We know that neither affirmation nor denial are as simple as that. But in matters of public morals Voltaire shocked and justly shook the Church.

Tolkien's 'Comic' Verse (including Clerihews)

Tolkien, who did not trust Williams's theology, wrote of him (in verse):

> When your fag [i.e., cigarette] is wagging and spectacles are twinkling
> when tea is brewing or the glasses tinkling,
> then of your meaning often I've an inkling,
> your virtues and your wisdom glimpse. Your laugh
> in my heart echoes, when with you I quaff
> the pint that goes down quicker than a half,
> because you're near. So, heed me not! I swear
> when you with tattered papers take the chair
> and read (for hours maybe), I would be there.
> And ever when in state you sit again
> and to your car imperial give rein,
> I'll trundle, grumbling, squeaking, in the train
> of the great rolling wheels of Charles' Wain.
> (Carpenter 126)

The presentation of Great Charles's Wain as a virtual juggernaut is in fact a description with such exactitude as to be virtually (what I have called) a "Tolkienian" pun on "Charles's Wain [Wagon]" – which is a traditional English name for the Big Dipper. (In fact, I might even claim my use of the word "juggernaut" in this context could qualify as a kind of "Tolkienian" pun.)

But Tolkien's more characteristic light verse of the period, also involving some punning, comes in the virtually classic "clerihews" he wrote (after the manner of Edmund Clerihew Bentley and G. K. Chesterton), about certain of the other "Inklings" in the late War years and perhaps slightly after. I should note here that the more I have read about the T.C.B.S. and especially the "Great Twin-Brethren" Christopher Wiseman and John Ronald Tolkien, the more similarity I see to the slightly earlier schoolboy club with its twin-brethren of Gilbert Chesterton and Edmund Clerihew Bentley – the brethren who invented the clerihew.

Three of Tolkien's clerihews are in Carpenter's *The Inklings* (177, 186, 187), respectively on Owen Barfield:

> Mr Owen Barfield's
> Habit of turning cartwheels
> Made some say: 'He's been drinking!'
> It was only 'conscientious thinking'.

Gervase Mathew:

> The Rev. Mathew (Gervase)
> Made inaudible surveys
> Of little-read sages
> In the dark Middle Ages.

Charles Williams:

> The sales of Charles Williams
> Leapt up by millions,
> When a reviewer surmised
> He was only Lewis disguised.

That last, as Carpenter notes, was entirely nonsense, though penetrating commentary on how Lewis was shepherding Williams's reputation. Technically, in rhyme at least, the Mathew clerihew may be the best, but the other two are wittier. Finally (Tolkien, *Letters* 359) on Coghill, referring to verses he wrote under the name of Judson, on the Norwood Report:

> Mr. Nevill Judson Coghill
> Wrote a great deal of dangerous doggerill.
> Practical progressive men
> Called him little poison-pen.

We may set these against a clerihew written by one of the form's originators (in fact, by the Grand Originator, Edmund Clerihew Bentley), on an author sometimes linked with the Inklings, Dorothy L. Sayers:

> Miss Dorothy Sayers
> Never cared about the Himalayas.
> The height that gave her a thrill
> Was Primrose Hill.

From the original (1893?) collection of clerihews (*The First Clerihews*, 1982), I would add two for our viewing. Both have a significance for members of the Inklings (though it is highly unlikely they ever saw them – but they are very early examples, undimmed by time).

Given C.S. Lewis's dislike of Henty (his brother, Major Lewis, also an Inkling, rather liked him), we have (Bentley 25):

> G.A. Henty
> Has written more books than twenty.
> Isn't it sad?
> They're all so bad

Or, anticipating the concerns of Charles Williams (detective-fiction reviewer) and J.R.R. Tolkien, we have (Bentley 43):

> Conan Doyle
> Ought to be boiled in oil.
> He makes no reference to gnomes
> In "The Adventures of Sherlock Holmes."

The form is catching, following the Tolkienian rule that one's first reaction to a piece of literature may be to write something in the same form oneself. Here's mine on Tolkien:

> John Ronald Tolkien
> Had a soul keen
> Not on being Etonian or Harrovian
> But Tea Club Barrovian.

Appendix I at the end of this paper contains more of my clerihews, for what they are worth. As I say, the form is catching, and historically so in Tolkien fan-circles.

In contradistinction to Tolkien, C.S. Lewis's best humourous verses (I believe) are classic Gilbertian nonsense ("Awake! My Lute," printed in Chad Walsh's *C.S. Lewis: Apostle to the Skeptics*). Note that this is "Lewisian" and "Carrollian" ("LewisCarrollian"?) nonsense rather than Dysonian nonsense (as in the "roaring cataract"). We'll come back to that later.

> I stood in the gloom of a spacious room
> Where I listened for hours (on and off)
> To a terrible bore with a beard like a snore
> And a heavy rectangular cough,

> Who discoursed on the habits of orchids and rabbits
> And how an electron behaves
> And a way to cure croup with solidified soup
> In a pattern of circular waves;

Till I suddenly spied that what stood at his side
Was a richly upholstered baboon
With paws like the puns in a poem of Donne's
And a tail like a voyage to the Moon.

Then I whispered, 'Look out! For I very much doubt
If your colleague is really a man.'
But the lecturer said, without turning his head,
'Oh that's only the Beverage Plan!'

As one might have foreseen, the whole sky became green
At this most injudicious remark,
For the Flood had begun and we both had to run
For our place in the queue for the Ark.

Then I hardly know how (we were swimming by now),
The sea got all covered with scrum.
Made of publishers' blurbs and irregular verbs
Of the kind which have datives in -um;

And the waves were so high that far up in the sky
We saw the Grand Lobster, and heard
How he snorted, 'Compare the achievements of Blair
With the grave of King Alfred the Third,

And add a brief note and if possible quote,
And distinguish and trace and discuss
The probable course of a Methodist horse
When it's catching a decimal bus.'

My answer was 'Yes'. But they marked it N.S.,
And a truffle fish grabbed at my toe,
And dragged me deep down to a bombulous town
Where the traffic was silent and slow.

Then a voice out of heaven observed, 'Quarter to seven!'
And I threw all the waves off my head,
For the voice beyond doubt was the voice of my scout,
And the bed of that sea was my bed.

(We know Lewis's father enjoyed Gilbert and Sullivan – he quotes the "Modern Major-General" in a letter to his young son circa 1912 (in Cording 98) – these verses appear to have some trace-origins of "When You're Lying Awake" in *Pirates of Penzance*.)

Some Other Inklings' Humour: Coghill, Dyson, Lord David

It would seem Lewis's humour derived from family humour (and older male members of his family – his brother and father and uncles), while Tolkien's was from his school-fellows (and perhaps from Father Morgan), since he had only a younger-brother and an aunt or two (of whom Jane Neave was most important) in his family. Coghill's family's sense of humour can be found in Somerville and Ross (*Irish R.M.*), Lord David's family was more serious than most, and Hugo Dyson was the nearest thing the Inklings possessed to a stand-up comic (or comedian).[3] But all of them engaged in word-play (Lord David perhaps the least). It happens that the most successful joke (for want of a better word) or pun or word-play was set up by Coghill in his *The Masque of Hope* (1948), where along with some excellent humourous lines (many delivered by Kenneth Tynan in the role of Fear), the great design of the Masque is to apply Shakespeare's lines on Princess Elizabeth (later Queen Elizabeth I) *in toto* to Princess Elizabeth (thereafter to be Queen Elizabeth II) – with as few observers as possible knowing it (or perhaps not).

One reminiscence of Coghill and his humour, in a very different context, deserves note here: Dacre Balsdon writes of a day at Maefield's estate at Boar's Hill in the 1930s:

> that stifling afternoon in the Barn on Boar's Hill, not to be forgotten by anyone who was there. 'Beautiful-voiced maidens will now recite the poems of Yeats.' They did, beautifully. The trouble was that they never stopped. It was very hot and most of the audience was in the state of never wishing to hear another beautiful-voiced maiden again in his life, when, miraculously, the recitation stopped and instead, like a satyr play after the tragedies in ancient Greece, your wonderful burlesque of Henry VIII and his wives was acted. You could not have hoped for a more sympathetic audience. The London Mercury afterwards published it. It was one of the funniest things ever seen. (Lobdell, *Forgotten Leaves* 240)

And with that tribute to Coghill registered, we can turn to Hugo Dyson. There are well-known recollections of Dyson from the '60s, by John Carey (eventually Professor at Oxford), and from the '50s, the American Critic George Steiner,

---

3 Indeed, at the risk of an American stereotype, a stand-up Jewish comedian (his name was changed by deed poll from Henry Victor Dyson Tannenbaum to Henry Victor Dyson Dyson in 1905). See my essay "Hugo's Home?" in the *Proceedings* of the 2015 New York Tolkien Conference.

and a brief but highly interesting passage in Alastair Fowler's recollection of C.S. Lewis as Supervisor: From Carey we have – relevant to our topic here – a description of Dyson (in the '50s) as

> an Oxford 'character' [...] known for his wit. I always found him alarming. He was like a hyperactive gnome, and stumped around on a walking-stick which, when he was seized by one of his paroxysms of laughter, he would beat up and down as if trying to drive it through the floor. It brought to mind Rumpelstiltskin driving his leg into the ground in the fairy tale.

He was, Carey goes on to say, on a good day,

> the funniest man I ever met [...], second only to Peter Ustinov who could do mimicry as well, although he always seemed more 'rehearsed', whereas Dyson was famous for his spontaneity. It was said that, one evening in Merton when there was duck on the menu, and the bird served was not duck but pheasant, he remarked, 'Ah, *le mallard imaginaire*'.[4]

One curiosity concerning the Inklings is the story Hugo Dyson told of his days at Ottoline Morrell's soirées he attended in the 1920s: At Garsington, Dyson had encountered

> all the people whom secretly one would have most desired to meet – and, as so often happened to a shy insignificant person, when one did meet them one was filled with a kind of terror. They were kindly enough, but I found them alarming. They weren't, most of them, my weight. I do remember finding Virginia Woolf immensely beautiful and immensely frightening; and one of my *fears* – I don't think I was quite alone in this – was that she would speak to me one day (but she never did). (Carpenter 97n)

Now this in itself is not curious – Dyson told the story on the BBC in 1971, and it was clearly an often-told story. What is more curious, perhaps, is that another member of the Inklings wrote the introduction to Carolyn Heilbrun's *Lady Ottoline's Album* (1976), a pictorial memoir of the soirées at Garsington, that being Lord David Cecil (whose picture, taken by Lady Ottoline, is in the album).

Now Lord David's attendance at Garsington gave him the opportunity for the detailed observation of daily (or at least week-endly) life there – the kind of observation that is at the root of Stephen Potter's *(Sense of) Humour*. But his

---

4 From my forthcoming essay "Hugo's Home?" which further argues my view of Dyson as the sad Clown who tragically missed his greatest opportunity to know a great literary figure and who grew (or declined) into a caricature of himself in his resident years at Oxford 1945-63.

great achievement in the field is his monumental *Max: A Biography* (1964), the authorized biography of the (largely expatriate) gentle English humourist and caricaturist, Sir Max Beerbohm (1872-1956). Sir Max was an associate of both Sir Winston Churchill (1874-1965) and of Lord David's uncle, Lord Hugh Cecil (1869-1956), Lord Quickswood from 1941. Lord David (1902-1986) was thirty years younger than Sir Max, dying at the same age of 83 thirty years after, but his gentle humour (even gentle satire) was a nearly perfect match for the elder man's gentle humour (even gentle satire). And his biography of "the incomparable Max" is humourous in precisely the Stephen Potter sense of *humour*.

Lewis's pen-portraits tended toward the sharply satirical – or even the simply sharp – from his early years (consider the portrait of Harry Weldon as Feverstone in *That Hideous Strength* – which has its origins in the '20s – or as far back as Boxen). Tolkien's satire was a kind of general satire of human nature, not as sharp as Lewis's. Charles Williams was more likely to satirize literary forms than individuals (his opening to *War in Heaven* is virtually a satire on the openings of English mystery novels circa 1930). Barfield kept most of his satire directed at himself (*This Ever Diverse Pair*) or perhaps at literary forms. I see little satire (and little but serious scholarly writing) from the pen of Charles Wrenn. Coghill's satire as translator of Chaucer is, of course, largely Chaucerian – but his translations of Langland are broader satire, as their originals are. Dyson, considered the most humourous – and funniest – of all the Inklings, and perhaps their greatest wit, falls oddly here. Finally, Warren Lewis was not a humourous writer or – mostly – a satirist, nor was Dom Gervase Mathew.

A Note on a Later Inkling: John Wain

Nor was Christopher Tolkien (b. 1923), nor – at least in the Inklings context – his approximate contemporary, John Wain (1925-1994). This last point deserves a little attention – after all, Wain's first novel *Hurry on Down* (1953) is described as a comic picaresque story about an unsettled university graduate who rejects the standards of conventional society (see the entry on Wain in Wikipedia), and his best-known critical work is on Dr. Johnson (1974), a kind of avatar of British humour – if not as a writer at least as a subject. But Wain among the

Inklings is perhaps best typified by his collection of verses whose publication was supported by the Inklings.

The publication is John Wain, *Mixed Feelings: Nineteen Poems* (printed in the School of Art, University of Reading, 1951, in an edition of 120 copies, completed October 31, 1951). The list of subscribers before publication shows 67 names, including those of Nevill Coghill, Esq., H.V.D. Dyson, Esq., Roger Lancelyn Green, Esq., C.G. Hardie, Esq., Dr. R.E. Havard, C.S. Lewis, Esq., Major W.H. Lewis, and Professor J.R.R. Tolkien. My copy (number 42) has no original owner's signature, but a card used as a marker bears the name and address of Roger Lancelyn Green. Other non-Inkling names among the pre-publication subscribers (names I recognize) include Mrs. Anne Wain, Arnold Wain, Esq., Kingsley Amis, F.W. Bateson, Esq., Professor D.J. Gordon, A.A. Hartley, Esq., Frank Kermode, Esq., J.B. Leishman, Esq., Professor Edith Morley, W.W. Robson, Esq., and Miss Mary Salu. Edith Moreley, I recall, wrote the original (warning) review of Hugo Dyson's perhaps slightly *outré* volume *Augustans and Romantics*.

I have also seen for sale a copy of *Nineteen Poems* with the signature of John Masefield, so we know who at least one non-subscriber (before publication) was who wound up with a copy. (It will be remembered that the Poet Laureate was a long-time friend of Nevill Coghill. Whether W.H. Auden, another long-time Coghill friend, likewise wound up with a copy, I cannot say.)

The particular importance of this slim volume for our purposes here lies in the last six poems, numbers XIV-XIX, each bearing the title "Who Speaks My Language" after the numeral. The subject is words and being in rhyme, the poems show a good deal of word-play, which falls into our subject here. I quote Number XVII, the fourth of John Wain's "Who Speaks My Language" poems.

> And then there is the question of how far
> You can expect the Common Man to share
> Your own concern with words and what they are.
> The shades of meaning hover in the air,
> But when you want to point to one precisely,
> The others cannot see them glowing there.
> You dare not speak too primly or concisely
> Because your hearers for their simple needs

> Feel that a few crass gestures will do nicely,
> Words being just a feeble kind of deeds.
> It puzzles them that you should spend your time
> Coaxing the wind to touch strategic reeds;
> And like the rope trick boy, they think, you climb
> Up nothing, and achieve a senseless poise;
> Reasoning thus: a poem is a rhyme,
> And language quite a useful kind of noise.

Now this, in the verse, seems not savagely satiric – but the views of the "Common Man" (note the capitals) are satirized, and there is surely satire in "Words being just a feeble kind of deeds." Moreover, I suggest the scansion of the penultimate line virtually dictates a full two syllables for "poem" – which is not only satiric but sarcastic. The importance of these lines, indeed these poems, to an on-going Inklings discussion of language and human nature I have elsewhere suggested in my Guest of Honor paper for the 2016 New York Tolkien Society Conference, "Three Inklings and the Sciences of Language: C. L. Wrenn, CSL, JRRT, and the 'Kalends-of-Greece' Collaboration." Here this example is designed to warn us of this Inkling's approach to "humour" – something we might call *suaviter in modo fortiter in re* – but better, perhaps, *leviter in modo graviter in re*.

My copy apparently once belonged to Roger Lancelyn Green, who was not only a member of the Inklings at least in the post-War years, but a member whose later academic study included Lewis Carroll, and who has himself discussed the Inklings. Lewis Carroll is, of course, a humourist, as a writer of Nonsense – very academic Nonsense, one might say. (After all, Charles Lutwidge Dodgson was an Oxford Tutor, and Alice Liddell, for whom he invented the stories of Alice, was his Dean's daughter, and the Dean was Liddell of Liddell and Scott's *Lexicon* – still used in my time in college.) I have looked in Roger Lancelyn Green's reminiscence of Lewis in James Como's *Remembering C.S. Lewis* – he is a noted Carroll scholar – only to find that Lancelyn Green records virtually nothing of what Lewis said when (Como 343) they talked about children's books – or indeed on pretty much any other subject. He does however record one joke told by Lewis, of the young room-service waiter who surprised a lady and gentleman (bride and groom) "in the act" – the well-known story whose punch-line is "Your early morning tea, gentlemen" (Como 345).

The Awfulness of *Irene Iddesleigh*

In fact, the best-known example of Lewis's sense of humour (as opposed to his wit) is the fact that reading the excessively awful novel *Irene Iddesleigh* aloud could reduce him – and those engaged in the process with him – to helpless laughter. Tolkien (and Wrenn) apparently participated in this ritual, though the ritual was essentially Irish – as was the authoress (at least Northern-Irish), Amanda McKittrick Ros (Anna Margaret Ross, *née* McKittrick, 1860-1939). Here are the first three paragraphs of the opening chapter of what has been called the worst novel ever written in English. The point of Lewis's reading being to see how far any reader could get without collapsing into helpless laughter at the book's sheer awfulness.[5] (Those who wish to try the whole chapter without breaking down in laughter will find it in Appendix II.)

> 'Sympathise with me, indeed! Ah, no! Cast your sympathy on the chill waves of troubled waters; fling it on the oases of futurity; dash it against the rock of gossip; or, better still, allow it to remain within the false and faithless bosom of buried scorn.'
>
> Such were a few remarks of Irene as she paced the beach of limited freedom, alone and unprotected. Sympathy can wound the breast of trodden patience,–it hath no rival to insure the feelings we possess, save that of sorrow.
>
> The gloomy mansion stands firmly within the ivy-covered, stoutly-built walls of Dunfern, vast in proportion and magnificent in display. It has been built over three hundred years, and its structure stands respectably distant from modern advancement, and in some degrees it could boast of architectural designs rarely, if ever, attempted since its construction. (*Irene Iddesleigh*)

'Fantastication' and Holy Wit

One point we might note here. Peter Bayley, one of a small group of post-War undergraduates who met with Lewis and Dyson in 1946-47 refers (Bayley 168) to "Dyson's incredible energies of wit, wordplay, and conversational fantastication" – and we should note also any references, direct or implicit, to the fantastic in Lewis's humour. Did Lewis carry out the same "fantastication" as Dyson? The accounts of his humour by Bayley and Derek Brewer (another of that small

---

5 Note that Lewis had a kind of proprietorial interest in Amanda McKittrick Ros – his father was her solicitor, to whom she had given a copy of her [self-published] *magnum opus*, first [1897] edition.

group) suggest that Lewis relied on "intelligence, knowledge, learning, zest, wit, and witty quotation" (Bayley 139) – though I note the follow-up remark (Bayley 145) that his "conversation sparkled with quotations and references that poured out as inadvertently as the jewels from the mouth of the good girl in the fairy tale [...] He would stop and look hard and seriously into space as he evolved a new thought, then change rapidly into beaming good humour." This strikes me as describing the same process, so to speak, by which the "fantastication" came about. And here I would note a passage in *Out of the Silent Planet* (117), describing Malancandrian humour:

> Apparently the comic spirit arose chiefly from the meeting of the different kinds of *hnau*. The jokes of all three were equally incomprehensible to him. He thought he could see differences in kind – as that the *sorns* seldom got beyond irony, while the *hrossa* were extravagant and fantastic, and the *pfifltriggi* were sharp and excelled in abuse – but even when he could understand all the words he could not see the points. He went early to bed.

Lewis, I think (in Ransom's *persona*) would like to have had the hrossa gift for "fantastication" – rather than the "Seronian" irony (Lewis got tired of writing the ironic/satiric *Screwtape Letters*). We know Dyson's penchant for – and ability in – "fantastication." But what of Tolkien? It is time perhaps to round this paper off by returning to its original focus on Tolkien. And we find – what? Have we any of Tolkien's work that proceeds through a process of fantastication, with zest, wit, wordplay, even bordering occasionally on a "cataract of nonsense" (though with Tolkien, unlike Lewis or – apparently – Dyson, it would not be a "roaring cataract." Tolkien didn't roar: Lewis did, and Lewis said that Dyson did.)

The answer is yes, and it is found in the most neglected of Tolkien's minor works, *Mr. Bliss*. Let me begin by going back to a source lying behind this considerably neglected work. Here is something sounding not unlike a Tolkienian story, of young Pippo, the donkey, and the fruit. It was when he was about eight years old that young Pippo's parents briefly left him alone in a courtyard. He saw a donkey laden with fruit and jumped on its back. With Pippo on his back, the donkey bolted, and donkey, fruit, and Pippo tumbled together into a deep hole, Pippo on the bottom. His parents hastened to the spot and extricated him, not dead, indeed entirely uninjured.

One may hear echoes of this in the story of *Mr. Bliss*, though there it is mixed with Knight and Day and Mr. Bliss's motorcar, as first Mr. Day's barrow-load of cabbages and then Mrs. Knight's donkey-cart-load of bananas are struck by Mr. Bliss's car. You will recall, Mr. Bliss turns to the right and runs into Day with a barrow-load of cabbages and turns to the left and runs into Knight with a donkey-cart-load of bananas, and winds up piling the bananas on top of the cabbages and Knight on top of Day, and tying the donkey behind the car.

Pippo was in fact Pippo Neri, San Filippo Neri (St. Philip Neri 1515-1595), the Apostle to the Romans and founder of the Oratories. In Father Morgan's guardianship of Ronald and Hilary Tolkien, I discern the figure and indeed the example of Philip Neri, and since the classic life of Philip Neri includes this story just told, I suspect young Ronald Tolkien heard it. Here is what Cardinal Newman, founder of Birmingham's Oratory, had to say on his great exemplar.

Philip Neri (he said) had

> as the idea of his mission, not the propagation of the faith, nor the exposition of doctrine, nor the catechetical schools; whatever was exact and systematic pleased him not; he put from him monastic rule and authoritative speech, as David refused the armor of his king [...] He came to the Eternal City and he sat himself down there, and his home and his family gradually grew up around him, by the spontaneous accession of materials from without. He did not so much seek his own as draw them to him. He sat in his small room, and they in their gay worldly dresses, the rich and the wellborn, as well as the simple and the illiterate, crowded into it [...] And they who came remained gazing and listening till, at length, first one and then another [... came to follow him.] (Newman n.p.)

He refused the armor of his king. (He had of course his own weapon, of a lowlier kind.)

Philip Neri was the joking saint who shaved half his beard to be a fool for Christ and had his reader read jokes to him for meditation (and who drew all kinds to him in the room he chose). One could almost think of him in hobbit terms (hobbitually – to echo the "hobbit-forming" pun), and one remembers that Tolkien said (of himself) that he was himself a hobbit.

Now it was a Roman more than any English saint (Philip Neri), a Spanish (and Welsh) not an English priest (Father Francis Morgan), and a Portuguese shining city on a hill (Lisbon on the voyage to England from South Africa) and not an English city that played their roles in Tolkien's early years. But after and upon that, more and more, the English language (with all its puns and wordplay, all its home-grown humour) transposed to the intersection of the Timeless Moment, England and Always. And the humour remained in or at least bordering – marching with – that Timeless Moment.

After all, Christ was a humourist, a wit – think of "Whose image and superscription are these?" and the follow-up, or the advice to treat one's enemy well so as to heap coals of fire upon his head, or the reference to John and James bar-Zebedee as Boanerges (= Suns of Thunder = Sons of Zeus = Castor and Pollux, the Great Twin Brethren, the Heavenly Trouble-Makers).

And, moreover, isn't the Girabbit a piece of "fantastication" – along with Day and Knight and cabbages and bananas and the motorcar (not unlike the little car in the old Monopoly game, but in fact older, since it dates back to a toy car of Christopher's, as *Roverandom* does to a toy dog)? I think of Coghill's great tribute to Tolkien as Langland, and I am tempted to write (and wildely, of course, will give in to temptation):

> In a somer seson / what softe was the sonne
> I shope me in shroudes / as I a shepe were
> In herenet as an hobbite / but holy of werkes
> Went wyde in this world / wondres to here.[6]

In a sense, of course, punning is on the edge of fantastication – and, by the way, it is scarcely accidental that the illustrator and co-author of *The First Clerihews* was the great "fantasticator," the man who habitually raised paradoxysms of laughter by his wordplay, medievalist, mystery-writer, Roman Catholic, a man who published Charles Williams in his *Weekly*, whose Orthodoxy and Everlasting Man greatly influenced Lewis, still a living literary (even cultural) presence in the early days of the Inklings, and apart from Lewis's coeval in death (who wrote *Profiles in Courage*) the only author of my time fully identified by his initials, GKC himself. (The reader may find a punning transposition in the lines quoted, or at least a bit of wordplay.)

---

6 Cf. Langland's original: *In a somer seson / what softe was the sonne / I shope me in shroudes / as I a shepe were / In habite as an heremite / unholy of werkes / Went wyde in this world / wondres to here.*

In *The Lord of the Rings*

The one point we have not yet discussed here is humour (in other than the Potter sense) or comedy (in other than the Northrop Frye sense), or comicality, the comic, or even jokes in *The Lord of the Rings*. There is in fact little enough of any of these, and most of that little a carry-over from *The Hobbit*. But there is wit. For example, consider the interchange between Gandalf and Merry in the chapter on "The Palantir" in *The Two Towers* (Saruman has referred to Merry and Pippin as the "cut-throats and small rag-tag that dangle" (*LotR* 188) at Gandalf's tail):

> 'Are we riding far tonight, Gandalf?' asked Merry after a while 'I don't know how you feel with a small rag-tag dangling behind you; but the rag-tag is tired and will be glad to stop dangling and lie down.'
>
> 'So you heard that?' said Gandalf. 'Don't let it rankle. Be thankful no longer words were aimed at you. [...] A sneer from him, Meriadoc, is a compliment, if you feel honoured by his concern.'
>
> 'Thank you!' said Merry. 'But it is a greater honour to dangle at your tail, Gandalf. For one thing, in that position one has the chance of putting a question a second time. Are we riding far tonight?'
>
> Gandalf laughed. (*LotR* 193)

After all, again, as I said just before, wit is not out of place in the Gospels, and Christ was witty (in both the modern and mediaeval senses). There is humour in the portrayal of the Mithrandir who recollects that yes, he was called Gandalf once. There is wit (and kindwit) in Merry and Pippin (particularly with Gandalf), and mother-wit one might say in Sam. But *The Lord of the Rings* is not carnival; it is not a children's book; it is not (except in a greatly extended sense) a Christmas book – and at that it is pre-Christmas. The career of Saruman (and his name as Sharkey, "a term of affection, possibly") is humorously etched, and the Hobbits, even at the end of all things, retain a certain comicality. And Gollum bites off more than he can chew. And he comes to his end with a last despairing wail "*Precious!*"

As for the story's end, and this too leads us to play on words, there are three endings, or four – "Well, I'm back, he said" (*LotR* 1031), followed immediately by "The End" – and then "There at last when mallorn-leaves were falling and spring had not yet come, she laid herself to rest upon Cerin Amroth, and there is her green grave, until the world is changed, and all the days of her life are utterly forgotten by men that come after, and *elanor* and *niphredil* bloom no more east of the Sea" – followed by "Here ends this tale, as it has come to us from the South; and with the passing of Evenstar no more is said in this book [i.e. the *Red Book of Westmarch*] of the days of old." (*LotR* 1063)

Here is a second ending, but we must still remember that the great tales have no end. We go on.

> But when King Elessar gave up his life Legolas followed at last the desire of his heart and sailed over Sea [...] We have heard tell that Legolas took Gimli Glóin's son with him, because of their great friendship, greater than any that has been between Elf and Dwarf. If this is true it is strange indeed [...] But it is said Gimli went also out of desire to see again the beauty of Galadriel; and it may be that she [...] obtained this grace for him. More cannot be said of this matter. (*LotR* 1081)

But a little more is said – for the great tales indeed do not end easily, if at all:

> In this year [1541 S.R.] on March 1st came at last the Passing of King Elessar. [...] Then Legolas built a grey ship in Ithilien, and sailed down Anduin and so over Sea; and with him, it is said, went Gimli the Dwarf. And when that ship passed an end was come in Middle-earth of the Fellowship of the Ring. (*LotR* 1098)

It is not, I suppose, punning, but wordplay it clearly is, and the great tale that has no end, has yet four endings, of which the latest in time comes second in the book. Is this a matter of humour? It is not comic, certainly, nor risible, nor comical, though it might be considered Comedic (Frye's sense), as part of a *penseroso* sorting-out of matters. But let me suggest a slightly different coign of vantage from which to regard this matter. Let me suggest that each one of these is properly an end – to the whole story of *The Lord of the Rings* ("'Well, I'm back,' he said") – to the "Tale of Arwen and Aragorn" ("There at last, when mallorn-leaves were falling and spring had not yet come ...") – to the story of "The Fellowship of the Ring" ("And when that ship passed, an end was come in Middle-earth to the Fellowship of the Ring").

The stories are all true, including the reasons ascribed for the actions, even though the narrator (the voice is the Professor's) hedges the conclusions with scholarly reticence and self-deprecation, less comic than (but similar to) his reference elsewhere to the Four Wise Clerks of Oxenford. What is it other than Tolkien's excellent humour that sets the greatest novel of its time in the form of a hobbit-annotated edition of a medieval chronicle (and he was himself a hobbit)?

Appendix I: More Cherihews

> Clive Staples Lewis
> Third-personally said "What's true is
> As a name 'Clive Staples' lacks –
> He's Jacks!"

> Charles Williams
> Would have planted psylliums and trilliums
> Had he known they would have grown
> Around the Logothete's throne.

> Henry Victor Dyson Dyson ("Hugo")
> Told his fellow Inklings, "As you go
> Through life enjoy good liquor, my jokes, yourselves –
> But for me, I'm tired of elves."

> Lord Edward Christian David Gascoyne-Cecil
> It will turn out (I would guess)'ll
> Have known everyone in three centuries, or more –
> Or, from Dorothy Osborne the 20th made four.

[For the next two, I apologize profusely if the references are slightly over-arcane. But "live long and prosper" in context seems particularly appropriate for my friend Owen – and he did write a science-fiction novel. And Coghill's Aunt Edith Somerville (1858-1949) did, with her cousin, write the Irish R. M. stories – on which I was brought up.]

> Arthur Owen Barfield
> Trekked a runcible evolving star-field
> And heard Lear's cat Old Foss purr
> "Live long and prosper."

> Nevill Kendal Aylmer Coghill
> In youth followed the R. M. over fog-hill and bog-hill,
> But in the end, perforce, though with hesitance,
> (Magisterially) changed his residence.

C. L. Wrenn
Said "I'm having drinks with some men –
At the B & B the glasses are tinkling –
And when I'll be home, I haven't an inkling."

Appendix II: Chapter I or *Irene Iddesleigh*

'Sympathise with me, indeed! Ah, no! Cast your sympathy on the chill waves of troubled waters; fling it on the oases of futurity; dash it against the rock of gossip; or, better still, allow it to remain within the false and faithless bosom of buried scorn.'

Such were a few remarks of Irene as she paced the beach of limited freedom, alone and unprotected. Sympathy can wound the breast of trodden patience,--it hath no rival to insure the feelings we possess, save that of sorrow.

The gloomy mansion stands firmly within the ivy-covered, stoutly-built walls of Dunfern, vast in proportion and magnificent in display. It has been built over three hundred years, and its structure stands respectably distant from modern advancement, and in some degrees it could boast of architectural designs rarely, if ever, attempted since its construction.

The entrance to this beautiful home of Sir Hugh Dunfern, the present owner, is planned on most antique principles; nothing save an enormous iron gate meets the gaze of the visitor, who at first is inclined to think that all public rumours relative to its magnificence are only the utterances of the boastful and idle; nor until within its winding paths of finest pebble, studded here and there with huge stones of unpolished granite, could the mind for a moment conceive or entertain the faintest idea of its quaint grandeur.

Beautiful, however, as Dunfern mansion may seem to the anxious eye of the beholder, yet it is not altogether free from mystery. Whilst many of its rooms, with walls of crystal, are gorgeously and profusely furnished, others are locked incessantly against the foot of the cautious intruder, having in them only a few traditional relics of no material consequence whatever, or even interest, to any outside the ancestral line of its occupants.

It has often been the chief subject of comment amongst the few distinguished visitors welcomed within its spacious apartments, why seemingly the finest rooms the mansion owned were always shut against their eager and scrutinizing gaze; or why, when referred to by any of them, the matter was always treated with silence. All that can now be done is merely to allow the thought to dwindle into bleak oblivion, until aroused to that standard of disclosure which defies hindrance.

Within the venerable walls surrounding this erection of amazement and wonder may be seen species of trees rarely, if ever, met with; yea, within the beaded borders of this grand old mansion the eye of the privileged beholds the magnificent lake, studded on every side with stone of costliest cut and finish; the richest vineries, the most elegant ferns, the daintiest conservatories, the flowers and plants of almost every clime in abundance, the most fashionable walks, the most intricate windings that imagination could possibly conceive or genius contrive. In fact, it has well been named 'The Eden of Luxury.'

Dunfern mansion was handed down as an heirloom since its purchase by Walter, third Earl of Dunfern, in 1674; and since then has been tenderly cared for internally, and carefully guarded externally, by the skillful hands of noted artisans. The present owner is only son of Sir John Dunfern, by Irene, adopted daughter of Lord and Lady Dilworth, of Dilworth Castle, County Kent.

About the Author

JARED CHARLES LOBDELL (born 1937) is an American writer and teacher of Literary Criticism (and many other fields). As such, he has published several studies and articles about various fantasy and science-fiction writers, like J.R.R. Tolkien, C.S. Lewis and George Orwell.

Abbreviations

LotR: TOLKIEN, *The Lord of the Rings*

Bibliography

BARFIELD, Owen. *This Ever Diverse Pair*. London: Gollancz, 1950.

BENTLEY, E.C. et al. *The First Clerihews*. Oxford: Oxford University Press, 1982 [assembled 1893].

BLISH, James. "Probapossible Prolegomena to Ideareal History." *Foundation* 13 (1978): 6-11.

CARPENTER, Humphrey. *The Inklings*. London: Unwin Paperbacks, 1981.

CECIL, Lord David. *Max: A Biography*. London: Constable, 1964.

COMO, James. *Remembering C. S. Lewis*. 2nd ed., San Francisco: Ignatius, 2005.

CORDING, Ruth James. *C.S. Lewis: A Celebration of His Early Life*. Nashville: Broadman & Holman, 2000.

FRYE, Northrop. *Anatomy of Criticism*. Princeton: Princeton University Press, 1957.

GALLONIO, Antonio [d. 1605]. *Life of St. Philip Neri*. San Francisco: Ignatius, 2005 [Rome 1600].

HEILBRUN, Carolyn. *Lady Ottoline's Album: Snapshots and Portraits of Her Famous Contemporaries (and of Herself)*. New York: Knopf, 1976.

LEWIS, C.S. "The Dark Tower." in *The Dark Tower*. New York: Macmillan, 1982.

The Great Divorce. London: Bles, 1945.

Out of the Silent Planet. London: Bles, 1938.

Perelandra. London: Bles, 1943.

The Pilgrim's Regress. London: Sheed & Ward, 1935.

Screwtape Letters. London: Bles, 1941.

That Hideous Strength. London: Bles, 1945.

LOBDELL, Jared. "Three Inklings and the Sciences of Language: C.L. Wrenn, CSL, JRRT, and the 'Kalends-of-Greece' Collaboration." Guest of Honor paper for the 2016 New York Tolkien Conference, Conference *Proceedings* forthcoming from MythInk 2017-18.

"Hugo's Home?" Forthcoming in the *Proceedings* of the 2015 New York Tolkien Conference (MythInk 2016-17).

"An Irish Friendship in English Lit." In *Leaves from a Forgotten Smial*. Staten Island: MythInk, 2015. 200-263.

Rise of Tolkienian Fantasy. LaSalle and Chicago: Open Court, 2005.

sv "*Mr. Bliss*" (442-43), "*Roverandom*" (528-29),"*Welsh Language*" (706-7) in Michael D.C. DROUT (ed.). *J.R.R. Tolkien Encyclopedia: Scholarship and Critical Assessment*. New York: Routledge, 2006.

NEUBAUER, Lukasz. "Plain Ignorance in the Vulgar Form: Tolkien's Onomastic Humour in *Farmer Giles of Ham*." *Laughter in Middle-earth. Humour in and around the Works of J.R.R. Tolkien*. Ed. Thomas HONEGGER and Maureen F. MANN. Zurich and Jena: Walking Tree Publishers, 2016. 89-104.

NEWMAN, John Henry. *The Idea of a University*. e-book. [1854]

PEVSNER, Nikolaus. *Englishness of English Art*. New York: Praeger, 1954.

POTTER, Stephen. *Sense of Humour*. London: Reinhardt, 1954.

ROS, Amanda McKittrick [Anna Margaret Ross, *née* McKittrick]. *Irene Iddesleigh*. Belfast, 1897.

SHIPPEY, Tom A. *Tolkien: Author of the Century*. Boston: Houghton Mifflin, 2001.

SMITH, Laura Lee. "'This is, of course, the Way to talk to Dragons': Etiquette-Based Humour in *The Hobbit*." *Laughter in Middle-earth. Humour in and around the Works of J.R.R. Tolkien*. Ed. Thomas HONEGGER and Maureen F. MANN. Zurich and Jena: Walking Tree Publishers, 2016. 107-132.

TOLKIEN, John Ronald. *Mr. Bliss*. Boston: Houghton Mifflin, 1983.

Farmer Giles of Ham. Boston: Houghton Mifflin, 1949.

The Hobbit. London: Allen & Unwin, 1937.

The Letters of J.R.R. Tolkien. Ed. Humphrey CARPENTER with the assistance of Christopher TOLKIEN. London: HarperCollins, 2006.

The Lord of the Rings. First published 1954-55. 50th anniversary one volume edition. Boston: Houghton Mifflin, 2004.

The Monsters and the Critics. Ed. Christopher R. TOLKIEN. Boston: Houghton Mifflin, 1984.

and Donald SWANN. *The Road Goes Ever On: A Song Cycle*. Boston: Houghton Mifflin, 1967.

Roverandom. Ed. Wayne G. HAMMOND and Christina SCULL. Boston: Houghton Mifflin, 1998.

WAIN, John. *Mixed Feelings: Nineteen Poems*. Printed in the School of Art, University of Reading, 1951, in an edition of 120 copies.

WALSH, Chad. *C.S. Lewis: Apostle to the Skeptics*. New York: Macmillan, 1949.

WILLIAMS, Charles. *The Arthurian Poems of Charles Williams: Taliessin through Logres and The Region of the Summer Stars*. Cambridge: D.S. Brewer, 1982.

The Descent of the Dove: A Short History of the Holy Spirit in the Church. First published 1939. Eugene, OR: Wipf and Stock Publishers, 2016.

Tim Kirk
Homeless Orc

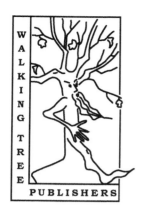

Walking Tree Publishers
Zurich and Jena

Walking Tree Publishers was founded in 1997 as a forum for publication of material (books, videos, CDs, etc.) related to Tolkien and Middle-earth studies.

http://www.walking-tree.org

Cormarë Series

The *Cormarë Series* collects papers and studies dedicated exclusively to the exploration of Tolkien's work. It comprises monographs, thematic collections of essays, conference volumes, and reprints of important yet no longer (easily) accessible papers by leading scholars in the field. Manuscripts and project proposals are evaluated by members of an independent board of advisors who support the series editors in their endeavour to provide the readers with qualitatively superior yet accessible studies on Tolkien and his work.

News from the Shire and Beyond. Studies on Tolkien
Peter Buchs and Thomas Honegger (eds.), Zurich and Berne 2004, Reprint, First edition 1997 (Cormarë Series 1), ISBN 978-3-9521424-5-5

Root and Branch. Approaches Towards Understanding Tolkien
Thomas Honegger (ed.), Zurich and Berne 2005, Reprint, First edition 1999 (Cormarë Series 2), ISBN 978-3-905703-01-6

Richard Sturch, *Four Christian Fantasists. A Study of the Fantastic Writings of George MacDonald, Charles Williams, C.S. Lewis and J.R.R. Tolkien*
Zurich and Berne 2007, Reprint, First edition 2001 (Cormarë Series 3), ISBN 978-3-905703-04-7

Tolkien in Translation
Thomas Honegger (ed.), Zurich and Jena 2011, Reprint, First edition 2003 (Cormarë Series 4), ISBN 978-3-905703-15-3

Mark T. Hooker, *Tolkien Through Russian Eyes*
Zurich and Berne 2003 (Cormarë Series 5), ISBN 978-3-9521424-7-9

Translating Tolkien: Text and Film
Thomas Honegger (ed.), Zurich and Jena 2011, Reprint, First edition 2004 (Cormarë Series 6), ISBN 978-3-905703-16-0

Christopher Garbowski, *Recovery and Transcendence for the Contemporary Mythmaker. The Spiritual Dimension in the Works of J.R.R. Tolkien*
Zurich and Berne 2004, Reprint, First Edition by Marie Curie Sklodowska, University Press, Lublin 2000, (Cormarë Series 7), ISBN 978-3-9521424-8-6

Reconsidering Tolkien
Thomas Honegger (ed.), Zurich and Berne 2005 (Cormarë Series 8), ISBN 978-3-905703-00-9

Tolkien and Modernity 1
Frank Weinreich and Thomas Honegger (eds.), Zurich and Berne 2006 (Cormarë Series 9), ISBN 978-3-905703-02-3

Tolkien and Modernity 2
Thomas Honegger and Frank Weinreich (eds.), Zurich and Berne 2006 (Cormarë Series 10), ISBN 978-3-905703-03-0

Tom Shippey, *Roots and Branches. Selected Papers on Tolkien by Tom Shippey*
Zurich and Berne 2007 (Cormarë Series 11), ISBN 978-3-905703-05-4

Ross Smith, *Inside Language. Linguistic and Aesthetic Theory in Tolkien*
Zurich and Jena 2011, Reprint, First edition 2007 (Cormarë Series 12), ISBN 978-3-905703-20-7

How We Became Middle-earth. A Collection of Essays on The Lord of the Rings
Adam Lam and Nataliya Oryshchuk (eds.), Zurich and Berne 2007 (Cormarë Series 13), ISBN 978-3-905703-07-8

Myth and Magic. Art According to the Inklings
Eduardo Segura and Thomas Honegger (eds.), Zurich and Berne 2007 (Cormarë Series 14), ISBN 978-3-905703-08-5

The Silmarillion - Thirty Years On
Allan Turner (ed.), Zurich and Berne 2007 (Cormarë Series 15), ISBN 978-3-905703-10-8

Martin Simonson, *The Lord of the Rings and the Western Narrative Tradition*
Zurich and Jena 2008 (Cormarë Series 16), ISBN 978-3-905703-09-2

Tolkien's Shorter Works. Proceedings of the 4th Seminar of the Deutsche Tolkien Gesellschaft & Walking Tree Publishers Decennial Conference
Margaret Hiley and Frank Weinreich (eds.), Zurich and Jena 2008 (Cormarë Series 17), ISBN 978-3-905703-11-5

Tolkien's The Lord of the Rings: Sources of Inspiration
Stratford Caldecott and Thomas Honegger (eds.), Zurich and Jena 2008 (Cormarë Series 18), ISBN 978-3-905703-12-2

J.S. Ryan, *Tolkien's View: Windows into his World*
Zurich and Jena 2009 (Cormarë Series 19), ISBN 978-3-905703-13-9

Music in Middle-earth
Heidi Steimel and Friedhelm Schneidewind (eds.), Zurich and Jena 2010 (Cormarë Series 20), ISBN 978-3-905703-14-6

Liam Campbell, *The Ecological Augury in the Works of JRR Tolkien*
Zurich and Jena 2011 (Cormarë Series 21), ISBN 978-3-905703-18-4

Margaret Hiley, *The Loss and the Silence. Aspects of Modernism in the Works of C.S. Lewis, J.R.R. Tolkien and Charles Williams*
Zurich and Jena 2011 (Cormarë Series 22), ISBN 978-3-905703-19-1

Rainer Nagel, *Hobbit Place-names. A Linguistic Excursion through the Shire*
Zurich and Jena 2012 (Cormarë Series 23), ISBN 978-3-905703-22-1

Christopher MacLachlan, *Tolkien and Wagner: The Ring and Der Ring*
Zurich and Jena 2012 (Cormarë Series 24), ISBN 978-3-905703-21-4

Renée Vink, *Wagner and Tolkien: Mythmakers*
Zurich and Jena 2012 (Cormarë Series 25), ISBN 978-3-905703-25-2

The Broken Scythe. Death and Immortality in the Works of J.R.R. Tolkien
Roberto Arduini and Claudio Antonio Testi (eds.), Zurich and Jena 2012
(Cormarë Series 26), ISBN 978-3-905703-26-9

Sub-creating Middle-earth: Constructions of Authorship and the Works of J.R.R. Tolkien
Judith Klinger (ed.), Zurich and Jena 2012 (Cormarë Series 27),
ISBN 978-3-905703-27-6

Tolkien's Poetry
Julian Eilmann and Allan Turner (eds.), Zurich and Jena 2013
(Cormarë Series 28), ISBN 978-3-905703-28-3

O, What a Tangled Web. Tolkien and Medieval Literature. A View from Poland
Barbara Kowalik (ed.), Zurich and Jena 2013 (Cormarë Series 29),
ISBN 978-3-905703-29-0

J.S. Ryan, *In the Nameless Wood*
Zurich and Jena 2013 (Cormarë Series 30), ISBN 978-3-905703-30-6

From Peterborough to Faëry; The Poetics and Mechanics of Secondary Worlds
Thomas Honegger & Dirk Vanderbeke (eds.), Zurich and Jena 2014
(Cormarë Series 31), ISBN 978-3-905703-31-3

Tolkien and Philosophy
Roberto Arduini and Claudio R. Testi (eds.), Zurich and Jena 2014
(Cormarë Series 32), ISBN 978-3-905703-32-0

Patrick Curry, *Deep Roots in a Time of Frost. Essays on Tolkien*,
Zurich and Jena 2014 (Cormarë Series 33), ISBN 978-3-905703-33-7

Representations of Nature in Middle-earth
Martin Simonson (ed.), Zurich and Jena 2015, (Cormarë Series 34),
ISBN 978-3-905703-34-4

Laughter in Middle-earth
Thomas Honegger and Maureen F. Mann (eds.), Zurich and Jena 2016
(Cormarë Series 35), ISBN 978-3-905703-35-1

Julian Eilmann, *J.R.R. Tolkien – Romanticist and Poet*, forthcoming

Claudio Testi, *Holy Pagans in Middle-earth*, forthcoming

There and Back Again. Interdisciplinary Perspectives on J.R.R. Tolkien and his Works.
Monika Kirner-Ludwig, Stephan Köser, Sebastian Streitberger (eds.), forthcoming

Music in Tolkien's Work and Beyond
Julian Eilmann and Friedhelm Schneidewind (eds.), forthcoming

Beowulf and the Dragon

The original Old English text of the 'Dragon Episode' of *Beowulf* is set in an authentic font and bound in hardback as a high quality art book. Illustrated by Anke Eissmann and accompanied by John Porter's translation. Introduction by Tom Shippey. Limited first edition of 500 copies. 84 pages. Selected pages can be previewed on: www.walking-tree.org/beowulf

Zurich and Jena 2009 , ISBN 978-3-905703-17-7

Tales of Yore Series

The *Tales of Yore Series* provides a platform for qualitatively superior fiction that will appeal to readers familiar with Tolkien's world:

The Monster Specialist

Sir Severus le Brewse, among the least known of King Arthur's Round Table knights, is preferred by nature, disposition, and training to fight against monsters rather than other knights. After youthful adventures of errantry with dragons, trolls, vampires, and assorted beasts, Severus joins the brilliant sorceress Lilava to face the Chimaera in The Greatest Monster Battle of All Time to free her folk from an age-old curse. But their adventures don't end there; together they meet elves and magicians, friends and foes; they join in the fight to save Camelot and even walk the Grey Paths of the Dead. With a mix of Malory, a touch of Tolkien, and a hint of humor, The Monster Specialist chronicles a tale of courage, tenacity, honor, and love.

The Monster Specialist is illustrated by Anke Eissmann.

Edward S. Louis, *The Monster Specialist*
Zurich and Jena 2014 (Tales of Yore Series No. 3), ISBN 978-3-905703-23-8

Tales of Yore Series (earlier books)

Kay Woollard, *The Terror of Tatty Walk. A Frightener*
CD and Booklet, Zurich and Berne 2000, ISBN 978-3-9521424-2-4

Kay Woollard, *Wilmot's Very Strange Stone or What came of building "snobbits"*
CD and booklet, Zurich and Berne 2001, ISBN 978-3-9521424-4-8

Information for authors

Authors interested in contributing to our publications can learn more about the services we offer by reading the "services for authors" section of our web pages.

http://www.walking-tree.org/authors

Manuscripts and project proposals can be submitted to the board of editors (please include an SAE):

Walking Tree Publishers
CH-3052 Zollikofen
Switzerland

e-mail: info@walking-tree.org

Walking Tree Publishers, Zurich and Jena, 2016